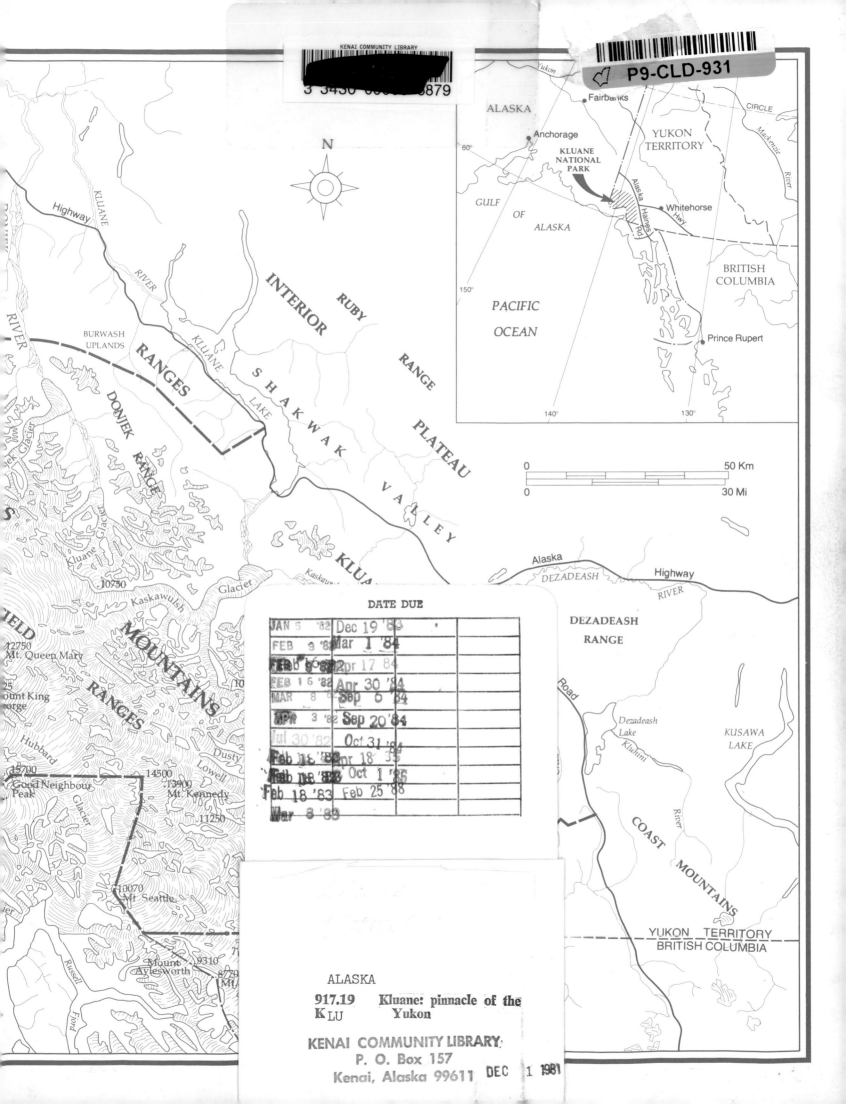

KENAI COMMUNITY LIBRARY

3 3430 000 0879

P9-CLD-931

DATE DUE

JAN 5 '82	Dec 19 '8	
FEB 9 '8	Mar 1 '84	
Feb 16 '82	Apr 17 '84	
FEB 16 '82	Apr 30 '84	
MAR 8 '8	Sep 6 '84	
Apr 3 '82	Sep 20 '84	
Jul 30 '82	Oct 31 '84	
Feb 18 '82	Apr 18 '85	
Feb 18 '82	Oct 1 '86	
Feb 18 '83	Feb 25 '88	
Mar 8 '83		

ALASKA

917.19   Kluane: pinnacle of the
K LU   Yukon

KENAI COMMUNITY LIBRARY
P. O. Box 157
Kenai, Alaska 99611   DEC 1 1981

KLUANE
PINNACLE OF THE YUKON

KLUANE PINNACLE

PROPERTY OF
KENAI COMMUNITY LIBRARY

OF THE YUKON

John B. Theberge, Editor

With the Assistance of George W. Douglas

Line Drawings by Mary Theberge

1980
DOUBLEDAY CANADA LIMITED
Toronto, Canada
DOUBLEDAY & COMPANY, INC.
Garden City, New York

Library of Congress Catalog Card Number: 80-1078

ISBN: 0-385-17122-6

Copyright © 1980 by John B. Theberge

All rights reserved

FIRST EDITION

Printed and bound in Canada by the Hunter-Rose Company

Design by Robert Burgess Garbutt

The photograph on page 157 is of the Dezadeash Valley;
photographer Roland Wickstrom.

COLOR PHOTOGRAPH CREDITS

Monty Alford: 60, 61
Garry Clarke: 8
Michael Cobus: 9
William Dekur: 13, 62, 66
George Douglas: 29, 37
Geological Survey of Canada, William Dekur: 5-7
Jeff Green: 10, 50
Manfred Hoefs: 14, 19, 27, 31, 42, 45, 58
Dewitt Jones: 4
Stephen Krasemann: 35, 36, 46, 65
David Murray: 11, 24, 25, 30, 33, 34, 38, 53
Sebastian Oosenbrug: 51
Chris Perrin: 18, 47
John Theberge: 3, 12, 15-17, 20-23, 26, 28, 32, 39-41, 43, 44, 48,
49, 52, 54-56, 59, 63, 64
Andy Williams: 57
Walter Wood: 1, 2

The contributors dedicate this book to the Arctic Institute of North America and the National and Provincial Parks Association of Canada, the former for its scientific achievements spanning decades of study in the St. Elias Mountains, the latter for its public lobby for protection of the land as a national park. People in both nonprofit organizations desire that the beauty and wonder of the St. Elias Mountains be appreciated not only by those who have been privileged to work or live there, but by everyone who shares an interest in our natural heritage.

FOREWORD

THIS BOOK IS about Kluane National Park — an area of some 8,500 square miles (22,015 square kilometers) in the southwest corner of the Yukon, which includes one of the world's largest nonpolar icefield systems, outstanding glaciers, and Mount Logan, which is the highest mountain in Canada.

For me, it is difficult to express adequately in words the emotion I felt the first time I had the privilege to fly over this part of the Yukon Territory and see the magnificence of the snow-capped mountains, the green and turquoise color of the lakes, the splendor of the forests, and the vastness and unspoiled nature of the landscape. It was not difficult to decide that this territory must be preserved unspoiled for future generations.

While it is now more than 17 years since I entered public life, I consider my proudest moment to be February 22, 1972, when I was able to announce the expansion of Canada's national parks system to northern Canada and the creation of the first three national parks north of the 60th parallel — Kluane in the Yukon, and Nahanni and Baffin Island (Auyuittuq) in the Northwest Territories.

It was at that moment, as Minister responsible for National Parks, that I was able to ensure that thousands of square kilometers of unique Canadian wilderness will be preserved in their natural state in perpetuity for the enjoyment of future generations of Canadians and indeed of all mankind.

As Minister of Indian Affairs and Northern Development for over six years, I developed a very close affinity with northern Canada and came to be a strong believer in the philosophy of balanced development. Northern Canada is large enough to accommodate both the resource development that is essential for the economic well-being of all Canadians and the need for conservation of our natural heritage, which is just as essential for the quality of life of a society.

As Minister responsible for National Parks, I made the decision that there will never be mineral development in the spectacular landscape of Kluane National Park, just as the Virginia Falls on the South Nahanni River will never be the site of a hydro-electric development.

As I look back in my ministerial career up to the present, one of my greatest satisfactions comes from the creation of 10 new national parks, the expansion of the area of land dedicated to national parks by almost 50 percent, and the extension of the National Parks system to every province and both territories.

At a time when Canadians are more and more preoccupied with problems related to economics, we must never forget the need to enrich the quality of life in a nonmaterial way. By that I mean the world of nature, the world of our environment, and the world of our heritage. It is this world which is the subject of this book.

The Honourable Jean Chrétien

"WILD AND WIDE ARE MY BORDERS" *

THE ST. ELIAS Mountains form the highest range in North America, a rugged landscape of snow-clad peaks jutting up from the largest icefield outside polar regions in the world. Together with the green tundras and abundant wildlife in their foothill Kluane Ranges, they represent one of the world's great natural treasures. Here is a museum of nature, a showplace of hundreds of millions of years of evolution, and one of the world's most spectacular national parks, listed as a World Heritage Trust Site of global significance, Kluane.

This book not only portrays and describes an unusual landscape but also tells how the land works. The mountains are still rising, even migrating; the glaciers are transporting vast tonnages of rock daily, building dams, creating lakes, destroying rivers; wildlife populations are cycling, with checks and balances that sometimes work, sometimes fail.

Man's trail of history, too, has been unique, from 8,000-year-old archaeological sites where he squatted beside campfires eating the meat of giant bison, to the gold-rush days and a share in the Klondike glamour, to the mountaineering conquest of pinnacles like Mount Logan, the highest in Canada (5,951 meters; 19,525 feet).

For years the St. Elias Mountains have attracted scientists seeking to reveal the mountains' origins and workings. How did they evolve? How do living things adapt to the harsh environment on and near their icy slopes? What have been the experiences of men who entered the region and learned to live in harmony with

* R. W. Service

ix

Mount Logan, highest mountain in Canada, from the south. (Walter Wood)

it? Because of the studies of these scientists, woven into the text, this book is one of the most comprehensive accounts of natural and human history ever written about a northern environment.

Sixteen scientist-writers have contributed to this book, each stressing the most interesting and significant aspects of his subject. But they all express the common observation, even after their years of experience and study, that for every question answered a host of new questions arises. Because of this, all have developed a respect for the forces of nature that are at work in the region, and this feeling they have tried to convey. Perhaps the respect commanded by the St. Elias Mountains, where nature's forces seem to be on display, can encourage a similar respect for nature everywhere.

The book is organized into three parts: "The Elements," dealing with the mountains, the glaciers, and the climate; "The Living Things," about the flora, birds, mammals, and fish; and "Man," including accounts of prehistoric man and modern man, the history of mountaineering and flying, and a description of some easy climb-ing routes in the Kluane Ranges. The chapters are self-contained and need not be read consecutively. Some events, however, such as the gigantic volcanic explosion of 1,220 years ago, form part of more than one chapter and are described in greatest detail where first mentioned.

Common names are used for plants, except where none exist, and for fish, birds, and mammals. Since common names are sometimes misleading, scientific names are provided, in an appendix, for all species mentioned.

All measurements are given in both Imperial and metric units. The unit preferred by the author is given first, followed by the approximate equivalent in the other system.

Some readers will, no doubt, have a chance to visit the St. Elias Mountains and Kluane National Park, and suggestions for them are given in a brief appendix. The park is easily accessible, fronting along the Alaska and Haines highways. Most readers, however, will not be so lucky; for them we hope to convey, through our profile of knowledge and through pictures, a sense of the beauty and wonder that is there.

John Theberge

ACKNOWLEDGMENTS

P EOPLE WHO WORKED toward this publication but whose names do not appear are: Ken de la Barre, formerly of the Arctic Institute of North America, who helped with the book's initial conception; Tom Fairley, freelance editorial consultant whose scrutiny improved the text and photo selection; Betty Jane Corson of Doubleday Canada Ltd. who conceptualized the book's final form.

The map on the endpapers and the maps at the openings of chapters 9, 10, 11, and 14 were prepared at the Environmental Studies Cartography Centre, University of Waterloo, Waterloo, Ontario, by Gary Brannon and Barry Levely. Figures 1, 2, 3, 4, 5, 8, and 11 were prepared by Ann Ball. Figures 6, 7, 9, and 10 were drafted by Nancy Young.

The authors of the chapter entitled "The Story of the Rocks and Glaciers" would like to thank C. J. Dodds, G. H. Eisbacher, J. G. Souther, and J. W. H. Monger of the Geological Survey of Canada; P. B. Read, consulting geologist; E. M. Mac-Kevett, Jr., and G. Plafker, Jr., of the United States Geological Survey. H. Gabrielse and D. J. Tempelman-Kluit constructively criticized the manuscript. Concepts of the glacial and neoglacial lakes and of major drainage reversals originated with E. D. Kindle and H. S. Bostock formerly of the Geological Survey of Canada.

Photos were kindly provided by the Geological Survey of Canada (6), Yukon Archives (6), Public Archives of Canada (2), Parks Canada (1), and the Inland Waters Directorate (1).

CONTENTS

PART THREE **Man**

KLUANE
PINNACLE OF THE YUKON

Mount St. Elias. (Walter Wood)

Part One
THE ELEMENTS

INTRODUCTION

I N THE ST. ELIAS Mountains, 20 peaks crest more than 4,200 meters (14,000 feet), 20 more peaks crest over 3,600 meters (12,000 feet), and hundreds exceed 3,000 meters (10,000 feet). Towering over all stands majestic Mount Logan, 5,951 meters (19,525 feet), Canada's highest mountain and one of the world's most extensive massifs. The St. Elias Mountains dwarf all other mountain ranges in North America; only one mountain stands higher than Mount Logan: Mount McKinley, 6,193 meters (20,320 feet), in Mount McKinley (Denali) National Park, Alaska.

There are other giants, like Mount St. Elias at 5,489 meters (18,008 feet), long thought to be North America's highest mountain because, unlike Logan and McKinley, it was visible to the first explorers along the Pacific coast; Mount Luciana at 5,226 meters (17,147 feet); and King Peak at 5,173 meters (16,970 feet).

More than 2,050 glaciers are found in the section of the St. Elias Mountains that lies within the 22,015 square meters (8,500 square miles) of Kluane National Park. From the icefield that straddles the divide between the Pacific Ocean and the Yukon River flow many of the world's largest and longest valley glaciers outside the polar regions: Hubbard Glacier, 112 kilometers (70 miles); Walsh Glacier, 97 kilometers (60 miles); Kaskawulsh, Logan, and Lowell glaciers, 72 kilometers (45 miles).

These huge mountains and vast glaciers make their own weather, at times causing winds and snowstorms among the fiercest imaginable. But, for the foothill Kluane Ranges, the higher mountains to the west can also create warmth and semi-arid conditions.

This is a land of extremes.

2

1. THE STORY OF THE ROCKS AND GLACIERS

Richard B. Campbell & Vern N. Rampton

THE ST. ELIAS Mountains form not only the highest but also the youngest major range in Canada. They support icefields and glaciers greater in extent than those of any other subarctic region in the world. Travelers on the Alaska and Haines highways near Kluane National Park are impressed by the formidable front of mountains, their peaks crowned by small icecaps, to the southwest of the broad valley known as the Shakwak Trench, through which the highways run. These are the Kluane Ranges; they rise abruptly from the trench's wide, interconnected valleys. Deep in the mountains, and separated from the Kluane Ranges by the discontinuous, relatively low Duke Depression, are the Icefield Ranges, comprising the main body of the St. Elias Mountains and embracing all of their great peaks (Figure 1). To the north and east of the trench is the subdued

Lowell Glacier calving icebergs into the Alsek River. Black stripes are medial moraine gravels on the ice. (Walter Wood)

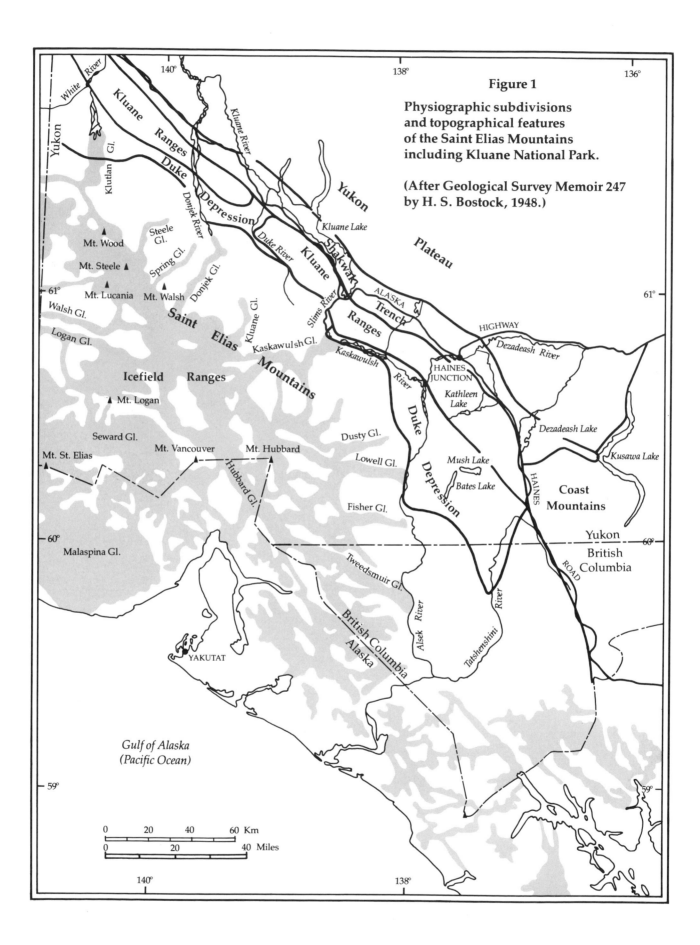

Figure 1

Physiographic subdivisions
and topographical features
of the Saint Elias Mountains
including Kluane National Park.

(After Geological Survey Memoir 247
by H. S. Bostock, 1948.)

Kluane Ranges from kilometer 1627, Alaska Highway, approaching town of Haines Junction. (Phil Upton)

topography of the Yukon's high Interior Plateau.

It is the mountains, however, that draw the eye of the traveler, who may speculate why the rugged peaks and ridges, with intervening, narrow, steep-walled valleys, are in such marked contrast to the more rounded mountains and trough-shaped valleys to the east. He may wonder what lies in the region beyond the mountain front, where Mount Logan and other great peaks and ridges, sheathed with ice and snow, rise from valleys inundated by icefields and glaciers. He may ask, "How did it all form?"

Geological Time and Processes

The oldest known rocks in the St. Elias Mountains are of Ordovician age—in absolute terms, about 500 million years old (Figure 2). This is not an excessive length of time in the history of the earth, whose most ancient rocks are about 3,500 million years old. But such a time span is beyond the human imagination. If years on earth are considered as seconds on some extraterrestrial

FIGURE 2. Geological timetable.

Era	Period	Epoch	Time millions of years
Cenozoic	Quaternary	Recent	0.1
		Pleistocene	3.0
	Tertiary	Pliocene	5.0
		Miocene	22.5
		Oligocene	37.0
		Eocene	55.0
		Paleocene	65.0
Mesozoic	Cretaceus		140.0
	Jurassic		200.0
	Triassic		230.0
Paleozoic	Permian		280.0
	Carboniferous		346.0
	Devonian		395.0
	Silurian		435.0
	Ordovician		500.0
	Cambrian		570.0
Precambrian			3 500 + ?

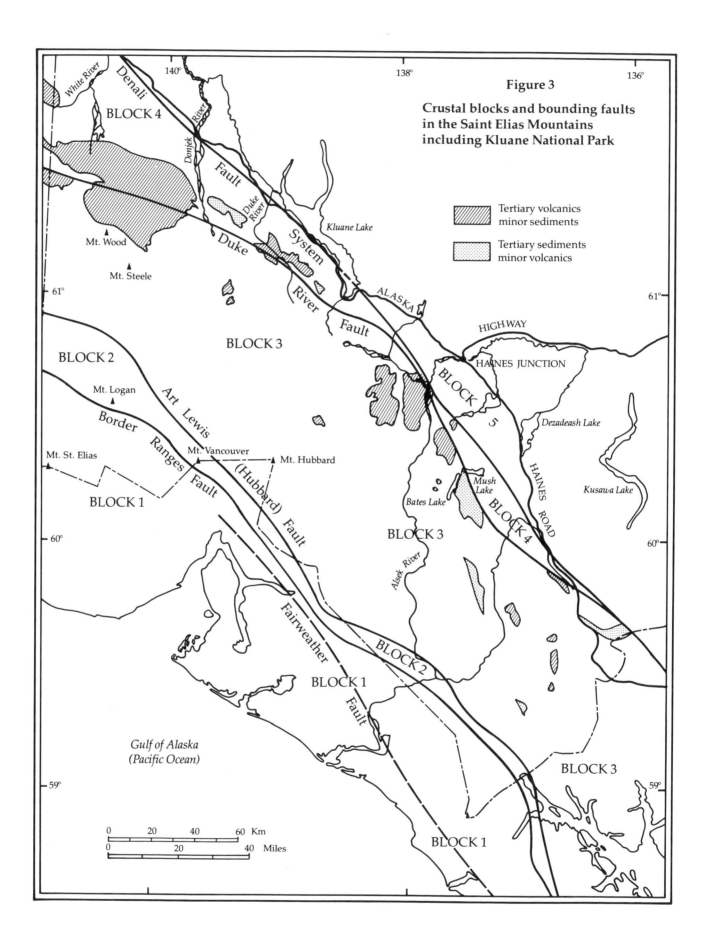

Figure 3

Crustal blocks and bounding faults in the Saint Elias Mountains including Kluane National Park

Tertiary volcanics minor sediments

Tertiary sediments minor volcanics

White River

Denali

Donjek River

BLOCK 4

Fault

Duke River

Kluane Lake

Mt. Wood

Duke

System

Mt. Steele

River

Fault

ALASKA

61°

61°

HIGHWAY

BLOCK 3

HAINES JUNCTION

BLOCK 2

Art Lewis

Mt. Logan

BLOCK 5

Dezadeash Lake

Border

Ranges

Fault

Mt. Vancouver

Mt. Hubbard

Mt. St. Elias

(Hubbard) Fault

BLOCK 1

Mush Lake

Kusawa Lake

Bates Lake

BLOCK 3

60°

Fairweather

Alsek River

BLOCK 4

HAINES ROAD

60°

BLOCK 2

BLOCK 1

Fault

BLOCK 3

Gulf of Alaska
(Pacific Ocean)

59°

59°

0   20   40   60 Km

0   20   40 Miles

BLOCK 1

140°   138°   136°

clock, then the earth's oldest rocks were formed about 112 years ago, the Ordovician period dawned about 16 years ago, man's total existence on earth has occupied perhaps less than 35 days, and a human lifetime is but 70 seconds. By this clock, the advances and retreats of the Pleistocene glaciers — the great ice age — occurred during the last 36 days.

The youngest known rocks in these mountains are late Tertiary and were formed about five million years ago (57 days on our special clock). Thus, the total span of time represented by rocks in the St. Elias Mountains is about 500 million years. Many other mountains in Canada, and elsewhere in the world, contain rocks that span even greater lengths of time.

In other Canadian ranges the forces in the earth's crust that warp, break, and finally uplift the rocks appear to have completed their work; they are quiescent, while the erosive powers of water, ice, and wind continue to wear the mountains away. In the St. Elias Mountains and sister ranges on the Pacific margin in nearby Alaska, the earth's crust remains active today, and the mountains may still be rising in defiance of the erosive forces working constantly to reduce them. Spectacular manifestations of this crustal unrest are the volcanic eruptions and the great earthquakes that have occurred in this century near the margin of the northern Pacific.

Earthquakes are associated with what geologists call "faults." Faults are long, deep fractures in the earth's crust between blocks of rock that shift periodically in relation to one another. Major faults, along which blocks of crust may have moved hundreds and even thousands of miles, have had a profound influence on the St. Elias Mountains. Some of the faults in this region are apparently dead, but others are active and abrupt movement occurs periodically, with accompanying earthquakes. The story of the crustal blocks and their bounding faults is a major part of the geological history of the mountains.

The mountains may be divided into five huge crustal blocks, or plates, each bounded by faults (Figure 3). The faults belong to major systems of fractures in the earth's crust that extend from the Alaska Panhandle through the St. Elias Mountains into eastern Alaska. All of the faults are geologically young and bear similarities to the well-known San Andreas fault of California, which underlies part of San Francisco.

The geological history of the individual crustal blocks is determined by studying the older, pre-Tertiary rocks. The Tertiary rocks are not separated according to the crustal blocks upon which they lie (Figure 3), and their geological history will be discussed separately.

The Migrating Mountains

The oldest rocks of the mountains are confined to the central crustal block (Figure 3) between the Duke River and Art Lewis faults. They range in age from Ordovician to Carboniferous (500 million to 300 million years). First a thick pile of volcanic rocks accumulated, and these are recognizable now only in the southeastern part of the mountains. Subsequently, extensive sheets of sedimentary rocks, including shale, limestone, and sandstone, were deposited on top of the volcanic rocks. Thick, gray to creamy-buff limestone strata of Devonian age (400 million years) stand out prominently. These rocks may have formed in shallow water in much the same way that corals are building the Great Barrier Reef off Australia today. They are extensively exposed in the more rugged mountains and in the ridges among the high icefields and are familiar to those who have climbed in the regions of the upper Fisher, Lowell, Kaskawulsh, Donjek, and Spring glaciers, or in the Centennial Range or west of Mount Wood.

Late in the Devonian period of rock formation, the Paleozoic strata were heated and warped or folded. The increased temperature and pressure caused new mica minerals to be crystallized in the rock, and shale and sandstone became slate and schist. Finally, local masses of partly melted rock material penetrated upward into the folded strata above and slowly crystallized into granite rocks in bodies of greatly varying size and shape. Because granite rocks are relatively resistant to erosion, they form most of the high peaks of the St. Elias Mountains. Examples are the Hubbard-Alverstone-Kennedy massif, Mount Steele, Mount Walsh, and Mount Logan.

After the emplacement of the granite rocks, there is a long and obscure period in the history of the central block; it must have included episodes of uplift, erosion, and displacement on the bounding faults. Finally, in the Tertiary period, sedimentary and volcanic rocks were deposited locally upon the older rocks.

Toe of the Donjek Glacier. (Parks Canada, Ron Seale)

The histories of the flanking crustal blocks, interestingly, have little in common with that of the central block; their rocks are mainly younger and generally not as intensely folded or recrystallized. The adjacent blocks (Figure 3, blocks 2 and 4) are similar to one another and are characterized by Carboniferous, Permian, and Triassic volcanic and sedimentary rocks that are younger than most if not all of the strata of the central block. Into them, from below, rose even younger Mesozoic and Tertiary granite masses. The rocks of block 2 are well exposed in the ridge between the Logan and Walsh glaciers and in adjoining eastern Alaska, where they have been studied in detail in the Kennicott area. The rocks of block 4 are known to those who have explored the front ranges of the mountains to the west of Kluane Lake. Great gray outcrops of limestone,

deposited 200 million years ago, occur along the Duke River, about 19 kilometers (12 miles) southwest of Burwash Landing. This limestone is of the same age as that which contains the rich Kennicott copper ore, in Alaska.

Thus, the flanking blocks are remarkably different from the central one. There is evidence to suggest that no rocks similar to those that form the bulk of the flanking blocks (2 and 4) were ever deposited on the older strata of the central block; and, as well, that the older rocks of the central block never formed a basement beneath the strata of the flanking blocks.

What of the blocks on the margins farthest from the central core (Figure 3, blocks 1 and 5)? Both contain thick layers of shale, sandstone, and conglomerate that were originally deposited on the ocean floor in deep water between 90 and

160 million years ago (Jurassic and Cretaceous). These rocks are younger than those commonly found elsewhere in the mountains. Following deposition, they were folded, and granite was pushed up into them. Summer travelers on the Alaska and Haines highways are familiar with the dark brown and grey rocks (block 5) on the lower slopes and among the glaciers and peaks of the rugged mountains from Jarvis River south to the border of British Columbia.

Geological studies to the northwest, in Alaska, have shown that blocks 4 and 5, although separated by a major fault, have much common geological history. The Jurassic and Cretaceous sedimentary rocks of block 4 were deposited at least partly upon a basement of Triassic and older rocks similar to those of block 5. Blocks 1 and 2, on the other hand, have little in common. The deep-water sedimentary rocks along the coast probably do not rest on a basement of rocks similar to those characteristic of block 2. The two southwesterly blocks therefore have very different geological histories.

Sedimentary rocks such as conglomerate, sandstone, and shale were formed from gravel, sand, and mud derived by erosion of a source above sea level. The older rocks in the central part of the mountains (block 3) apparently were not a source of, nor were they covered by, the younger sedimentary material found in the adjacent blocks. The implication is that block 3 was not nearby when the sedimentary rocks on the margins of the mountains were deposited.

How is it that the crustal blocks, bounded by faults, are so different from their immediate neighbours? A reasonable speculation is that individual blocks have moved great distances in relation to each other, along the bounding faults, and that some of the blocks that are face to face today came from very different regions. Where the blocks came from and the timing of their arrival are impossible to determine with present data. It is particularly difficult to speculate about the origin of the central block. The geological history of its strata seems to be unparalleled in western North America. Hence, if the central block came to its present location from a great distance to the south, its place of origin is obscure. Some have argued that it came from the latitude of northern California, moving along a series of faults that bounded the coast, much as today. Others have suggested that it moved, or was rafted, as a micro-continent across the Pacific Ocean from some part of Asia or Australia. Still others believe that the movement was, at the most, some tens of miles and that, in continental or global terms, the rocks of the central block are not seriously out of place.

Hubbard-Alverstone-Kennedy massif from across the upper Lowell Glacier. (Walter Wood)

Whatever the case may be, the data on which to base an answer are not yet at hand, and we can only say that the block has moved substantially in relation to those now near it.

There is evidence to suggest that some of the other blocks have moved vast distances. Measurements of certain magnetic properties of Triassic volcanic rocks in Alaska, similar to the rocks of blocks 2 and 4, indicate that the volcanic rocks that are now north of the 60th parallel may have come into being at least as far south as the 20th parallel. They must therefore have moved hundreds or even thousands of miles after they were formed 200 million years ago by the cooling of molten lava.

When did the blocks move? The easternmost rocks (block 5) seem to be securely attached to the region to the east of the St. Elias Mountains and hence may be considered to have been stationary relative to the other blocks. Movement or slippage along the Denali fault carried block 4 horizontally northwestward past block 5 for a distance of at least 320 kilometers (200 miles). This fault activity began between 30 and 100 million years ago. It continued, periodically, at least until about five million years ago. The extent of the displacement along the Duke River fault is not known but may be more than 320 kilometers (200 miles). This fault was active

until about 10 million years ago and its movement may have begun 100 million years ago. The potentially enormous but unknown displacement on the Art Lewis fault probably was completed more than 80 million years ago. The Border Ranges fault was active about 60 million years ago and has long been dormant. Finally, near the coast, there is the Fairweather fault, which is active today; abrupt movements along its course have triggered major earthquakes in historical times. The Fairweather may be the beginnings of a new crustal block boundary.

The St. Elias Mountains are a gigantic geological jigsaw puzzle, most of whose pieces moved into place in the last 50 million years — very recently, in geological terms. But that is only one chapter in their history.

The Mountains Are Raised

From about 60 million years ago until 20 million years ago (Figure 4), the various crustal blocks of the mountains, some still moving, were above sea level except for parts of them in the region near the coast in Alaska; but there were no high mountains. Rivers flowed in broad valleys through a gently rolling land, some of them from northeast to southwest out of what is now the

FIGURE 4. Chart of events in the geological history of the St. Elias Mountains for the last 60 million years.

Age in millions of years	Events
60	
15	Volcanism. Lava covers part of land. Alaska volcanoes active to near present. — Regional uplift. Erosion carves land into present mountains and valleys. — Major Faulting
10	Local glaciation begins. Climate cools.
3	Major ice age begins
present	

Mountains, carved from flat-lying lava flows, rise on the north above the rough, debris-covered surface of the lower Steele Glacier. (Geological Survey of Canada, William Dekur)

interior of the Yukon and British Columbia, and building up, here and there, thick flood-plain deposits of gravel, sand, and mud. A warm, perhaps subtropical, climate encouraged the growth of lush vegetation, and layers of woody material were entombed in places within the flood-plain sediments. These layers subsequently became coal seams, some of which may be seen today at Amphitheatre Mountain and along the upper part of Sheep Creek.

Perhaps as much as 25 million years ago (see Figure 4), molten rock rose to the surface from vents and fissures, signaling the beginning of vast outpourings of lava and volcanic ash. The lava flows are now well exposed along the Steele Glacier and Steele Creek, on the middle reaches of the Duke River, and along the Dusty River. There has been no very recent volcanic activity in the Canadian part of the mountains; the most recent known flows there occurred six million years ago. But in Alaska, just west of the Klutlan Glacier, there are numerous young volcanic craters. Around 98 A.D. and again around 758 A.D., explosive volcanic activity blew several cubic miles of white volcanic ash from a small vent in the hillside beside the glacier. Much of the ash settled nearby in deposits several feet thick, particularly in the White River valley, and fine material from the second explosion was carried by the prevailing westerly winds for hundreds of miles, into the central Yukon. This ash forms a prominent white line that is visible along road cuts and in the cut banks of the Donjek, Yukon, Pelly, and other rivers. The age of the deposits was determined by the analysis of carbon isotopes from plant material buried by the ash.

On the surface of lava flows, sediments were deposited along stream channels and in swamps. These sediments, which were subsequently covered by more lava, contain coal and in places fossil logs more than 30 centimeters (12 inches) in diameter, attesting to a much warmer climate than today's. These sedimentary rocks contain none of the fragments that one would expect to find in them if streams carrying gravel and sand had been able to flow from some nearby nonvolcanic mountains. This, with the evidence of a warm climate, indicates that, as recently as 15 or 20 million years ago, the St. Elias Mountains did not exist.

About 10 million years ago the St. Elias Mountains began to rise (Figure 4). Coal layers are absent in strata between the younger lava flows,

indicating that moderating winds from the Gulf of Alaska were no longer influencing the inland climate. At about that time, also, on the Alaska coast below the St. Elias Mountains, deposits made by glaciers of what is called "till" first appear. The glaciers may have flowed, not only to the sea, but also toward the interior where volcanic activity continued; some smaller glaciers may have developed here and there on the high volcanic mountains.

As the land rose, the erosive forces began to carve valleys into it, leaving intervening mountains and ridges, and the landscape we see today began to take shape. The more resistant rocks remain as the highest peaks; they, together with the entire region, may be rising still, in steady conflict with the forces of erosion. In many places, most of the old, gently rolling surface has been eroded away; only scattered remnants of it remain, some of them visible as tiny patches high in the mountains. For example, on the ridge between the Donjek and Duke rivers, immediately east of the terminus of the Donjek Glacier, conglomerate was deposited in a low area but is now perched high above the modern valleys.

The uplift was not uniform in rate or extent from place to place. This led to tilting and warping of the original subdued surface. The old surface is preserved under Tertiary sedimentary and volcanic rocks and can best be seen near Amphitheatre Mountain and in the rolling upland country to the west of Bates Lake, that is, along the Duke Depression.

The uplift, and perhaps the volcanic activity, is probably related in some way to the processes that brought about the movement of the great crustal blocks. With the development of the mountains and the onset of glaciation we come to the Pleistocene glacial epoch and the last chapter in the story of what made the mountains we see today.

Carved by Ice and Water

As the Kluane Ranges rose up and were eroded, several large streams were able to keep pace with the uplift, down-cutting valleys that constituted great gaps from one side of the ranges to the other. These gaps are now occupied by the White, Donjek, Slims, Jarvis, Dezadeash, and Tatshenshini rivers and by the Kathleen Lakes.

The valley west of Dezadeash Lake is another such gap. Likewise, too, the Alsek River managed to cut its way through the rising Icefield Ranges, and so, in spite of the great mountain barrier, it flows through a deep gorge to the ocean.

Possibly three million years ago the period of major continental glaciation began (see Figure 4). Glaciation began much earlier in the St. Elias Mountains, but there, too, the maximum glacial advances occurred during the Pleistocene epoch. As elsewhere, there were several major glacial stages separated by long intervals during which the climate may have been warmer than that of today. Evidence of early Pleistocene glaciation, and warm nonglacial intervals, is rare within the St. Elias Mountains because of the intense, continuous erosion and the more recent extensive, still-existing glaciers. In the Shakwak Trench and the Duke Depression, however, sedimentary deposits have provided evidence of glaciations older than 100,000 years. These were followed by a warm period and by at least two cooler periods when the ice advanced again.

Much of the present topography of the St. Elias Mountains and of the Shakwak Trench was shaped by erosion and by the scour of moving ice during the two more recent Pleistocene glaciations, between 100,000 and 12,500 years ago, and by later erosion, which still goes on. During the two recent Pleistocene glaciations, which were separated by a warm interval, glaciers within the mountains expanded until they overflowed most of the major valleys. Some high peaks deep in the mountains, and most of the peaks and high ridges near the Shakwak Trench, stood above the ice as islands of rock, called "nunataks." Streams of ice flowed out through the great gaps in the Kluane Ranges, joining together in the Shakwak Trench and partly filling it. Just as today, the major accumulation of ice was in the high mountains near the coast, a region of heavy snowfalls. The glaciers flowing down the leeward side of the mountains entered a region of light precipitation.

From the southern end of Kluane Lake, the ice moved in a northwesterly direction along the Shakwak Trench, into the large, flat area around Snag. Two distinct moraines of rock debris carried by the ice mark the outer limits of the two glacial advances, and these are plainly visible around the basin and on the adjoining hillsides. The ice of the last advance reached a thickness of about 915 meters (3,000 feet) at the site of Haines Junction, where its surface was at an elevation of about 1,525 meters (5,000 feet) above sea level. It stood at about 1,860 meters (6,000 feet) above sea level at the southern end of Kluane Lake, and the surface sloped from there to the southeast and the northwest along the Shakwak Trench. The tops of the rounded mountains to the northeast of Kluane Lake were not glaciated. Remnants of an old plateau, they exhibit a type of erosion peculiar to this environment. A combination of frost action and what might be called "slope creep" has created the vertical sides of castles, or tors, of bedrock on the tops of the ridges. Some of these are visible from the highway across Kluane Lake.

As the Pleistocene glaciers grew, reached their maximum, and eventually retreated, they had a profound influence on the drainage patterns. Periodically, sections of some valleys became choked with ice, and their streams were thus dammed. This damming occurred, notably, in the valley of the Alsek River, where Pleistocene glaciers flowing from the west impounded vast lakes. The most noteworthy of the Pleistocene lakes, the Glacial Lake Champagne, formed during the retreat of the last major ice advance; it reached an elevation of about 760 meters (2,490 feet) above sea level in tributaries of the Alsek River, including the Dezadeash and Kathleen river valleys. The site of Haines Junction was under more than 150 meters (490 feet) of water. Silt beds, deposited in the lake, are well exposed in highway cuts and along the Dezadeash River west of Haines Junction. Old beaches, or strand lines, marked by benches of beach sand and gravel, are visible here and there on the hillsides along the highway east of Haines Junction. As the glaciers retreated, and the Alsek River was able to resume its course to the ocean, the lake was drained. Many of the small tributary valleys were ice-free during the period when the major valleys were occupied by glaciers, and the drainage of these small valleys was ponded in glacial lakes. Sediments that were deposited in one such lake are exposed in terraces along Bullion Creek.

Large rivers, laden with gravel, sand, and mud, issued from the glaciers. At times, these rivers created wide flood plains coated with mud and silt in various parts of the Shakwak Trench. When the flats were dry, the wind picked up great clouds of dust from them, just as it does today from the flats of the Slims and Donjek

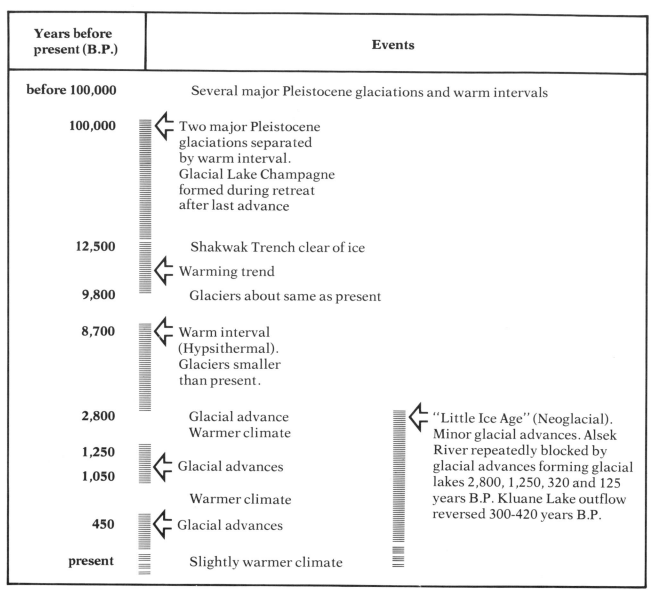

Years before present (B.P.)	Events
before 100,000	Several major Pleistocene glaciations and warm intervals
100,000	Two major Pleistocene glaciations separated by warm interval. Glacial Lake Champagne formed during retreat after last advance
12,500	Shakwak Trench clear of ice
	Warming trend
9,800	Glaciers about same as present
8,700	Warm interval (Hypsithermal). Glaciers smaller than present.
2,800	Glacial advance / Warmer climate — "Little Ice Age" (Neoglacial). Minor glacial advances. Alsek River repeatedly blocked by glacial advances forming glacial lakes 2,800, 1,250, 320 and 125 years B.P. Kluane Lake outflow reversed 300-420 years B.P.
1,250	
1,050	Glacial advances
	Warmer climate
450	Glacial advances
present	Slightly warmer climate

FIGURE 5. *Chart of the glacial chronology and related events during the last 100,000 years in and near the St. Elias Mountains.*

rivers. The dust accumulated, here and there, in deposits called "loess." Loess deposits may be seen along the highway south of Kluane Lake.

The glaciers had retreated out of the Shakwak Trench by about 12,500 years ago and had been reduced to their present size by about 9,800 years ago (Figure 5). The estimate of 12,500 years was determined by the analysis of carbon isotopes from plant material buried by glacial sedimentary deposits. The estimate of 9,800 years was arrived at by the analysis of carbon isotopes from grass buried by wind-blown loess near the present terminus of the Kaskawulsh Glacier.

The Warm Interval (The Hypsithermal)

Between 8,700 and 2,800 years ago the climate of the world was slightly warmer than it is at present, and glaciers were less extensive. The terminus of the Kaskawulsh Glacier was at least 21 kilometers (13 miles) up the valley from its present position. Today, the meltwater from the glacier drains off on either side of a pile of glacial morainal debris just beyond the snout of the ice; part of it flows south via the Kaskawulsh River to the Alsek River, and part goes northeast via the Slims River to Kluane Lake and the Yukon River system. During the warm period, when the glacier's terminus was far up the valley of the Kaskawulsh, the pile of morainal material did not exist, and Kluane Lake drained through the Slims River and into the Alsek River system to the Gulf of Alaska.

To the Present (The Neoglacial)

Since the warm period, the great valley glaciers have advanced several times — about 2,800 years ago, again between 1,250 and 1,050 years ago, and finally in the period that started 450 years ago (See Figure 5). New, chaotic piles of rocky moraines were deposited by glaciers at various points beyond their present termini. The dates of these advances were obtained by the analysis of carbon isotopes from wood and plant material from trees and other plants that were overridden by ice and buried by glacial deposits. Another dating technique that has been used, for the youngest of the moraines, is based on the measurement of certain circular lichens that increase in diameter with age and have been

Snout of spatulate-shaped rock glacier at southern edge of Kathleen Lake. (Geological Survey of Canada,William Dekur)

Terminal moraines of the Kaskawulsh Glacier, fount of the Slims River. (Walter Wood)

found growing on rock surfaces that were fresh and clean at the time they were dumped in the moraine. This technique permits the dating of various valley glacial moraines that have been deposited during the last 450 years.

Rock glaciers and debris-covered glaciers, formed during the Neoglacial period, are common in the northeastern part of the St. Elias Mountains. Rock glaciers are streams of broken rock that flow down a slope and, at the bottom, form lobes, or tongues, similar to those of ice glaciers. Rock glaciers are fed from above by steep cliffs that provide a continuous source of material. Debris-covered glaciers are similar to rock glaciers in appearance, but in fact they are true ice glaciers completely covered by broken rock. Some rock glaciers may once have been debris-covered ice glaciers. Remarkable examples of rock glaciers and debris-covered glaciers are visible from the road between Haines Junction and Dezadeash Lake.

The lakes that were formed behind glacial

dams in the Neoglacial period are of special interest. When the Kaskawulsh Glacier reached its maximum advance, 300 to 420 years ago, it dammed the drainage of Kluane Lake which was then southward through the Slims River to the Alsek River. This caused the level of the lake to rise, and the water finally began to escape from the northern end, where it cut a new channel, the present Kluane River, and flowed into the Yukon River system as it does today. By the time the glacier receded, leaving a pile of morainal debris, the new channel was low enough that flow out of the southern end of the lake did not resume. During the period when the level of the lake was raised, two distinct beach benches, where driftwood may still be found, were formed four and 13 meters (13 and 43 feet) above the present water level. The benches are particularly obvious on the open, grassy slopes northeast of the southern part of the lake, and may be seen from the highway.

The largest lake formed during the period was

Mount Logan, pinnacle of the Yukon (1).

ABOVE: Mount St. Elias (2).
RIGHT: Chilkat Pass after summer storm (3).

Icebergs in the Alsek River (4).

ABOVE: Lowell Glacier (5).
ABOVE RIGHT: Kaskawulsh Glacier (6).
BELOW RIGHT: Kluane Range near Kathleen Lake (7).
FAR RIGHT: Mount Wood across Rusty Glacier (8).

TOP: Summer melt on the Lowell Glacier (9).
ABOVE: Clouds building over Icefield Ranges (10).
RIGHT: Surging Jackal Glacier (11).

Three views of the Slims River.
BELOW: Summer dust storm (12).
RIGHT: Delta (13).
BOTTOM: Winter (14).

Neoglacial Lake Alsek, which was created repeatedly during the last 2,800 years, each time the Lowell Glacier dammed the Alsek River. The lakes flooded the Alsek, Kaskawulsh, Dusty, and Dezadeash river valleys and certainly flooded the site of Haines Junction. A series of beach deposits, or strand lines, is beautifully preserved along the northern side of the Dezadeash River where it cuts through the Kluane Ranges just west of Haines Junction. Driftwood still lies on the younger beaches, which are well above the river level. Various strand lines between 640 and 670 meters (2,100 and 2,200 feet) in elevation were formed either 2,800 or 1,250 years ago; the shores of these lakes have not yet been firmly separated. The lower beaches were built about 320 and 125 years ago. As a result of the most recent major flooding, a sharp trim-line, below which the trees were killed, was produced in the forest along the Alsek River. Younger trees have begun to grow below this line. Tales of the recent lakes were told to early geologists by the Indians. A minor surge of the Lowell Glacier produced a small, short-lived lake at its terminus in 1953.

Evidently, Neoglacial Lake Alsek drained quickly and perhaps many times during the life of a single glacial dam. The violent rush of water out of the lake basin created large current-formed dunes and scour hollows up to six meters (20 feet) deep in the gravel on the bottom of the valley. These features are visible on the bare gravel terraces along the Alsek and Dezadeash rivers. Downstream from the Lowell Glacier, the Alsek River must have been a raging torrent for several days each time the lake drained.

With minor climatic cooling, a major surge of the Lowell Glacier might well re-create Lake Alsek and cause flooding far up the Dezadeash and other valleys to an elevation of about 610 meters (2,000 feet) above sea level.

Glaciers can move vast amounts of material, as the ancient glacial deposits attest. A spectacular modern example is provided by the Kaskawulsh Glacier, with its high, chaotic terminal moraines, the long narrow piles of rock debris in the lateral moraines at its edges, and its medial moraines. A drink from the Alsek or Slims rivers, which seem to be almost solid with silt and mud, will give a vivid indication of the volumes of rock debris that are moved by the ice and discharged into the meltwater streams. With such vast and active transport going on, it is small wonder that the glaciers have influenced the shape of the mountains so profoundly in a relatively brief span of time.

The St. Elias Mountains provide a spectacular example of changes that have occurred in one short, recent interval in the vast reaches of geological time. That changes continue today seems certain — perhaps imperceptibly slowly to us, but quickly indeed in the perspective of earth history.

2. THE GLACIERS: NATURE'S SCULPTORS

Richard H. Ragle

WHAT IS A GLACIER? It can be defined in different ways, but basically the term *glacier** denotes a snow-fed body of land ice that persists year after year and shows evidence of past or present flow. But because *ice* is truly a rock, and *snow*, like a beach sand, is a sediment, a glacier can also be considered a rock formation with a sedimentary veneer. In 1890 G. Frederick Wright wrote, "To the ordinary man of science, water is a mineral and ice is a rock; but to the glacialist both are fluids."[1]

Descriptions of glaciers can be found in eleventh-century Icelandic sagas, but it was not until the 12th century that literature recorded that glaciers are dynamic. Indeed they are, but not quite like Mark Twain expected when in 1880 he traveled in the Swiss Alps:

"I marched the Expedition down the steep and tedious mule-path and took up as good a position as I could upon the middle of the glacier—because Baedeker[2] said the middle part travels the fastest. As a measure of economy, however, I put some of the heavier baggage on the shoreward parts to go as slow freight."

Little progress was noted that afternoon and evening by Mr. Twain, so the next day Baedeker was again consulted:

---

* Technical terms in the text are italicized the first time they are used. Definitions are found in the Glossary of Terms, at the end of this chapter.

1. Wright, G. F., *The Ice Age in North America* (New York: D. Appleton and Company, 1890).

2. Baedeker, K., *Handbook for Travelers. Switzerland, and the Adjacent Portions of Italy, Savoy and the Tyrol* (Leipzig: Firm Publishers. 8th Remodelled Edition, 1879).

"... I hunted eagerly for the timetable. There was none. The book simply said the glacier was moving all the time. This was satisfactory, so I shut up the book and chose a good position to view the scenery as we passed along. I stood there some time enjoying the trip, but at last it occurred to me that we did not seem to be gaining on the scenery. I soon found a sentence which threw a dazzling light on the matter. It said, 'The Gorner Glacier travels at an average rate of a little less than an inch a day'. I made a small calculation: 1 inch a day, say 30 feet a year; estimated distance to Zermatt, 3 and one-eighteenth miles. Time to go by glacier, a little over five hundred years! I said to myself, 'I can walk it quicker—and before I will patronize such a fraud as this, I will do it!'"[3]

3. Clemens, S. L., *Mark Twain. A Tramp Abroad* (Hartford: American Publishing Company, 1880).

Glaciers cover nearly 6 million square miles (15,400,000 square kilometers) or nearly 11 percent of the earth's surface and account for about 80 percent of all our fresh water. During the last million or 2 million years there have been periods when there was almost three times as much ice as at present, and other periods when there was somewhat less. By best estimate, there is 26 times more fresh water stored in today's glaciers than contained in all the earth's lakes, rivers, groundwater basins, and in the atmosphere.

Most of the earth's *glacier ice* is found on the Antarctic continent, the island of Greenland, and on the Canadian and other circumpolar islands. Yet, with the exception of Australia, all continents have glaciers, and glaciers occur at almost all latitudes.

Glaciers come in many forms and sizes. The world's largest is the Antarctic *Ice Sheet* with an

Mid Kaskawulsh Glacier showing medial moraines. (Russ Kinne)

Highland glacier between the north arm of the Kaskawulsh Glacier (upper left) and Hubbard Glacier (lower right). Only the highest peaks, nunataks, rise above the glacier. Photo encompasses nearly 200 square miles (500 square kilometers) of glacier surface. (Walter Wood)

area exceeding 5.4 million square miles (14 million square kilometers). Smallest are *glacierets*, or *cirque glaciers*, of which there are many in Kluane National Park. These can be as small as an acre in area and many can be seen at the lower elevations where they are sustained in protected north-facing amphitheaters carved out by ice action from the face of a mountain peak. At the higher elevations glaciers may fill neighboring valleys until the ice overflows and merges to become an intermontane glacier or highland glacier with only the highest peaks (*nunataks*) and ridges rising above the glacier surface. The vast *icefield* that spreads across the top of the St. Elias Mountains is composed of many highland and *transverse glaciers* that flow outward from the uppermost region to funnel down valleys and become *compound valley glaciers*. Some, called *tidewater glaciers*, terminate at the sea like the Hubbard Glacier which has its *source* in the Icefield Ranges of the Park and ends in tidewater in Disenchantment Bay near Yakutat, Alaska. Others, called *piedmont glaciers*, flow out onto relatively flat land fronting the mountains; an example is the

Malaspina Glacier, which is an Alaska extension of the Seward Glacier in the Park and which is exceptionally large covering nearly 1,475 square miles (3,775 square kilometers), an area equivalent to four-fifths the size of Lake Manitoba and large enough to easily accommodate the State of Rhode Island.

Anatomy of a Glacier

Glaciers are the product of a continuous accumulation of snow. Snowflakes fall through the atmosphere at below-freezing temperature (32°F, 0°C) as a crystal mineral and in the form of a hexagon. Johannes Kepler in about 1609 wrote an essay, *De niva sexangula* (*The Six-cornered Snowflake*). It was not printed, however, until 1611 and not translated from the Latin into English until 1966.[4] In it he was first to ask the question "cur semper sexangula?", why always six-

4. Kepler, Johannes, "The Six-cornered Snowflake." Translation of *De niva sexangula* by Johannes Kepler, c. 1611. In Latin. Translation by Colin Hardie, with essays by B. J. Mason and L. L. Whyte (Oxford: Clarendon Press, 1966).

cornered? By surmising its regularity to the geometric close packing of globules of condensed moisture, he introduced a principle that took three and a half centuries to prove. In 1912 the answer for near-perfect symmetry of minerals was found by Max von Laue, Nobel Prize winner in physics. His work in X-rays proved to be the starting point on research into crystal structure.

In a matter of days or months after deposition, depending upon the temperature and other processes, *snow* is transformed from a crystal into a sediment of rounded grains called *firn* (Figure 6). In a matter of years or decades under ever-increasing pressure from deeper burial of overlying layers of firn and *englacial* temperature fluctuations, the mass becomes a *monomineralic* (single-mineral) rock called glacier ice. With more accumulation and depending upon steepness of valley slope, ice will flow normally under the force of gravity.

A glacier has an "upstream" zone upon which snow accumulates (gain) each year and a "downstream" zone where snow and ice ablate (loss) by melt and evaporation. The two zones are separated by the annual snowline (*firn limit*) — the line between annual income and expenditure. Economy minded, a glacier strives to maintain a

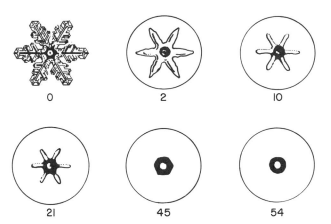

FIGURE 6. *Details of the gradual change of a hexagonal snow crystal. (Modified from H. Bader, "Snow and Its Metamorphism," Cold Regions Research and Engineering Laboratory, Hanover, New Hampshire.)*

balanced budget and is sensitive to both surplus and deficit. Should the upper section gain more snow than is removed from the lower section, the glacier will thicken and the excess weight accumulated will tend to promote expansion. On the other hand, if in the lower section net loss is greater than net gain in the upper section, a glacier will contract. Glaciers that overexpand during "prosperous" years will generally fall

Firn line shown by light upper and dark lower zones on the central arm of the Kaskawulsh Glacier, August 1967. A tributary glacier enters from the left, bringing medial moraines into the central arm. (Phil Upton)

back, recede, and lie quiescent during the following "depression." In other words, a glacier will strive to adjust to its environment.

Glaciers can be either *temperate* (warm) or *polar* (cold). Polar glaciers are further divided into high-polar and subpolar, their definition depending upon the degree of melting that occurs at the end of the *ablation* (summer) season. In polar-type glaciers there is no significant melting of the firn in the *accumulation* area and the temperature at depth is below freezing, but in temperate glaciers melting of firn in the accumulation zone occurs and its temperature is close to the freezing point throughout its entire mass.

A glacier's anatomy may also vary with elevation. For instance, a valley glacier whose source is at 18,000 feet (5,486 meters) but whose *terminus* is near sea level can be a cold-type glacier in its upper part and then become a warm-type glacier at a somewhat lower elevation. Figure 7 is a schematic cross-section of the zones of accumulation and ablation in a glacier and differentiates cold and warm parts.

Active Ice

Glaciers are in a state of either noticeable activity or passivity. Occasionally a glacier will become dormant and may even disappear — and on occasion even reappear. Or a glacier may all of a sudden become very active and *surge* forward.

The movement of glaciers has been recognized for more than 700 years and observed qualitatively for more than 100 years. Only within the last three decades, however, have quantitative theories appeared to explain mechanisms of glacier flow. How does ice flow, and what are the mechanics of the process?

Except for the phenomenon of surge, *climate* is the most popularly recognized factor influencing the size and movement of glaciers. Climate governs precipitation and temperature, both of which strongly influence accumulation and ablation of ice. Just as rivers and streams have annual budgets that are dependent upon amount of rain, glaciers have budgets that depend upon the accumulation and ablation of snow. Over a

FIGURE 7. *Schematic diagram illustrating zones of a glacier. (Modified from C. S. Benson, Research Report 70, Cold Regions Research and Engineering Laboratory, Hanover, New Hampshire.)*

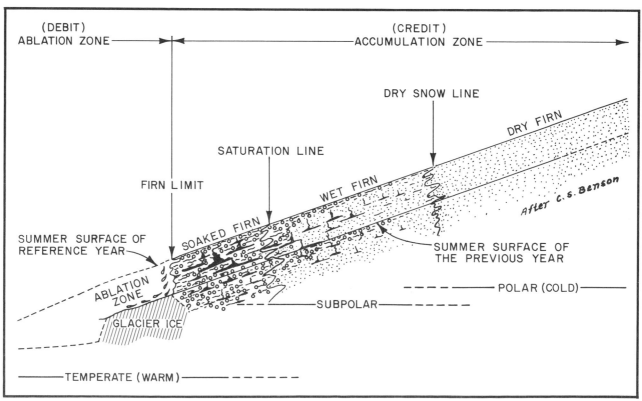

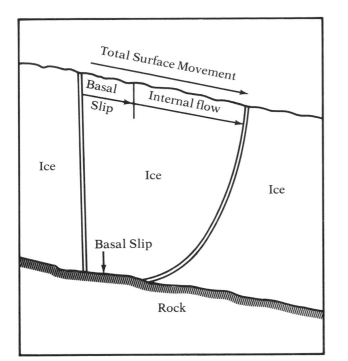

FIGURE 8. *Schematic illustration of the two flow
components—sliding of the ice mass on the rock bed,
and internal shearing of the ice masses. (After
R. P. Sharp, "Glaciers," Condon Lectures, Oregon State
System of Higher Education, Eugene, Oregon.)*

five-to-ten-year period the health of a glacier is
considered in terms of its economy—net volume
gain minus net volume loss. The resultant mass
of the glacier influences its speed of flow and,
indeed, much of its "reason" and ability to flow.
So, too, does the shape of the valley, its slope and
channel shape, resistance along the edges and at
the glacier *sole*, or contact with the bottom rock,
temperature of the ice, and amount of water at
the base of the glacier.

Normal motion is most likely due to a number
of mechanisms but is most often represented by
the sum of two: internal flow within the mass of
ice itself plus the basal slip of the glacier over its
rock floor. Figure 8 illustrates the two basic flow
components.

Except when a glacier surges, glacier ice flows
as a visco-plastic material—an intricate combination of *liquid flow* and *plastic deformation*.
Disturbance to the flow by an obstacle on the
valley floor, such as a rock mound or ledge, is
often reflected on the glacier surface in the form
of a dome or terrace, or an *icefall*. Although not
proven, it appears reasonable that the degree to

which topography of the glacier's bed influences
the surface relief of a glacier depends in some
measure on the height and extent of the obstacle
and the depth of ice. If the obstacle is large—if
for instance there is a steep dip (*rock step*) along
the glacier bed and the glacier is relatively thin,
crevasses will appear at the surface (Figure 9).
They occur in a number of different forms, from
a narrow crack to a nearly vertical, broad transverse or longitudinal rift. Seldom have crevasses
been found to be more than 200 feet (60 meters)
deep.

There are periods during the normal activity
of a glacier when its steady-state flow is disrupted by a phenomenon called a *kinematic
wave*. This is a surface wave that travels down
the glacier at a velocity somewhat greater than
the velocity of the ice mass itself. In nature, rates
of accumulation and ablation of snow and ice
and the temperature of the ice change with time.
There are short-term seasonal changes, year-
to-year changes, and long-term variations due to
climatic change. The sum of these variables is
the cause of a mass-balance disturbance that
will stimulate a kinematic wave to occur much
the way a catastrophic downpour of rain will
initiate a surface wave of water to travel down a
river more rapidly than the river's current.
Glacier waves are seldom recognized by the
traveler or alpinist, but they can be identified on
photographs and their down-glacier velocity cal-
culated by successive photogrammetric surveys.

Small alpine valley glaciers may move only
inches a day while larger valley and *outflow
glaciers* or the *ice streams* found in Greenland

FIGURE 9. *A cutaway schematic diagram showing chief
features of a glacier and associated moraines.*

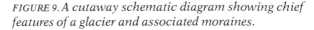
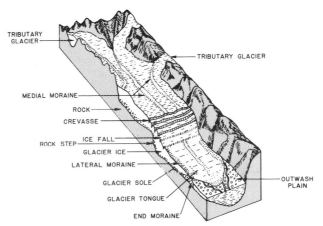

and Antarctica may move a few feet a day or tens of feet a day respectively. Table 1 gives some surface velocities, taken from mid-glacier, of some typical glaciers in the world. Table 2 gives velocities for some of the glaciers in the Kluane National Park.

Table 1 / *Glacier Surface Velocities*[5]

Glacier	Type	Place/country	Approx. measured velocity
Rink	outlet	West Greenland	88 ft. (27 m)/day
	outlet	West Greenland	26 ft. (8 m)/day
Columbia	valley	Alaska, U.S.A.	10 ft. (3 m)/day
Denman	ice stream	Antarctica	9 ft. (3 m)/day
Franz Josef	valley	New Zealand	7 ft. (2 m)/day
Taku	valley	Alaska, U.S.A.	2 ft. (0.6 m)/day
Fox	valley	New Zealand	1 ft. (0.3 m)/day
Bashkara	valley	Caucasus, U.S.S.R.	3 in. (8 cm)/day
Baltora	valley	Karakorum, Kashmir	9 in. (22 cm)/day
Styggedal	valley	Jotunheim, Norway	3 in. (8 cm)/day
Blomstrandbreen	valley	Spitsbergen	7 in. (18 cm)/day
Blue	valley	Washington, U.S.A.	10 in. (25 cm)/day
Lemon Creek	valley	Alaska, U.S.A.	3 in. (8 cm)/day
South Cascade	valley	Washington, U.S.A.	2 in. (5 cm)/day
Thompson	outlet	Axel Heiberg Island, N.W.T., Canada	7 in. (18 cm)/day
White	outlet	Axel Heiberg Island, N.W.T., Canada	4 in. (10 cm)/day
Crusoe	outlet	Axel Heiberg Island, N.W.T., Canada	4 in. (10 cm)/day
Barnes	ice cap	Baffin Island, N.W.T., Canada	1 in. (3 cm)/day
Saskatchewan	valley	Alberta, Canada	8 in. (20 cm)/day
Athabasca	valley	Alberta, Canada	4 in. (10 cm)/day
Salmon	valley	British Columbia, Canada	4 in. (10 cm)/day
South Leduc	valley	British Columbia, Canada	3 in. (8 cm)/day

Table 2 / *Glacier Surface Velocities in Kluane National Park*

Glacier	Type	Approx. measured velocity
Kaskawulsh (upper basin)	highland	18 in. (46 cm)/day
(north)	outlet	19 in. (48 cm)/day
(confluence)	valley	16 in. (41 cm)/day
"Hubbard Extension"	outlet	14 in. (36 cm)/day
Rusty	valley	1 in. (3 cm)/day
Backe	valley	8 in. (20 cm)/day[6]
Trapridge	valley	2 in. (5 cm)/day

5. Mellor, M., *Snow and Ice on the Earth's Surface*, U.S. Army Cold Regions Research and Engineering Laboratory, Science and Engineering Monograph II-C1, 1964.
6. Waning period of surge, which probably began about 1963.

Surging Glaciers

While glaciers are very sensitive to climate, many of them experience very sudden and spectacular movement that is not related specifically to climate. Instead, this sudden movement is thought to be more controlled by dynamic conditions within a glacier together with an "uncoupling" of the near-freezing glacier ice from the bedrock valley floor. Instances of glaciers displaying sudden, rapid, down-valley movement amounting to several miles in a few months, or up to as many as three years, have been reported for more than a century. A glacier that has exhibited normal movement or has been in a passive state for tens of years will suddenly be "triggered" and advance at a rate of from 10 to a hundred times normal. This rapid flow is known as *glacier surge* and although not fully understood, it is believed to be a periodic phenomenon created by a build-up of ice in the upper part of a glacier. In Kluane National Park more than 60 glaciers have been identified as surge-type, and they represent approximately 35 percent of all surge-type glaciers identified in western North America.

The Steele Glacier, a surge-type glacier, occupies a valley along the northwest boundary of Kluane National Park. Prior to beginning its dramatic advance in the fall of 1965, it lay very nearly dormant for many decades, moving only a few inches per day. Yet, nearly two years later, during the summer of 1967, the surging down-valley movement of Steele Glacier could easily be heard rumbling past the glacier camp of the Yukon Alpine Centennial Expedition. The glacier was traveling past the camp at an average surface velocity of 40 feet (12 meters) a day and, in two years, had traveled more than 5 miles (8 kilometers) down its valley.

Surges appear to occur in cycles with a periodicity somewhat related to the size of a glacier, and are separated into three major classes: Class I: large, high speed; Class II:

Steele Glacier as it "surges" down valley, February 1967. (Inland Waters Directorate, Environment Canada, Monty Alford)

Table 3 / *Four Characteristic Measurements on Six Selected Glaciers Known to Have Surged in Kluane National Park*

Glacier	Class	Approx. max. velocity	Approx. displacement	Approx. duration	Cycling period
Walsh	I	50 ft. (15 m)/day	7.0 mi. (11 km)	6 yrs.[+]	50 ± 10
Steele	I	55 ft. (17 m)/day	5.6 mi. (8 km)	3 yrs.[+]	100 ± 10
Tweedsmuir	I	15 ft. (5 m)/day	0.5 mi. (0.8 km)	7 mos.	(?)
Kluane	II	(?)	1.2 mi. (2 km)	(?)	19 ± 1
Backe	III	3 ft. (1 m)/day	0.2 mi. (0.3 km)	6 yrs.±	(?)
"Upton"	III	(?)	0.4 mi. (0.6 km) (?)	2 yrs.[+]	(?)

medium, moderate speed; and, Class III: small, steep glaciers that show small displacement yet large relative to their size. Table 3 lists six of the surging glaciers in or near Kluane National Park, the class of glacier and characteristics.

Some glaciers surge only every century or more; others every few decades. The periodicity may vary by several years depending on any one glacier's response to climate, its size and shape, and its response to the dynamic conditions existing within the glacier and at the bottom ice/rock interface. After a surge the cycle makes a fresh start, with snow accumulation building up in the upper zone while the lower zone melts downward and stagnates until the time comes when the critical balance between zones is exceeded and another surge occurs.

Surging glaciers can be recognized by the ice being severely crevassed and broken up into blocks and spires, by sheared margins and truncated *tributary glaciers*, by a lowering in the upper zone of the surface of the main glacier of as much as 400 feet (120 meters), a bulging, overriding, advancing front, and often times by the appearance of large volumes of muddy water produced by melt from friction along the bottom ice-rock interface. These characteristics are unique to surging glaciers and thus easily distinguished from those of normal fast-moving and advancing glaciers.

Glaciers and Climate

Climate may exert either a constructive or a destructive influence on a glacier. In response to a slight lowering of the earth's surface temperature or a slight rise, a glacier will either expand and advance or shrink and retreat.

The scientists who observe and study glaciers

recognize that they grow or diminish as changes occur in precipitation, wind, cloud cover, and energy received from the sun. But they also recognize that the relative significance of weather factors is influenced in turn by a glacier's geographic location and orientation, its dimensions, morphology, and its land-water relationship. Likewise, interplay between meteorological observations is involved and consequently add complexities to understanding the link between climate and glacier fluctuations.

Glaciers are usually in the process of adjusting and readjusting to meteorological conditions, which may vary considerably from year to year and which may in turn cause correspondingly large variations in glacier balance. It is difficult, therefore, to detect long-term climatic trends from a single glacier's annual budget, which is mostly concerned with accumulation and ablation. Yet, by integrating weather conditions over an interval of time equal to decades or even centuries, a glacier's dynamic response to meteorological circumstances will be represented. Thus an averaging of the fluctuations of many glaciers may very well be useful for monitoring climatic trends and for gaining an understanding of a glacier's dynamic response to climate. In time, close monitoring may lead to our ability to turn back to weather records of the past and thereby predict future glacier behavior. This could be of particular importance to those countries where during the past fifty or so years dams and power plants have been built in areas near glaciers that are healthy and active.

Man is now more than ever before the instrument influencing cause and effect on our environment, and glaciers are very sensitive to change. The budget balance and health of a glacier adjust to and reflect its environment. Glacier economics are thus becoming more and more important to man.

Sculpture

As one approaches and travels past Kluane National Park one cannot help but be awed by the magnificence and magnitude of the scenery. The grandeur of alpine sculpture appears everywhere. The sculptors are the glaciers that, using for tools the rock debris embedded in the glacier sole, have gouged out great *U-shaped valleys* and chiseled on the bedrock testimony of a moving glacier's abrasive power. Evidence is imprinted in the form of rounded and polished rock sur-

faces called *glacial polish*, and of *glacial grooves, striations* and *chattermarks*. These features are apparent along the bedrock valley walls and often on rocks and boulders that have been transported down valley by glacier and river action and by *mass wasting*. Some small tributary valleys, long abandoned by glacier ice, can be seen high on the steep walls of the main valleys and accordingly are called *hanging valleys*. During the summer these high valleys are green with alpine vegetation, and over their lips cascade spectacular waterfalls. Other elements in the shaping of mountains and valleys are the rivers and streams, snow, *frost wedging*, and the action of growing plants. Figure 10 illustrates some of the sculpture of a typical glaciated area and fea-

FIGURE 10. *A sketch showing some of the features in the park resulting from glaciation. (After R. Streiff-Becker.)*

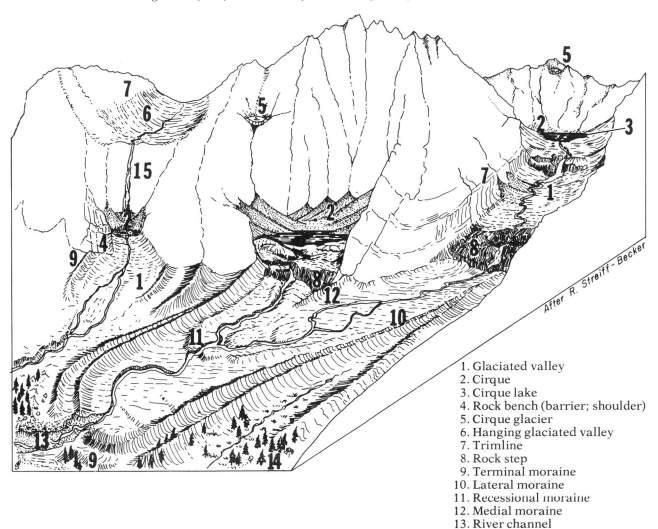

1. Glaciated valley
2. Cirque
3. Cirque lake
4. Rock bench (barrier; shoulder)
5. Cirque glacier
6. Hanging glaciated valley
7. Trimline
8. Rock step
9. Terminal moraine
10. Lateral moraine
11. Recessional moraine
12. Medial moraine
13. River channel
14. Encroaching forest
15. Waterfall

tures seen when driving by or hiking through the valleys and passes of the Kluane Ranges.

In the high, central region of the St. Elias Mountains, the Icefield Ranges provide many spectacular examples of the influence of glaciation on the shaping of the topography. And then one need only view the Kaskawulsh Glacier in its classic U-shaped valley and its vast and hummocky moraines (see photograph on page 16) in order to sense the immense amounts of material that are being moved by ice. Likewise, during the high melt period in late summer, a dipper of water from the Alsek, Slims, or Donjek rivers will appear milky and the surface of the rivers almost viscous with silt and mud — another indication of the rock debris (*rock flour*) that is moved down valley by the ice and discharged into the meltwater streams. With such extremely active and efficient transport, it is small wonder that the glaciers of Kluane National Park have so profoundly influenced the shape of the mountains.

GLOSSARY OF TERMS

Ablation All processes by which snow, firn, or ice is lost from a glacier, principally by melting and evaporation.

Accumulation All processes that add snow or ice to a glacier.

Alpine Referring to any high mountain or range of mountains modified by severe glacial erosion to resemble the European Alps.

Chattermark Small crescent-shaped scars chipped from a bedrock surface by rock fragments carried in the base of a glacier. The points of the crescent generally extend in the direction of ice movement.

Cirque A deep, steep-walled, crescent-shaped, glacier-carved recess high on the side of a mountain and commonly at the head of a valley glacier.

Cirque glacier A small glacier occupying an amphitheatre-like recess high on the side of a mountain, and produced by the erosive activity of ice.

Cirque lake A deep, almost circular lake, occupying a cirque where there was once a cirque glacier.

Climate The sum of all the various weather elements of a region which have prevailed over a long period of time.

Col A deep saddle-shaped pass across a sharp ridge between two sharp mountain peaks.

Compound valley glacier A glacier composed of two or more individual valley glaciers flowing from tributary valleys.

Crevasse A crack, fissure, or rift in a glacier, ice cap or ice sheet caused by movement of the ice over an uneven bed.

Englacial Pertaining to the inside of a glacier. That contained or carried within the body of a glacier.

Firn An aggregate of small grains transitional between snow and glacier ice. Old snow which has existed through at least one summer.

Firn limit The highest level on a glacier to which the snow cover recedes at the end of the melting season. The state of equilibrium between accumulation and ablation.

Firn line The regional snow line on a glacier at any one time during the melting season.

Flow lines A descriptive term pertaining to a glacier's surface appearance which exhibits a continuity of motion.

Frost wedging The roll played by ice in the mechanical dislodgement and disintegration of jointed rock. Ice acting as a wedge.

Glacial grooves A wide furrow carved in bedrock by rock fragments embedded in the bottom ice of a moving glacier.

Glacial polish A smooth, usually curved or rounded surface produced on bedrock by the abrasion of fine debris at the bottom of a moving glacier.

Glacial striation A thin furrow, usually long and oriented in the direction of ice movement, scratched on a bedrock surface by rock fragments embedded in the bottom of a glacier; also seen on boulders and other rock fragments that have been transported by a glacier.

Glaciated valley A U-shaped valley that shows signs of glacial erosion. A valley that has been modified by a glacier.

Glaciation The formation, movement, and recession of glaciers. Also the erosive action of glacier ice.

Glacier A mass of ice originating on land by the accumulation and recrystalization of snow and firn and showing evidence of past or present motion.

Glacieret A very small glacier on a mountain slope or in a cirque.

Glacier ice A consolidated aggregate of recrystalized snow and refrozen meltwater that forms in a glacier.

Glacier surge See *Surge*.

Glacier tongue   The long narrow extension of the lower part of a valley glacier.

Glaciology   The scientific study of all aspects of snow and ice including their physical and dynamic properties. The science that treats quantitatively the whole range of processes associated with all forms of solid existing water.

Hanging glacier valley   A glaciated valley separated by a cliff or very steep slope from the main glacier valley.

Highland glacier   A semi-continuous glacier system covering the highest or central position of a mountainous area and reflecting in part the undulating land surface below.

Horn   A high steep-walled mountain peak shaped like a pyramid by the headward erosion of glaciers.

Ice   The solid state of water; specifically the dense substance formed by the freezing of water or the recrystalization and compaction of fallen snow.

Ice cap   A dome-shaped expanse of snow and ice covering all of the summit area of a mountainous region and spreading outward in all directions. Ice caps are generally accepted as having an area less than 50,000 sq km (19,300 mi²).

Icefall   The part of a glacier that becomes severely crevassed as it flows over a very steep slope on the glacier bed.

Icefield   An extensive mass of land ice covering a mountain region consisting of many interconnected valley and other types of glaciers, covering all but the highest peaks and ridges.

Ice sheet   A very large, thick glacier forming a continuous cover of snow and ice that buries all but the highest mountains and flows outward in all directions. Ice sheets are more than 50,000 sq km (19,300 mi²) in area.

Ice stream   A relatively narrow zone within an ice sheet or ice cap and not constrained by exposed rocks where the flow is more rapid than in adjacent zones. See *Outlet Glacier*.

Intermontane glacier   A glacier formed by the confluence of several valley glaciers and occupying a trough between several mountain ranges or ridges.

Kinematic wave   A disturbance in the normal flow of a glacier that propagates downstream at a velocity greater than the ice velocity.

Liquid flow   The movement of a liquid that is usually of low viscosity.

Massif   A very large topographic and structural feature in a belt of uplifted rock commonly formed of intrusive igneous or metamorphic rock.

Mass wasting   The dislodgement and transfer downslope by gravity of rock and soil material.

Metamorphism   Snow (the sediment) metamorphism is a change of texture and a rearrangement of grains, an evolution beginning with the deposition of snow and ending only when it has ceased to exist, either by ablation or by changing to glacier ice.

Ice (the rock) metamorphism involves the physical change and adjustment imposed by temperature and pressure and further densification of ice grains subjected to deformation.

Mineral   A naturally occurring chemical element or compound formed as a product of inorganic processes and usually having a characteristic form.

Monomineralic   A rock composed of essentially a single mineral, e.g. ice.

Moraine   Rock debris deposited by a glacier along its lateral (side) or terminal (end) parts. The joining of two lateral moraines where two valley glaciers coalesce gives rise to a medial (middle) moraine.

Nunatak   An isolated bedrock peak or ridge that projects above the surface of a glacier and is surrounded by glacier snow and ice.

Outflow glacier   See *Ice Stream*.

Outlet glacier   A glacier issuing from an ice sheet or ice cap through a mountain pass or valley, constrained to a channel or path by exposed rock.

Outwash plain   A broad accumulation of rock fragments, sand and fine materials gently sloping away from a glacier terminus or terminal moraine and deposited by meltwater streams.

Piedmont glacier   The thick expanded terminal portion of a valley glacier which descends from a highland area onto a broad lowland at the base of steep mountain slopes.

Plastic deformation   In glaciology, the movement and deformation of glacier ice that does not involve failure by rupture.

Polar glacier   A glacier whose temperature is below freezing to considerable depth, or throughout its mass, and on which there is no melting even in summer.

Rock bench   A glacier-carved bench (niche) produced on the valley side consisting of more resistant rock than that adjacent to it.

Rock flour   A very fine powder of pulverized rock formed when stone fragments embedded in the bottom ice of a glacier abrade the underlying rock.

Rock step   A steep slope produced by an outcrop of a resistant rock. A ledge in the floor of a glacier valley.

Scree   A layer of broken and angular rock fragments on a steep mountain slope derived from rock cliffs above. See *Talus*.

Snow A form of ice composed of small, white, delicate, often branched or star-shaped hexagonal crystals of frozen water.

Sole The lower part or basal ice of a glacier, often containing rock fragments and dirty in appearance.

Source The highest region or area of origin of a glacier. The high accumulation zone.

Striation See *Glacial Striation*.

Surge The displacement and down-valley movement of glacier ice resulting from very rapid flow.

Talus A heap of fallen rock fragments usually coarse and angular that have accumulated at the base of a slope. See *Scree*.

Temperate glacier A glacier in which the firn and ice at the end of the ablation season are near the melting point. Its temperature is in fact close to 32°F (0°C) throughout except in winter when its upper part freezes to a depth of 6 to 10 ft.

Terminus The lower margin or extremity of a glacier.

Tidewater glacier A glacier which terminates in the sea most often ending with a high ice cliff.

Tongue See *Glacier Tongue*.

Transverse icefield Highland ice which has completely filled the valleys on both sides of a major topographic divide but whose flow extends downslope in opposite directions.

Tributary glacier A glacier that flows into a larger glacier.

U-shaped valley A valley carved by glacial erosion and typified by steep valley walls and a broad, nearly flat valley floor.

Valley glacier A glacier flowing down between the walls of a mountain valley in all or part of its length. A glacier usually originating in a cirque and confined to a single valley, e.g. alpine glacier.

3. CLIMATE: THE SUPREME RULER

Melvin G. Marcus

RESEARCH ACTIVITIES WERE moving at a fast pace at the Kluane Lake base camp of the Arctic Institute's Icefield Ranges Research Project. The late July days were balmy, as temperatures climbed into the 20s Celsius (70s Fahrenheit), and only a few fair-weather clouds occasionally blocked the sun. The scientists were taking advantage of the fine weather and long summer days.

Only 145 kilometers (90 miles) to the southwest and 5,000 meters (16,000 feet) higher up, six field workers were at the same time caught in a blizzard just below the summit of Mount Logan. A full day's travel from the Mount Logan Research Station, they were prepared for such an emergency; they carried 10 days' extra food and fuel. The advantages of good planning and foresight were never better demonstrated. Before

this July storm abated, they were subjected to 175-kilometers (110 miles) per-hour winds, almost a meter (three feet) of snow, and temperatures constantly below −18°C (0°F). Under this barrage of cold blasts, they were pinned down for nine full days.

Such dramatic differences in conditions for work and survival between the project's highest and lowest research sites are common because the most distinctive aspect of climate in mountainous regions is its great variability over short spans of time and distance. Climatic variations are especially marked in the St. Elias Mountains, because within only 200 kilometers (125 miles) they rise from the Pacific shores to more than 6,000 meters (19,000 feet) and then drop to 760 meters (2,500 feet) in the continental interior. In fact, between the lowland and high-mountain extremes, there is a continuous spectrum of microclimates, each reflecting the complex, interrelated influences of altitude, topography, local exposure to sunlight, and regional weather patterns.

Altitude has a major influence on local climate. Changes in altitude are often viewed as climatically proportional to changes in latitude; for example, ascending a mountain slope is comparable to traveling toward the North Pole at sea level. In the St. Elias Mountains, within a 1,500–1,800-meter (5,000–6,000 feet) ascent from the Alaska Highway, one encounters sub-arctic, tundra, and ice cap climates (and associated vegetation). The same climatic transitions at sea level require a poleward journey of hundreds of kilometers. Altitude is an important climatic control, and not only because of its effect on temperature. Decreasing barometric pressure, reduced concentrations of water vapor and carbon dioxide, and increased reception of sunlight are some of the other significantchanges that occur with increases in altitude.

The St. Elias Mountains form the highest coastal mountain range in the world and present a massive barrier between the Pacific Ocean and the continental interior. The effects are striking. The range effectively divides the region into two moisture belts: the marine slopes along which water-laden Pacific air is cooled and deposited; and the semi-arid "rain shadow" zone of the leeward continental slopes. The barrier effect is so strong that the amount of precipitation at 800 meters (2,600 feet) on the marine slopes is at least 12 times that at the same altitude on the continental side; even at 2,000 meters (7,000 feet) the ratio is 3 to 1. The comparative impact of the two precipitation regimes on the behavior of glaciers and the run-off streams is impressive.

The internal arrangement and form of the mountains and valleys play a significant role in determining local climate. For example, the direction in which a slope faces affects temperature, humidity, and water retention at the surface. If one were to walk around a mountain, always holding the same elevation, one would encounter different local climates and corresponding differences in vegetation. This is best seen by comparing a shady north-facing slope with a sunny south-facing slope. The south side would be the drier and warmer of the two environments. Snow would melt earlier in the spring there, and begin to accumulate later in the

autumn, resulting in a longer growing season. On the other hand, warmer temperatures would lead to greater evaporation and transpiration, so that less water would be retained in the soil for plant use. The north slope, in comparison, would retain a late snow pack, would have less evaporation and more soil moisture, and would experience colder temperatures.

The local orientation of mountains and valleys can also be important because the way the terrain is arranged strongly influences wind speed and direction, cold-air drainage, and atmospheric heat exchange. The last named can significantly affect the regimes of glaciers and snowfields.

The factors that have been described—altitude, ocean-continent relationships, topography, terrain orientation, and form—all play significant roles in the generation of the many climates of the St. Elias-Kluane region. Other factors are also important. For example, the development and migration of the high- and low-pressure systems that form over both the Pacific Ocean and the continental interior is basic to the evolution of broad regional climatic patterns. Such factors, however, are best described in terms of the weather that visitors to Kluane National Park might expect to encounter. The following sections describe more fully the weather patterns in two key zones of the region: the easily accessible lowland valleys with their network of rivers and lakes, traversed by the Alaska Highway; and the mountain areas, accessible only to hardy and experienced outdoorsmen and mountaineers.

Lowland Climate

The climate of the lowland areas bordering the St. Elias Mountains on the north and east is typically continental and sub-arctic, although marine influences begin to emerge to the south along the Alsek River. Three weather stations in the Shakwak Valley—Burwash Landing, Kluane, and Haines Junction—provide representative data on temperature and precipitation (Table 4). Records have been maintained at these stations for only a few years. They typify the weather but do not provide an official climatic norm, which ordinarily requires at least 30 years of records.

The sub-arctic climatic regime shown by the

TABLE 4 / *Mean Monthly Temperature and Precipitation for Lowland Stations, Kluane National Park*

Station	Elevation (meters)		Jan.	Feb.	Mar.	April	May	June	July	Aug.	Sept.	Oct.	Nov.	Dec.	Year
Burwash	801	T(°C)	−27.7	−18.8	−12.5	−2.7	4.8	10.2	12.2	9.9	4.6	−3.6	−14.8	−21.7	−5.0
Landing		P(mm)	19	7	13	18	26	43	74	36	29	18	19	14	316
Kluane	786	T(°C)	−25.6	−13.7	−13.3	−2.3	4.6	9.1	11.8	9.9	5.8	−2.1	−11.7	−19.3	−3.9
		P(mm)	5	9	2	8	15	46	38	32	9	16	21	17	218
Haines	599	T(°C)	−26.27	−15.9	−10.2	−0.8	5.6	16.6	12.6	16.3	5.9	−1.6	−13.0	−20.6	−3.9
Junction		P(mm)	22	22	6	6	30	28	41	29	34	35	24	22	299

data from these three stations is one of extreme seasonal differences. A range of about 40°C (70°F) exists between the coldest and warmest months, as shown in Table 4. In fact, stations such as those at Snag and Dawson, which lie not far to the north of the St. Elias Mountains, have recorded the coldest temperatures in North America. That area is sometimes referred to as the continent's "cold pole," yet summer temperatures in the low 30s Celsius (90s Fahrenheit) have occurred there. Summer temperatures in the sub-arctic climate generally rise above 10°C (50°F) for one to three months, which provides sufficient heat for growth of the boreal forest. Mean monthly temperatures fall above and below freezing in roughly equal proportions. The daily temperature range does not, however, vary as greatly as the seasonal range, because of long winter nights and long summer days, which reduce fluctuations during the 24-hour period.

The sub-arctic lowlands adjacent to the St. Elias Mountains are classified as semi-arid. As Table 4 shows, the annual rainfall at the three stations ranges between 215 and 360 millimeters (8.5 and 12.5 inches). In lower latitudes, such small amounts of precipitation would result in desert landscapes and sparse vegetation. In the sub-arctic, very little water is lost to evaporation and transpiration, and almost all of the moisture that falls to the ground is therefore potentially available for use by plants. Furthermore, between six and eight months' precipitation is stored in snow and ice and is available to soil and plants later, during the growing season. As a general rule, the period of maximum precipitation occurs during the summer months, and the minimum during deepest winter. Figure 11 indicates the precipitation and temperature regimes at Burwash Landing, the wettest of the regional stations. The seasonal flow of weather throughout these sub-arctic lowlands is described next.

Spring and Summer

In early spring, daytime temperatures rise above freezing and the snow cover begins to disappear, first in the open stands of spruce and intervening muskeg flats with their darker, heat-absorbing surfaces. Here the snow absorbs and stores more and more heat as the sun remains above the horizon for longer periods. This heat, in turn, is conducted and reradiated back into the melting snow packs. The highly reflective ice cover on the ponds and lakes resists the solar heat. The result is a pattern of white circles and ovals upon a brown to dark green land.

The daytime air warms considerably by May and June, but temperatures still occasionally

FIGURE 11. *Mean monthly temperature and precipitation, Burwash Landing, Yukon.*

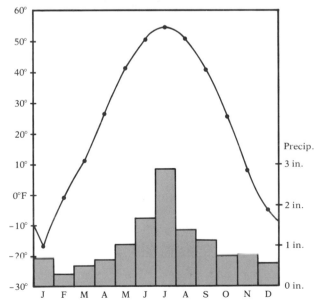

Towering series of lenticular clouds near Kluane Lake, August 1971. (Walter Wood)

drop below freezing at night. As spring advances toward the June 22 solstice, summer indicators begin to emerge. With the sun above the horizon for 16 to 20 hours a day (depending upon location and local horizons), the last of the lake ice disappears. The ice cover on Kluane Lake usually breaks up and moves northward during the first two weeks of June. Its overnight disappearance from the southern part of the lake is almost magical. Also, with longer, warmer days, the insect world awakens for the summer's work; the earlier appearance of a few flies and mosquitoes seems desultory in retrospect. Nights

seldom have frost now, and vegetation begins to bud and bloom.

Throughout this period the weather is generally clear along the interior valleys. Although clouds often trail eastward from the St. Elias Mountains, remnants of the moist Pacific air flow dissipate as the air warms along the continental slopes. Occasionally, however, storm systems will slide out of the northwest, following the interior valleys and bringing cool, moist air inland from the Bering Sea or Arctic Ocean. Typically, low clouds and intermittent rainfall last for one or two days. Only infrequently is the visiting air mass cold enough to result in snowfall. Side effects of these storms are the suspension of most light aircraft travel and the transformation of the Alaska Highway from dusty hardpan to slick gumbo.

As the weather warms into summer, puffy, fair-weather cumulus clouds begin to dot the skyscape. Later in the season these will build frequently into towering cumulo-nimbus systems that will bring turbulent winds and occasional thunder showers to the area. These showers are one reason why the annual maximum precipitation occurs in summer. Thunder and lightning are also associated with the cumulo-nimbus clouds, but mostly in the storms that develop east of the lowland valleys. Another source of summer moisture is maritime air derived from the "Aleutian Low," a pressure system that develops in the North Pacific Ocean. This system occasionally migrates eastward into the St. Elias area from its source region, spinning inland through lower access troughs such as the Alsek River valley and the White and Chilkat passes.

Among the striking weather features in the area are the high, lenticular (double-lens-shaped) clouds that develop to the lee side of the St. Elias Mountains. Often as many as six to 10 layers thick, they stand out in profile like arched stacks of pancakes against the sky dome. These clouds, which are associated with steep pressure gradients, tell a story of violent winds and tremendous horizontal shearing forces. Concurrently, strong and gusty winds flow down-slope on the continental side of the mountains, producing downdrafts that make it almost impossible for light planes to penetrate the alpine interior. These winds, sometimes referred to as Chinooks, bring relatively warm, dry air to the lower valleys, thus increasing evaporation throughout the region. If the winds persist for long periods, as they did in the spring and early summer of 1970, surface water and soil moisture supplies suffer serious depletions, causing damage to plant and animal communities.

Dust storms are one result of the summer climate in the lowland valleys. Indeed, large areas in the interior lowlands are mantled by fine loess dust that was transported to its present location by wind over the last several thousand years. In the Shakwak Valley, most of these sediments were derived from the dried, silty flood plains of the Duke, Donjek, and Slims

river valleys. Not as many dust storms occur today, although the Slims River valley still generates a number each summer. These storms usually occur after the late spring run-off has subsided and when there has been no precipitation for a week or more. Such conditions permit the surface of the Slims River outwash and delta to dry out, and the sediment particles then become available to wind erosion.

Small dust storms are apt to occur in the afternoon, almost any day when the surface is dry, borne by strong down-glacier wind that is funneled from the Kaskawulsh Glacier through the narrow corridor of the Slims River valley. When a strong Chinook is blowing as well, the dust storms sometimes produce zero visibility and extend to a considerable altitude along the southern shores of Kluane Lake. Miniature dust storms are caused almost every afternoon by vehicle traffic crossing the Slims delta area on the Alaska Highway. Down-valley winds pick up the disturbed road dust and carry it across the southwestern corner of the lake.

Autumn and Winter
Autumn comes with a rush in the Yukon subarctic. Occasional frosts are experienced by late August, and subfreezing temperatures occur on more than half the days in September. From the beginning of October until mid-May only a few days pass without the temperature dropping to the freezing point or below. Ponds and small lakes freeze quickly, and even Kluane Lake is completely covered by ice by mid-October or early November.

Autumn and winter are less cloudy than spring and summer. The climate is dominated by a pattern of calm to light winds and cold, clear days and nights—with daylight hours diminishing to only a few by December 21. At Kluane Station, for example, the winter solstice is characterized by twilight only. Because of topographic barriers, the sun never rises above the horizon.

Temperatures continue to drop as the nighttime hours lengthen, eventually down to the −40s Celsius (−40s Fahrenheit). Concurrently, the earth radiates its heat into the higher atmosphere, and as the surface terrain is cooled in this manner it causes the air immediately above it to cool also. This process is amplified through fall and winter, and cold air draining down from the glacierized mountains adds to the cooling effect.

The result is a pond of extremely cold air, which stagnates and becomes almost immovable.

This phenomenon is known as a temperature inversion because normal temperature-altitude relationships have been reversed. Instead of becoming cooler with altitude, the air becomes warmer. Such inversion layers sometimes achieve a thickness of more than 300 meters (1,000 feet) in winter. The temperature is actually warmer on the summits of 2,500-meter (8,000-foot) peaks than it is in the low-lying valley bottoms. The stability and persistence of these cold-air inversions is enhanced by the very cold and intense Mackenzie high-pressure system, which dominates northwestern Canada's climate for most of the winter.

Occasional storms bring snowfalls to the frozen sub-arctic landscape, but these prevail for only a few days each month. The total amount of snow that falls in the sub-arctic winter is remarkably small; an entire winter's production will typically range from 460 to 1,200 millimeters (18 to 48 inches) of dry snow, which translates to only about 46 to 120 millimeters (1.8 to 4.8 inches) of liquid water equivalent. Winter is indeed a dry season for these interior valleys. Despite light snowfalls, however, a dominant feature of the winter landscape is the white mantle of snow. Once fallen, the snow is stored in the sub-arctic deep-freeze until spring. Only wind, which blows the snow about and builds drifts, and internal compaction are likely to alter the appearance of the snow pack.

Thus, in the lowland valleys, the crisp, clear winter air and the long nights are only rarely interrupted by snowfall, blowing snow, high winds, or low visibility. When this does happen, the sub-arctic is to both man and beast one of the most inhospitable environments on the face of the earth.

Mountain Climates

Mountain climates are among the most complex in the world, as already indicated, because dramatic changes occur over both short horizontal and vertical distances. Except in the heavily populated alpine areas of Europe, however, the records of these variations are poor. Knowledge of the processes that create localized mountain climates is only just developing. In the St. Elias

Mountains, research has been directed at mountain climates, particularly during the summer, and this has produced quite a remarkable fund of information.

A network of summer weather stations was maintained from 1963 to 1971 within and adjacent to the St. Elias Mountains, as part of the Arctic Institute's Icefield Ranges Research Project and in cooperation with the Canadian Meteorological Service. These weather stations — some of which were manned and some of which were automatic — made it possible to trace the outline of a transmountain profile from the moist Pacific slopes, across the glacier-covered peaks and passes, to the semi-arid continental interior. Data collected at the manned stations, which are the focus of the following descriptions, typically included recordings or direct observations of maximum and minimum temperatures, precipitation, wind speed and direction, relative humidity and dewpoint, cloud cover and cloud type, visibility, and incoming solar radiation.

Kluane Lake Station was the anchor of the network on the continental side of the mountains. At an elevation of 786 meters (2,580 feet), it was at the southern end of Kluane Lake in the broad Shakwak Valley. Discontinuous spruce forests characterize the surroundings, changing to alpine meadows and tundra where the Kluane Ranges rise a short distance to the south and west.

Four stations were situated in the glacierized heart of the Icefield Ranges. Kaskawulsh Station (1,768 meters — 5,000 feet) stood on a medial moraine formed by the north and central arms of the Kaskawulsh Glacier. The glacier system is 6.5 kilometers (four miles) wide there and deeply entrenched. Surrounding peaks and ridges rise 1,200-1,500 meters (4,000-5,000 feet) above the glacier surface; smaller tributaries and hanging glaciers cascade steeply down to the main stream.

Divide Station was located at 2,652 meters (8,700 feet) on the hydrological divide between the Kaskawulsh and Hubbard glacier systems. The surrounding area is a broad upland of perennial snow and glacier ice. Only a few nunataks (rock islands) interrupt this gently undulating snowscape.

Seward Station (1,859 meters — 6,100 feet) had the greatest marine exposure in the network. Situated on a small nunatak near the eastern margin of the upper Seward Glacier, it overlooked a perennially snow-covered glacier basin some 1,300 square kilometers (470 square miles) in area. Although slopes are slight within the basin, surrounding peaks provide some of the most spectacular relief in the world. From the Seward Glacier surface (1,500-1,800 meters — 5,000-6,000 feet) rise such peaks as Mount Logan (5,951 meters — 19,525 feet), Mount St. Elias (5,489 meters — 18,008 feet), King Peak (5,173 meters — 16,970 feet), and Mount Vancouver (4,875 meters — 15,860 feet).

Mount Logan Station, which operated from 1968 to 1970, was the most unusual station in the network. At 5,365 meters (17,600 feet), it was the highest weather station ever operated in

North America. Located near the western end of Mount Logan's extensive and glacier-covered summit plateau, it provided data for an elevation at which there is only half as much air (and pressure) as at sea level.

The Rusty Glacier Station was less directly associated with the transmountain profile, but it was an important element in the observational network. Located at 2,165 meters (7,100 feet) on the lower end of a small interior glacier, it was generally representative of alpine environments ringing the Donjek River watershed. Two other stations that played an important part in the research program — Chitistone Pass in the Wrangell Mountains, Alaska, and Gladstone, a mountain site in the Ruby Range northeast of

Rusty Glacier, with cluster of tents of research camp (white dots), opposite the snout of advancing Backe Glacier. (Walter Wood)

Kluane Lake—are not presented in Table 5 because they fall well beyond the boundaries of Kluane National Park.

Only two seasons can be realistically identified for the high mountains: winter, when temperatures are below freezing, and summer, when temperatures are above freezing. The lengths of the two seasons vary with the altitude; that is, higher altitudes experience shorter summers. The vertical position of the freezing level determines how much summer or winter is experienced by any area. The freezing level is never static, but migrates vertically in both seasonal and daily patterns. In the St. Elias Mountains, its usual position is about 2,400 meters (8,000 feet) in midsummer. For six to seven months, however, freezing temperatures extend to the lowest valley locations.

Above-freezing summer temperatures prevail for about five months at 750 meters (2,500 feet) in the lowland valleys, for about three months at 1,350 meters (4,500 feet), and for one and one-half to two months at 1,800 meters (6,000 feet). At 2,400 meters (8,000 feet), temperatures above freezing will occur only on a few days, and above 3,000 meters (10,000 feet) it is unlikely that any mean daily temperature will ever exceed the

freezing point, which means that the higher interior zones of the St. Elias Mountains experience perpetual winter.

With these data it is possible to define roughly the climatic zones along the continental slopes. The sub-arctic climate zone extends to about 1,200 meters (4,000 feet), which is 450 meters meters (1,500 feet) above the valley bottoms. This altitude approximates the tree line for white spruce and willow shrubs. Above this, alpine meadows and tundra vegetation characterize a tundra-type climate to an upper limit of about 2,100 meters (7,000 feet). Monthly mean temperatures in this zone remain above freezing for one to three months, but do not exceed 10°C (50°F). An icecap-type climate occurs in the higher areas, which experience continuous winter conditions.

The pattern of July temperatures across the St. Elias Mountains, shown in Table 5, indicates that one weather station was in the sub-arctic zone (Kluane Lake), three were in the tundra zone (Kaskawulsh, Seward, and Rusty), and two fell within the icecap climatic region (Divide and Logan). Although July cloudiness was about the same at all locations, precipitation and relative humidity varied across the mountains.

Table 5 / *Mean July Weather at Research Stations in the St. Elias-Kluane Mountains*

Station	Elevation (meter)	Days of Record	Temperature (°C) Mean	Mean maximum	Mean minimum	Extreme maximum	Extreme minimum
Kluane Lake	786	279	11.7	16.7	6.1	25.6	−1.1
Kaskawulsh	1,768	85	4.4	7.2	3.3	14.4	−2.2
Divide	2,652	217	−1.1	3.3	−6.1	12.8	−16.1
Mount Logan	5,365	84	−18.3	−12.2	−23.9	−3.3	−34.4
Seward	1,859	49	2.2	5.0	−1.7	15.6	−4.4
Rusty	2,165	56	2.8	6.1	1.1	9.4	−3.9

Station	Precipitation (minimum)	Cloudiness (tenths— sky dome)	Relative Humidity (percent)	Mean Solar Radiation (langleys)
Kluane Lake	43	6	69	472
Kaskawulsh	15	6	78	514
Divide	103	7	86	620
Mount Logan	52	6	80	742
Seward	25	7	89	520
Rusty	146	7	76	443

The effect of altitude was also apparent in the July statistics for solar radiation. Table 5 shows that stations at low elevations receive less radiation from the sun than do the higher stations. This is because the thicker clouds and deeper atmosphere over Kluane Lake provide a more effective sunlight filter than is available at higher elevations. For example, filtering by the atmosphere over Mount Logan was so weak that 80 percent of the sun's incoming energy reached the station; by comparison, Kluane Lake received only 50 percent. It is one of nature's ironies that the massive inputs of solar heat at higher altitudes in the St. Elias Mountains have little effect on the landscape or the local climate; some 90 percent of the incoming rays are reflected by snow and returned to space. Pity the high-altitude traveler who is sunburned not only by the solar lamp above but also by rays from the ground below!

Because of inaccessibility and high costs, weather stations have not been operated in the interior of the St. Elias Mountains during the winter. Many meteorological events that have occurred in the winter, however, can be reconstructed. Pits are dug through the snow down to the previous year's summer surface. The exposed pit walls provide a chronological record of the previous winter's precipitation. Total water content can be determined by combining measurements of density and depth that have been made along this profile.

In this manner the dramatic differences in precipitation between marine and continental slopes were established. In May 1965, for example, we measured more than 5,800 millimeters (19 feet) of snow accumulation on the marine slope, which is equivalent to about 2,000 millimeters (6.5 feet) of liquid water. At the same altitude (1,764 meters — 5,788 feet) on the continental side, the winter's snowfall was only 1,645 millimeters (5.4 feet), with a liquid equivalent of 640 millimeters (2.1 feet). Precipitation eventually begins to decrease at higher elevations on the marine slope, but amounts in excess of one meter (three feet) of water equivalent occur all the way to 5,500 meters (18,000 feet) on the Mount Logan summit plateau. Furthermore, all this snowfall is locked into glacier nourishment because of constant subfreezing temperatures. It is easy to see why the marine slope glaciers have a high potential for growth and are able, in many cases, to flow all the way to the sea.

Even more details of winter climate may be extracted from the snow-pack record, but these require careful analysis of individual snow crystals, temperature profiles, and snow-pack stratification. Individual storms, wind periods, and occasional thaws can often be identified by these techniques. With the help of chemical analysis it is even possible to determine the region from which various storms and snowfalls came, but the details of winter climate are perhaps not important to a general description. It is sufficient to say that winter in the high St. Elias is cold, snowy, and, in higher elevations, without end.

Other complex interacting natural forces characterize this mountain region and produce many fascinating meteorological phenomena. Among these are the near-continuous Kaskawulsh Glacier winds, and the upper-level storm systems that strike from the Pacific and cause severe operational problems on Mount Logan and the other high peaks; blizzards can reduce visibility to zero and travelers become isolated in a world of white. Another phenomenon is the "white-out," perhaps the most frustrating condition for humans to handle. White-outs most commonly occur where there are overcast skies, diffuse illumination, and uniform snow cover. Depth perception is lost and it is difficult to navigate or walk over uneven ground; it is especially difficult to land an aircraft during a white-out. Ice fogs, too, cause visibility hazards. This condition can occur when water vapor is released into very cold air, even when the air is clear and calm.

This mountain region is among the world's most awesome and inspiring. Its glacierized and glaciated environment dazzles us with a multitude of landscapes. And behind each of these landscapes stands a climate — for it is the hot and cold and wet and dry of the atmosphere that ultimately shape the land, build and destroy the glaciers, bring water to lakes and rivers, and set the limits for survival of animals and plants. Climate everywhere is dynamic, complex, and continuously changing — and particularly in the St. Elias Mountains. Year-to-year and even day-to-day variations are amazing. If the climate of these mountains provides pleasure and comfort today, tomorrow it may bring pain and disaster to the unwary. In Kluane National Park it is wise to expect the unexpected.

Part Two
THE LIVING THINGS

Dall sheep ewe and her yearlings.
(Stephen Krasemann)

INTRODUCTION

IMAGINE FOR A moment a wilderness land without wildlife — no sheep grazing in the high grassy bowls, no morning chorus of bird song, no trout snapping at mayflies as dusk shrouds a crystal lake. And no mice scurrying through your food pack.

But that cannot be; wildlife is a product of the land; the two are inseparable. Rock minerals become soil nutrients. Soil nutrients make plants. Plants feed grazing animals. Grazers feed carnivores. And all living things die and return their nutrients to the soil, to be used again. The sun's energy fuels the system — solar explosions convert hydrogen into helium and in so doing release light energy. A very small part of the light converts water and carbon dioxide in the presence of chlorophyl into complex sugar molecules. In these molecules the remaining light energy is converted and locked up as potential chemical energy, to be released by the metabolic processes of plants, or used by animals or organisms of decay. Animals run, fly, swim with that energy, converting it eventually into heat, which dissipates into the environment and is gone. Energy flows only one way.

Plant and animal life offer only a short excursion for soil nutrients and solar energy. But that excursion, of which we are a part, is full of wonder, compounded by the mysteries of animal intelligence, of sensing the environment, of complex social behavior, of emotions — for all animals share all of these in varying degrees. Accompanying these higher levels of complexity in animals are the vital pathways and exacting requirements for life: access to just the right kinds of spawning areas, nesting habitats, denning or calving grounds; sufficient food, be it plant or animal; and environments in which population densities can be adjusted, both naturally, through direct mortality—disease, predation, periodic starvation, harsh weather—and in more subtle ways, through socially induced restraints upon breeding, genetic fluctuations in population aggression or vitality, and the physiological effects of overcrowding. All are part of the natural order.

The Kluane Ranges are rich in things that grow, run, fly, and swim. But these are part of the land only as long as we keep the land whole and do not violate their environmental needs or sever any vital pathways. With that care, the fragile flora and wildlife of the Kluane Ranges will always remain.

4. ICE-AGE MAMMALS, GLACIERS, AND MAN

Valerius Geist

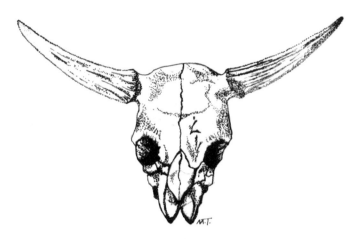

WE LIVE TODAY in a relatively warm intergla-
cial period, punctuated periodically by
short cold periods characterized by glacial
advances. The continental glaciers that once
covered the greater part of North America and
large areas of Europe and Asia have either
retreated to their origins or vanished altogether.

Continental glaciers of the sort we know to
have existed conjure up a picture of bleak desolation, of cold, snow, ice, and blizzards, of a
landscape alien to life. Yet recent discoveries
indicate that, far from being desolate and life-
less, the periglacial environments (areas
marginal to glaciers) were apparently regions of
great biological productivity, filled with life
forms so varied that they may have surpassed
the mammalian diversity of Africa. This biological richness attracted not one but two separate

waves of humans into the periglacial zones, first
the biologically highly specialized Neanderthal
man, and later, the more culturally specialized
late Paleolithic people, our ancestors.

For insights into life in regions near glaciers
we need not rely only on archaeological and
paleontological reconstructions. We can go
directly to some of the large St. Elias glaciers
and observe what is happening there today.
They show that the environments near large
glaciers are not hostile to life, and give us a clear
view of the same processes that once ruled
supreme at the edge of continental glaciers. In
the St. Elias Mountains, ice masses some 31,000
square kilometers (12,000 square miles) in
extent are located at a latitude sufficiently low
that they retain significant features of southern
periglacial environments.

On a late summer's day, hike along the big Lowell Glacier. You will find yourself hip deep in lush sub-alpine vegetation. You will see dense alder thickets and the orange berry clusters of the small mountain ash. You will inhale the scent of angelica and see the poisonous baneberry glow in the shade of the alders. Golden-crowned sparrows will chirp in willow bushes only a few meters away from the ever-rumbling glacier with its coat of rock debris and mud, its yawning blue cracks, its ridges and hollows, its gurgling waters and dripping ice caverns, and its colonizing herbs and grasses clinging to the soil that has collected in hollows in the ice.

Above the glacier, a band of mountain goats moves between ribbons of alder thickets, crossing the many steep avalanche gorges. Avalanches feed this glacier and tumble rock onto its craggy surface. On the glacier's rock rubble, gravel, and mud, you will find the tracks of mountain goats, and on its terminal moraine tracks of moose, wolf, and grizzly and black bear. Streamers of white goat wool wave in the breeze from branches of dwarf birch and shrubby cinquefoil that are rooted securely in the lateral moraine at the glacier's edge. Beyond the moraine, in the small, rich sedge meadows and willow flats, in the meadows of sub-alpine vegetation, and in the lower reaches of the avalanche gorges, you may see massive black bull moose with spreading antlers gorging themselves on willow leaves, sedges, fireweeds, and valerian, fattening up for the rut to come at the end of Indian summer. If you walk down the moraine to the end of the glacier, you may see a grizzly on a glacial outwash, foraging for soapberries that grow here in abundance or, on the way there, you may panic a black bear from a willow thicket nearby and watch him depart into the ever-present alders.

This is but one set of sights, for the glacial termini vary. One of the most astounding of these is the massive terminus of the Klutlan Glacier, the widest glacial terminus of continental Canada. Some 1,220 years ago a volcanic

Terminus of Klutlan Glacier. Directly below trees and shrub mat is ice. Foreground shows volcanic ash. (Valerius Geist)

Mammoth

Caribou have pounded deep trails along the Klutlan Glacier and its terminus, evidence of their regular movement deep along the glacier tongue to the snowfields beyond. The wealth of signs of large mammals in summer and their sighting in winter tells us how favorable glacier edges can be to life, for the large mammals are at the highest trophic level, the one most sensitive to the underlying ecosystem and the one most easily destroyed. There may be no other place on earth where large mammals live on a glacier as they do today on the Klutlan Glacier's terminus.

Though continental glaciers have retreated or vanished, the archaeological and paleontological record reveals their importance in shaping the life of the northern hemisphere. The successive advances of continental glaciers coincided with the appearance of some of the largest mammals ever to arise in the last 70 million years. The little ice ages of the Villafranchian, beginning probably some 4 million years ago, had already produced a multitude of giants—lions the size of oxen, cheetahs twice as large as those of today, hyenas and hunting dogs to dwarf modern descendants, a great variety of monstrous huge-antlered deer, and caprids, and even the largest giant among primates, *Gigantopithecus*. In the major ice ages that began some 1.8 million years ago, huge shaggy elephants, rhinoceroses, and bison emerged, as well as new waves of large-antlered giant deer and caprids, the most remarkable of the large-horned deer being the Irish elk and our moose.

eruption covered the terminus with a blanket of white volcanic ash. Today this layer has been eroded and lies unevenly distributed, but it appears to average more than half a meter in thickness over a wide expanse of the glacier. Vegetation has not only found a footing here but has developed into forests of white spruce and poplar, into alder thickets and wide flats covered by willows and dwarf birch. Here are moose, wintering right on the glacier. We find their browse marks, shed antlers, droppings, and tracks. We find the tracks of caribou and even skeletal remains of sheep. We find wolf tracks and flocks of ptarmigan—while but a few feet below is the blue ice of the glacier, and glacial water rushes past us over a stream bed on the ice, paved with cobbles, sand, and silt. The stream bed will eventually be an esker.

Mastodon

A variety of large carnivores followed, such as the cave bear, the cave lion, the cave hyena, the saber-toothed and scimitar cats, the dire wolf, and the large short-faced bear. We forget that we still have some of these giants, the like of which never walked the earth before the ice ages—the moose, the caribou, the wapiti, the big-horned sheep, and the ibex, as well as the grizzly, coastal brown, and polar bears. Extinct are curiosities such as a beaver the size of a bear, the many edentates (animals having few or no teeth) of elephantine proportions such as the ground sloth and the armored glyptodont, a short-faced carnivorous bear that was even larger than the grizzly, a great diversity of horses both small and large, and, of course, an offshoot of our own species, the peculiar, cold-adapted Neanderthal man. Some 29 species of large mammals and 34 species of small mammals once dwelled in the Alaska *refugium*, bordered in the south by glaciers from the St. Elias Mountains. Even today, these mountains harbor fourteen species of large mammals, a diversity not found anywhere else north of the 60th parallel, and in very few regions south of it.

Camel

Man himself came forth during the ice ages, repeating in his pattern of evolution what other mammalian lineages had done before. Such mammalian lineages arose from small tropical-forest-adapted forms and radiated from those forests into ever drier and colder habitats, increasing in body size and undergoing social adaptations—to culminate as the grotesque creatures of their respective lineages in the periglacial environments. These ice-age giants were characterized not only by large bodies, often by large antlers, horns, or tusks, and sometimes by behavior displaying sophisticated means of aggression and dominance, but also by brains that were large in comparison with those of pre-Pleistocene mammals.

Among some 163 species of primates, man is probably the third largest. Moreover, during the late Paleolithic, beginning some 40,000 years ago, the body and brain of our ancestors were, on average, considerably larger than those of present-day man. The late Paleolithic people, who are ancestral to us, had brains about 20 percent larger than ours.

We are beginning to understand some of the reasons for the evolutionary turmoil that characterized the ice ages. We can explain, for example, why on the oceanic side of the St. Elias Mountains in the vicinity of huge piedmont glaciers the brown bear reaches both gigantic dimensions and high population density. Near glaciers, bears have often reached such dimensions—though they have not always done so, as illustrated by the small grizzly bear of the dry lee side of the St. Elias Mountains. We can understand why some of the densest sheep populations on this continent roam deep into the ice fields on the continental side of these mountains.

In essence, some of the periglacial environments in low latitudes consist of "pulse-stabilized," highly productive ecosystems, particularly loess steppe (grassland growing on loess deposits) and sedge meadows. These exist particularly on the lee side of big glaciers, which weather systems cross after depositing their loads of moisture on the center of the glacier. They are subjected annually to pulses of rock dust and water liberated by the glacier. The glacier acts as a gigantic rock-grinding mill that scrapes rock dust off bedrock or engulfs rocks and grinds them in its interior, changing the rock dust into highly fertile silt. The silt is flushed out of the glacier by meltwater; the bigger the glacier, the more water and silt it spills out, and the more fertile is the silt since it is composed of the dust of many types of rock. The glacier acts essentially as a big disturber which, by means of annual floods and silt, sets the climax vegetation back to an earlier, immature, and far more productive stage.

When the flood waters subside in summer, the silt is left high on the once-submerged flood

Periglacial upland tundra at the foot of Mount Hoge. (John Theberge)

Four seasons of tundra.
BELOW LEFT: Winter (Chilkat Pass) (15).
BELOW RIGHT: Spring (Outpost Mountain) (16).
BOTTOM LEFT: Summer (Amphitheatre Mountain) (17).
BOTTOM RIGHT: Fall (18).

Four lowland environments.
TOP LEFT: Open spruce forest near Vulcan Creek (19).
MIDDLE LEFT: Alder Creek marsh (20).
BOTTOM LEFT: Floodplain of Quill Creek South (21).
ABOVE: Prairie openings east of Kluane Lake (22).

ABOVE AND TOP RIGHT: Adapting to windy conditions of arctic-alpine tundra with low-growth forms are *Dryas octopetala* (23), *Syntheris borealis* (24), and *Gentiana prostrata* (25).
LOWER RIGHT: Flexible stems resist strong wind. Monkshood or *Aconitum delphinifolium* (26); shooting star or *Dodecatheon frigidum* (27).

TOP: A mat-like growth form creates a favorable microclimate to avoid wind dessication. Moss campion or *Silene acaulis* (28) and hawk's beard or *Crepis nana* (29). MIDDLE: Pubescence reduces water loss. *Polemonium boreale* (30) and pasqueflower or *Pulsatilla patens* (31). ABOVE: Colonizer of gravel—*Dryas Drummondi* (32). TOP RIGHT: Colonizer of rock crevices—*Saxifraga oppositifolia* (33). LOWER RIGHT: Wildflower garden. *Arnica alpina* (yellow), *Hedysarum alpinum* (magenta), *Polemonium boreale* (blue) (34).

Tundra colors.
LEFT: *Vaccinium vitis-idaea* (35).
TOP: *Arctostaphylos alpina* (36).
ABOVE: *Xanthoria elegans* (37).

TOP LEFT: Willow ptarmigan (38).
LOWER LEFT: White-tailed ptarmigan (39).
ABOVE: Rock ptarmigan (40).
RIGHT: Ruffed grouse (41).
UPPER FAR RIGHT: Blue grouse (42).
LOWER FAR RIGHT: Sharp-tailed grouse (43).

Wandering tattler on its nest (44).

Horned grebes (45).

plains; it is dried by the sun and wind and is soon picked up by the gales that sweep down the glacier, regularly creating spectacular dust (loess) storms. These are experienced only on the dry lee side of glaciers. The silt is redeposited again and again by wind and water, moving ever farther from the glacier's margin. Each year a new pulse of silt is spewed out by the glacier and deposited on the silt of former years, much as the Nile deposits a new load of silt each year in its delta. Thus the glacier creates a pulse-stabilized ecosystem on its margins; if the pulses of water and silt were to be withheld, the productive plant communities would quickly revert to less productive tundra or boreal forest.

Thus, the secret of the great productivity of the pulse-stabilized loess steppes and sedge meadows in the periglacial zones lies in the rich fertile silt and loess, in the availability of water, and also in the sunny climate and the strong winds that prevail on the lee side of glaciers. These factors together create diverse plant communities with sharply defined borders.

The productivity of land close to glaciers is well illustrated by the information that was obtained at the former agricultural station at Haines Juncion, at kilometer 1,640 on the Alaska Highway. The station lay at the foot of the St. Elias Mountains. Despite a short summer it was possible to grow crops of oats and barley there equaling the best in Alberta. Vegetable gardening was uncertain due to the likelihood of summer frosts, but crops, particularly root crops, were still quite good. Beef cattle grazed there on native grasslands and were able to wean calves, some 250 kilograms (550 pounds) in weight, a surprisingly good performance.

The diverse assemblage of mammals in the periglacial environments of the various old glacial *refugia* is, in good measure, accounted for by the diverse assemblage of discrete plant communities. Archaeologists and paleontologists have long puzzled over the occurrences, at the same sites and strata, of bones of both tropical steppe animals and typical tundra animals. Thus, in Eurasia, the bones of jerboas—small jumping steppe rodents—have been found together with the bones of snow lemmings; the bones of saiga antelopes, horses, and steppe marmots have been found together with those of musk oxen, reindeer, and arctic foxes. Today, in Eurasia, these steppe and tundra creatures occur thousands of miles apart, the former in the

semi-deserts of central Asia, the latter in the arctic zones. Yet the question of how steppe and tundra animals occurred together in the past has a simple answer, as elementary ecological reconstruction shows: at the glacier's margin during continental glaciations a mosaic of tundra and loess steppe girdled the glacier. Such a mosaic still exists in the St. Elias region. The tundra is found on the upper elevations, on north-facing slopes, and the loess steppe is found in the warmer, drier valleys, particularly some distance from the glacier.

The bones of typical warm-climate creatures are also sometimes found mixed with those of tundra and steppe creatures. In some European digs the bones of aurochs, wild boar, red deer, and roe deer have been discovered together with those of cold-adapted mammals, and this indicates the presence of temperate forests close to tundra and cold steppe. This appears to be an incredible combination, but appearance can be deceptive. The loess beds were cut deeply by rivers, forming canyons which, in sun-exposed areas, protected from the cold glacial winds, held temperature inversions of warm air that rose along the river valleys from warm lowlands, permitting a deep intrusion locally, into the periglacial zones, of warmth-loving plants and animals.

Saiga antelope

Saber-toothed tiger

The great diversity of large carnivores such as brown bears, short-faced bears, lions, dire wolves, and saber-toothed cats may be explained by the diversity and abundance of large grazers. The carnivores largely vanished with the extinction of the large herbivores, although some, such as the scimitar cats and saber-toothed cats, may have vanished due to direct competition with man.

Another factor helping to support populations of large animals, in addition to the diversity of habitats and the high productivity of the fertile, perpetually immature periglacial ecosystem, was the abundance of mineral licks. Mineral licks characteristically form and are readily available at the glacier's edge, on the terminal moraine in shallow mineral-rich clay pans. Of greatest importance here is the ready availability of sulphate salts, such as magnesium or calcium sulphates. Only recently has it been discovered that ungulates can ingest inorganic sulphates, form sulphur-bearing amino acids within their digestive tracts, and absorb these directly into their bloodstreams. Therefore they are not dependent on organic sources, that is, on their forage, for these crucial structural amino acids. Sulphur-bearing amino acids are essential for growing massive coats of hair, horns, antlers, and hooves, and also strong tendons and connective tissues. The minerals probably also serve to strengthen the skeleton. This is very important for ungulates living off winter forage that is deficient in minerals, since these animals tend to dissolve their own skeletons to obtain metabolic salts.

Moreover, gestating females may raid their own skeletons for minerals needed to build the bones of the foetus. In spring the females may once again call on the mineral reserves of their bodies to supplement the mineral content of the milk—unless they have access to both a mineral-rich forage and mineral licks. In the winter and spring the skeletons of adults grow light, thin, and porous, but they are restored in summer when adequate forage and minerals are again available.

The winter climate in the vicinity of large glaciers is the most significant factor of all in the maintenance of large herbivores. Studies in Greenland indicate that a cold-air zone extends well beyond the fringes of the glaciers. Here the vegetation is quickly frozen in fall, and, being immediately in a "rain shadow," is covered only by a thin blanket of soft powdery snow; such snow is no major obstacle to herbivores. Moreover, much of the snow is blown away. Beyond the cold zone is a region where Chinooks penetrate and periodically clear the ground of snow, exposing vegetation. Again, this provides good winter forage for big animals. Beyond this zone, however, heavy snowfalls and periodic thaws create icing conditions that make the forage unattainable to herbivores.

As long as the glacier is large and advancing, Chinooks and an extensive cold zone may be expected at its continental margins; during glacial retreat this cold zone shrinks or disappears. Snowfalls, followed by thawing and frost, ice up winter ranges close to glaciers and ultimately lead to the collapse of populations of large grazers. Widespread favorable wintering conditions exist during glacial advances and glacial maxima because much of the vegetation is likely to be frozen in the green state—particularly along water courses—and thus to be of exceptionally high nutritional value. Rich animal populations exist as long as the glacier advances, making it possible for humans to hunt and colonize the adjacent zone.

An increase in icing conditions during deglaciation appears to lead to a reduction in grazing ranges and periodic starvation of herbivores, resulting in a decline in body size and an increase in the incidence of deformities. Fossil remains indicate that the Siberian mammoth suffered such afflictions before its extinction, some time at the end of the last glaciation. This theory would explain the destruction in the Alaska-Yukon *refugium* of herds of bison and horses during deglaciation. It is not surprising that the archaeological record reveals a grim struggle for survival by humans, following the retreat of the continental glaciers and the collapse of the rich periglacial ecosystems. Gone were the grasslands and the diverse herbivores, to be replaced by dense temperate forests with their scarcity of ungulates. Human populations declined sharply in Europe after the deglaciation: their physical development suffered, their bones became riddled with disease, and homicide and cannibalism were rampant. Archaeological evidence shows that craftsmanship, although technologically diversified, declined in comparison with that of the glacial period. Thus, with the withdrawal of large glaciers, the first dark ages descended on humans, amid a grim struggle to adapt and simply survive.

Why did modern humans do so well during the late Paleolithic, during glaciation, compared with their near-demise at the end of the glaciations? It must be noted that our predecessor, Neanderthal man, who flourished during the first major advance of the Würm glaciation, some 70,000-40,000 years ago, failed to survive the deglaciation that followed. He was totally tied to large mammals and, as these declined, he vanished. How is it possible that during glaciations our ancestors reached a degree of physical development that has not been reached by modern populations? They were athletic, with robust bones, were tall of stature, and had large brains. They practiced a culture whose products we admire to this day in the form of bold, stylized paintings and delicately carved figures of animals and women. They had musical scales and a lunar calendar and developed a craftsmanship with their tools that we can only admire. The late Paleolithic, beginning some 40,000-35,000 years ago, was modern man's first golden age, and it lasted in surprising continuity some four or five times longer than our period of recorded history.

Some sobering insights emerge when we reconstruct the life style of the late Paleolithic people from their bones, tools, and art, and, above all, by applying our knowledge of the ecology and behavior of large herbivores and of the ecology of cold-climate regions and periglacial environments. It seems unlikely that these people could have maintained their superb physical and intellectual development without consciously controlling their population size, in

order to maximize individual development. Individual development had to be maximized for the type of hunting strategies they required in order to kill, regularly, mammals that were very dangerous and relatively clever. Individual development could not be maximized without some system of mate selection that ensured genetic quality, at least to the extent of minimizing the effects of inbreeding. Here lies the origin of the kinship system, which presupposes a sound understanding of reproduction and the relationship between mating, pregnancy, and birth. Such a system may have involved social interactions within groups of individuals, leading to a refinement of a good many human activities such as music-making, dancing, complex speech, altruism, self-discipline, refined humor, cooperation, and sport. We took our final shape in the cold climates of the Mediterranean basin and Europe during the last major advances of the Würm glaciations. The study of periglacial ecology is thus one window on our own history, but the continental glaciers that penetrated to southern latitudes are gone.

Interesting as the glaciers of Greenland and Antarctica may be, they teach us less about life near glaciers than the ice masses of the St. Elias Mountains, which are located in a more benign climate where long hours of sunshine, annual floods, and the fertilizing effect of the loess generate great biological productivity.

In the St. Elias Mountains we can still see loess steppe and loess storms, forests growing on glaciers, shifting braided glacial streams, rich fauna and a trend to gigantism in the large mammals, exceptional floristic diversity, sharply bordered, mosaic-like plant communities, sharp contrasts in productivity between different plant communities on and off permafrost, sheep and mountain goats wintering above glaciers, moose wintering on glaciers, grizzlies congregating to feed on berries along glacial streams, salmon moving deep into the range to spawn in the tributaries of the silty glacial streams, and nunataks—ranges surrounded by ice—that still have small mammal populations and are occasionally visited by bears. Here lies a treasure of cultural insights, for the land speaks not only of its intrinsic worth but also of conditions in ages past that guided the ascent of man.

5. THE GREEN MANTLE

David F. Murray & George W. Douglas

THE SOUTHWESTERN CORNER of the Yukon Territory is oustanding for its richly varied terrain and vast complex of mountain ranges, with their extraordinary vertical relief from valley bottoms to mountain peaks, and strong climatic contrasts.

Due to the cooler temperatures that occur with increasing elevation, the vegetation on the mountain slopes exhibits strong vertical zoning: extensive forests of the montane zone from the valley bottoms up the slopes to about 1,000-1,300 meters (3,300-4,300 feet); a sub-alpine zone of tall shrubs and widely scattered white spruce; and a treeless alpine zone of low-growing vegetation above 1,500 meters (4,900 feet) up to the limit imposed by the permanent snowline.

The characteristics of the vegetation within each of these major zones vary locally according to the extent of bedrock outcrops and their susceptibility to erosion, the exposure of the slopes to the sun and the length of the snow-free period, and the texture, depth, and stability of the soil. Whether the soils were formed in place from the decomposition of bedrock or came from materials transported by glaciers, water, or wind strongly influences the texture of the soil and its water-holding capacity. Collectively, these aspects of the soil are of fundamental importance in determining differences in the landscape that govern the distribution of plant species.

Important to the diversity of today's plant habitats are the deposits of rock, silt, sand, and gravel left by the glaciers during their periods of stability and recession. The large moraines and

Tundra stream-side wildflower garden. (David Murray)

ice-carved features determine the form of the landscape, particularly along the valley walls and in adjacent portions of the valley bottoms. Even areas untouched by glacier ice were indirectly affected by glaciers as meltwater and wind action sorted and transported the till in the form of outwash and loess. Therefore, the patterns of vegetation we observe today reflect modern climatic and soil characteristics and also the legacy of past events. It is the interplay of past and present environments that must be appreciated in this region where geological events have so profoundly affected the landscape.

Extensive forests cover the valley bottoms and the lower mountain slopes. Most stands are coniferous, dominated principally by white spruce. When spruce forests are examined closely at a number of different sites, it becomes clear that all stands are not identical although they possess a common denominator of spruce trees. These stands may occur with pure white spruce canopies or mixed with other tree species, mainly quaking aspen. The spruce stands may have open or closed canopies with different shrub and herb undergrowth. On wet north- or east-facing slopes, dwarf birch and crowberry dominate the undergrowth. Greyleaf willow and soapberry are the most important undergrowth species on the moister sites, while the latter, along with bearberry, dominate dry open spruce stands. In addition to spruce forests, another type of forest is formed by balsam poplar on coarse, well-drained soils formed on river gravels.

While such a complexity of forest communities is often a function of varied topography, numerous small fires and some very large ones over the span of many centuries account for much of the large-scale checkerboard mosaic. What we see today are stands of different ages in various stages of recovery after fire. However, even stands of the same age can differ, since recovery depends also on the intensity of the fire and the susceptibility to burning of the species in the original forest. When, for example, a fire sweeps through white spruce, the trees are killed, whereas a quickly moving fire can leave buried stems and roots of many other species relatively undamaged, and from these parts new shoots will arise. Otherwise the plant cover must come from seed sources that survive the fires or from the adjacent unburned forest.

Fireweed, one of the most widespread "fire species" in northern North America, can flower profusely by the next summer. Travelers of the Alaska Highway know well the sight of entire hillsides of astonishing magenta, where blackened soil and tree trunks are evidence of very recent fire. Bearberry and shrubby willow also appear soon. In the Kluane region quaking aspen in pure stands is the most conspicuous forest type attributable to fire, but Scouler's willow is also able to regenerate or seed-in rapidly to form stands that can persist for fifty to one hundred years before white spruce is again dominant.

The forests are often interrupted by meadows, lakes, fens, and river systems. Areas that are poorly drained because of impervious soils or permafrost create continuously wet habitats. These fens are dominated by aquatic or semi-aquatic sedges, low shrubs, and an abundance of mosses; white spruce may also occur.

Particularly well developed in this region are vegetated openings, or meadows, where we would otherwise expect forest. These openings occur in two basic forms. One, on moist, finer-textured soils, has a relatively lush plant cover, and the grasses form a distinct turf; such areas are not unlike northern prairie and parkland. The other, on extremely dry sites, has coarser soils, sparse plant cover, and conspicuous bare ground. These are quite steppe-like and may have their closest equivalent in eastern Asia. The occurrence in these dry-soil communities of grasses, sedges, sages, and legumes is related to the abundance of rather coarse soils of glacial deposits, or to the extensive alluvium of the large rivers, or to the same sorts of soils that are found on beaches and on the wave-cut terraces of ancient lakes. In the Kluane drainage, steppe (grassland) vegetation has formed on steep dry bluffs that surround Kluane Lake and on the lower mountain slopes in the northern half of the park. Excellent examples may be seen at Sheep Mountain at the mouth of the Slims River, and also on the river alluvium of stabilized flood plains following shifts of the active river channel. These are circumstances that led to the development of the Duke Meadows, not far from Burwash.

The drainage of the Kluane watershed to the Yukon was only locally impeded by glacial activity. But the Dezadeash and Alsek rivers, which flow through the St. Elias Mountains to the Pacific Ocean, have been blocked by advancing glaciers at various times in the past. The result

Slims River Floodplain. (John Theberge)

was the formation of lakes dammed by ice. These lakes covered large areas to great depths, as indicated by the beach ridges complete with driftwood that are still in place well above the valley floor. The extensive beaches provide additional habitat for steppe vegetation, but the deep, fine-textured, generally more moist soils of the former lake beds account for the local abundance of prairie and parkland. It was the natural, lush, grassy openings in an old lake bed near Pine Creek that led to the development of the former agricultural experiment station beside the Alaska Highway just north of Haines Junction.

A special type of grassland occurs on the delta of the Slims River, which by the steady accumulation of silts has been expanding gradually into Kluane Lake. During periods of low water, large silt flats are exposed. Since the silts offer little surface drainage, water remains ponded in shallow depressions. During the hot dry summer the evaporation of these pools leaves the surface charged with carbonates, and what develops is a northern version of alkali flats. The vegetation is scant and the grasses occur characteristically in widely spaced bunches with a number of other herbaceous plants and occasional willows. The general impression is one of a youthful landscape, since the disturbance by frequent flooding prevents the establishment of a more complete vegetative cover. Of interest at this site is a population of a northern alkali grass, *Puccinellia nuttalliana*, far to the west of other known populations in the Canadian north and western Greenland, and a population of the maritime plantain, *Plantago maritima*, which is common in coastal British Columbia and Alaska but known inland in western North America at only two other stations, at Great Salt Lake, Utah, and in Wood Buffalo National Park, Northwest Territories.

The flood plains support more than just vari-

Sub-alpine zone. (Geological Survey of Canada, William Dekur)

ants of a grassland; stands of balsam poplar, thickets of tall willows, and even mixed stands of white spruce occur on portions of the flood plain that have not experienced major physical disturbance for a long time. It is the juxtaposition of forest stands, fens, silt flats, sand dunes, and gravel bars that make flood plains so diverse and interesting botanically. One can quickly appreciate the relationships between river process and consequent geomorphic features, and how these affect the development of soil and vegetation. Fluctuating water levels, which can occur daily as well as seasonally on these glacier-fed rivers, maintain ponds marginal to the channel and enrich the gravels with fine deposits. Down-valley winds sweep from the glacier termini, transporting clouds of loess that fall to the surface on valley floors many kilometers from the glacier front. It is an active

landscape. One wonders what will happen next. The river channel changes, leaving one area while eroding into another, simultaneously depositing new ground on one side while destroying it on the other. Deposits put down by the river long ago are reworked and sorted anew. The various levels of terraces and the extreme variability of the soils contribute to a grand array of sites and conditions. Some plant species flourish in or marginal to the flood plain, but few are restricted to it. The flora is borrowed from the forest and to some extent from the tundra, which in this region is never far removed from flood-plain conditions since riverine habitats ascend as a continuous, narrow strip from the valleys well into the mountains.

Above the montane forest is a tall-shrub zone — the sub-alpine zone. In the southern part of the Kluane region this zone is broad. Farther north it becomes relatively narrow. In the south, the tall shrubs (up to 4 meters — 13 feet) include willows, dwarf birch, and alder. The latter is lacking in the north, probably due to the drier and colder climate. Interspersed with the shrubby vegetation are meadows. These, too, change markedly from south to north. Lush herbaceous meadows, showing influences of coastal and mountain floristic elements, often predominate in the south. Important species in these moist meadows include false hellebore and Canadian bluejoint. The drier meadows are usually dominated by a fescue grass (*Festuca altaica*).

High up on the mountain slopes, the tall-shrub vegetation of willow and dwarf birch gives way to low shrubs, including the same dwarf birch and a different set of willow species from those encountered at lower elevations. The ericaceous shrubs (blueberry family) are best represented in the southern part of the park where white, yellow, and red heathers dot the landscape. Farther north, however, members of this family become sparse. Higher still, above 1,600 meters (5,200 feet), the erect shrubs become restricted to sheltered sites, and woody plants are only locally dominant. The so-called dwarf willows grow prostrate and extend their branches no higher than the surrounding herbaceous vegetation. This entirely treeless landscape is alpine tundra.

One must not construe the diminutive life form of these plants as simply a dwarfing of species that grow much larger in more favorable environments. True, the size and form of these plants are limited by the cold climate at high elevations, but these plants are genetically in tune with the rigorous conditions and flourish there. So fine is their adjustment that in many cases they do not do well at lower elevations. They possess a remarkable ability to tolerate

Cottongrass in a moist sub-alpine meadow. (John Theberge)

Active rock debris on upper slopes of Mount Hoge. (John Theberge)

freezing temperatures during the growing season, and many have means of growth and reproduction that ensure success in a short season. Not all of these adaptations are visible — that is, structural; they may affect only the metabolic processes. An alpine flora of over 200 taxa is ample testimony to the successful adaptation of plants to the limitations imposed by high altitude.

The various combinations of species, the "vegetation units," of alpine tundra are fully as diverse and complex as those of forests. In forests the mats of mosses, lichens, and herbs are overtopped by one or even two shrub layers, and the canopy is formed by the trees. Tundra vegetation appears at first glance to be a single layer. This is an oversimplification since there is a mat of mosses, lichens, and tiny herbs, a layer of taller herbs, and often one of low shrubs. The relative dimensions of the tundra layers and the presence of the same life form in each layer mean that communities are not as richly struc-

tured as forests. The sorting of plants into communities may go unrecognized by anyone unfamiliar with the plants as species. Vegetational boundaries are sharp and obvious where environmental gradients are steep, and changes in species composition occur over short distances. The abrupt changes in plant cover frequently coincide with the presence of land forms that are the products of cold-climate geomorphic processes and thus peculiar to tundra landscapes. Therefore, the description of vegetation patterns is closely tied to an accurate depiction of the physical environment at the ground surface and the few centimeters below it, where the bulk of the roots exist. The more you try to describe and explain the relationship between plant patterns and geomorphic processes, the clearer it is that one of the overriding considerations is the widespread vulnerability of the surface to disturbances caused by water, wind, frost, and the force of gravity.

Fragments from the rock outcrops on summits

and ridge crests accumulate over the millennia, and the resultant scree can cover entire slopes down to the valley bottom. Not only do the rocks fall and move down-slope individually, but the entire mantle moves; the instability is immediately evident to anyone attempting to traverse or climb the scree. At first glance these slopes appear utterly devoid of plant life. Access to them is often possible by following well-used Dall sheep trails, whereupon it becomes clear that plants, albeit widely scattered, inhabit the interstices of the scree. The surface of the rocks may be hot and dry, but beneath them the soil is cool and moist. The greatest difficulty for the plants lies in coping with the constant down-slope movement of the rocks. Many of the species are endowed with long, rapidly growing rhizomes. To dig out a plant by the roots, you are forced to burrow through the rocks a long way

up-slope; the cluster of flowers observed at the surface may be a long way from its roots. It is not unusual to find arctic poppies, mustards (*Draba ruaxes, Erysimum pallasii, Smelowskia borealis*), chickweeds (*Stellaria monantha, S. alaskana, Cerastium beringianum*), a fleabane daisy (*Erigeron purpuratus*), hawk's beard, and bladder fern tucked away here and there over the most immense screes. Small islands of closed vegetation can form below outcrops and large boulders that afford protection from encroachment by the scree as it moves inexorably down-slope.

Where upper slopes become more gentle, the movement of the scree is halted and the accumulation takes the form of a fan, or cone, on the side of the mountain. The midslopes are well vegetated, though bare ground may still be an important component of any community. Instability is still manifest in such features as stone

Solidification ridges, Observation Mountain. (David Murray)

stripes and stone- and turf-banked terraces. Frost action, the force of expansion generated by the formation of ice, disturbs the uppermost few centimeters of soil. Frost-heaving (perpendicular to the slope) and the subsequent settling (vertically downward) usually result in a net downward movement of the surface. Also, a loss of cohesive strength in the soil from excessive moisture is expressed in a slow down-slope movement at the rate of less than one centimeter to about three centimeters a year. The combined effect is the production of lobes and terraces, which when highly developed give slopes the appearance of a cake with icing dripping down the sides.

The rate of movement is slow and the surface mass travels more or less as a single unit; the plants are therefore able simply to "ride along," the vegetative mat intact. The surface irregularities of the lobes and terraces produce variations of habitat and preclude uniformity of vegetation. The bases of the lobes collect more snow during the winter than the exposed, windswept (perhaps even snow-free in winter) upper surfaces, thus assuring a more reliable supply of meltwater in the spring. These cooler, shaded, moist micro-habitats have a flora far different from that of the warm, sunny, dry tops and produce a cover of different colors that tends to heighten the physical differences.

Other evidence of frost-related processes abound even on relatively level ground with alpine tundra: upthrust rocks, sorted and unsorted stone circles; oblong patches of fresh soil in the otherwise continuous mats of vegetation; fresh and revegetated mud flows; slumps; and earthflows. Exposed soil is churned by the frequent growth and subsequent melting of needle ice. These features tell of events and conditions that determine the nature of seed beds, the perils for developing seedlings, and the instability to which the mature plants must be tolerant.

Special conditions occur where major irregularities serve as a catchment for snow. Depending upon the size and persistence of these late-lying snowbanks, the flora may be quite distinct. In extreme cases the snow lasts so long as to preclude any vegetation other than some scattered mosses. However, there is a group of plants capable of survival even when exposed for only a very brief growing season in the basins of snow accumulation areas at high elevations: mats of a prostrate willow, *Salix polaris*, the grasses

Phippsia algida and *Poa paucispicula*, a rush (*Luzula piperi*), a buttercup (*Ranunculus pygmaeus*), mountain sorrel, purple mountain saxifrage, and in some instances *Leutkea pectinata* and the moss heath (*Cassiope stelleriana*).

The snowbanks provide a special environment not only where they lie but also in areas below them that are irrigated by their meltwater as long as the snow persists. Snowflush sites provide some of the richest growths of sedges, with colorful herbs such as the monkshood, a valerian (*Valeriana capitata*), a buttercup (*Ranunculus nivalis*), and the rare and unusual spring beauty, *Claytonia bostockii*.

North-facing slopes receive less direct sunlight than other exposures, and there the snow generally remains longer over large areas. On these slopes a species of mountain avens (*Dryas octopetala*) and a white heather (*Cassiope tetragona*) form the closest thing to a heath in the northern section of the park. Where moister air masses from the Gulf of Alaska penetrate farther inland, the lower alpine slopes develop a more typical heath with an abundant species of blueberry (*Vaccinium uliginosum*) and a species of Labrador tea (*Ledum palustre*).

South-facing slopes at high altitudes have an interesting mix of species. On these warm and dry micro-sites are some of the montane taxa at their altitudinal limits, such as the grape fern, death camus, yarrow, a sage (*Artemisia alaskana*), a goldenrod (*Solidago multiradiata*), Jacob's ladder, *Androsace septentrionalis*, and *Penstemon procerus*.

The expanses of open tundra dwindle as you travel from the Kluane Ranges into the Icefield Ranges, where the terrain is dissected by glaciers and ice- and snow-covered peaks. Deep in the mountains the surface available for plants are few and often widely separated. Whereas in the Kluane Ranges glaciers are confined to cirques (deep, steep-walled basins), in the Icefield Ranges it is the mountains that occur as separate units in a matrix of the icefield. Mountain peaks that project through the glacier ice are called nunataks. Some nunataks show snow-free surfaces during the summer, and an inspection of a few of them has revealed a surprising number of flowering plants well above the snowline at 2,638 meters (8,650 feet)—and three most unexpectedly at 2,800 meters (9,200 feet).

Although the annual snowfall in these ranges

can be enormous, winds keep the actual accumulation low on the steep nunatak slopes and benches. There, the combined effects of sublimation and melt create both the bare spots and the meltwater necessary for a suitable seed bed in the mineral soil that has formed from these weathered rock surfaces. The nagging question is, of course, how the seeds arrived at these isolated points so far from the areas of continuous tundra. Whatever the explanation, seeds did arrive, and did germinate, and some of the seedlings survived to become mature plants. In this most inhospitable environment, the plants endure repeated freezing and frequentsnowfall during the growing season; nevertheless, many flower successfully and produce fruit with viable seed.

Changes in the flora that have taken place over many millennia can be pieced together only by inference, relying upon historical evidence of past climates and geological events. Plausible reconstructions are aided by geologists, who are providing increasingly detailed information on the extent of the glaciers and their positions at various times. The actual floristic details cannot be determined because the fossil record is meager, and we lack the ability to determine accurately the specific sources of pollen and plant macrofossils. Nevertheless, it is an intriguing exercise to wring as much information as possible from our few clues, on the understanding that our reconstruction includes both facts and tacit assumptions.

During glacial maxima the average annual temperature was undoubtedly cooler than at present, although we cannot be certain that all seasons were cooler. Warm, dry summers, even warmer and drier (but shorter) than today's, may have occurred in a full glacial environment. Pollen profiles from a number of places in Alaska and from near Snag suggest that the vegetation lacked spruce; at any rate, trees that might have been present failed to produce pollen as evidence. Tundra rather like the herb mats of the high slopes could have been the dominant vegetation then. There are some compelling arguments that this tundra was not like what we have today in most areas, but consisted of grasses and sedges and a high proportion of sages — an assemblage that has been called a steppe-tundra, or arctic steppe. This vegetation is being postulated for all of the immense unglaciated area in the Yukon and Alaska, based on abundant sage pollen in the paleontological record.

This view came about largely to account for the apparent abundance of horse, bison, and mammoth in the late glacial herbivorous fauna. These grazers occur in the fossil record with far greater frequency than browsing herbivores such as moose and to some extent caribou, which are so common in the north today, and this indicates a landscape that was a type of grassland, or at least an open parkland. Without evidence for spruces during this period, it is nevertheless possible that there were gallery forests along the river systems. The sudden disappearance of the large grazers from the fossil record in the post-glacial period, and the concomitant rise in the importance of browsers, coincides with the development of shrub tundra following the general amelioration of the climate. Therefore, it is presumed that the major type of vegetation 27,000 to 10,000 years ago was sage-rich grassland, or steppe-tundra, after which shrub tundra developed. Spruce did not appear in the general region until 8,000 years ago and may not have reached the Kluane area for another 2,000 years. For the last 5,000 or 6,000 years the vegetation (insofar as its history can be read from pollen remains) has been remarkably uniform, although we know that the climate has changed sufficiently for glaciers to respond with both advances and recessions during the last 5,000 years.

The flora of the southwestern Yukon shows affinities with several biogeographic areas: boreal forest, the western mountains and coast, the northern prairies, the arctic, and both steppe and mountain elements of northeastern Asia. A number of species show unusual distribution patterns. *Cassiope stelleriana*, *Fritillaria camschatcensis*, *Oplopanax horridus*, and *Vaccinium ovalifolium*, common along the coast, occur in the southern section of the park. On dry lowlands, *Erotia lanata*, *Erigeron pumilus*, *Townsendia hookeri*, and *Carex parryana* are found quite some distance from their main ranges in the prairie provinces. *Lewisia pygmacea*, *Arabis lemmonii*, and *Arabis lyalii* occur in the alpine zone, far from the Rockies of southern British Columbia and Alberta. The southern limits of the arctic taxa *Oxytropis arctica*, *Smelowskia calycina* subspecies *integrifolia*, *Braya purpurascens*, and *Thlaspi arcticum* are here in the Yukon or adjacent northern British Columbia. Localities for *Stellaria umbellata* and *Phippsia algida* have been found in snow beds high in the mountains that bridge gaps between Alaska and the southern Rockies, where both taxa are more common. The sedge *Carex sabulosa* is a wholly Asian plant except for its occurrence on terraces and sand dunes along the Alsek, Dezadeash, andKaskawulsh rivers (and at a similar site at Carcross, south of Whitehorse) where there are steppe-like assemblages of sages, juniper, legumes, and grasses. Similarly, on dry bluffs of Sheep Mountain and environs and along the Donjek River are the only North American populations of the Eurasian sage, *Artemisia rupestris*. Finally, the flora also includes a number of species believed unique to Alaska, the Yukon, and northern British Columbia. Such species as *Stellaria alaskana*, *Salix setchelliana*, *Aphragmus eschscholtzianus*, *Androsace alaskana*, *Castilleja yukonis*, *Artemisia alaskana*, *Aster yukonensis*, and *Claytonia bostockii*, found in the Kluane area are endemic to Alaska and the Yukon.

Thus, the flora is a marvellous blend of diverse elements; the difficulty lies in finding an explanation, particularly for the existence of outliers so far beyond their expected ranges. There are two basic proposals: one is that the distribution of these disjunct taxa was formerly more extensive, but that events of the past disrupted and essentially eradicated them, with these exceptions; the other is that these isolated populations are the result of post-glacial, long-distance dispersal. A third possibility is, of course, that we know too little about the actual range of these species and that the disjunctions we observe are reflections of our current ignorance.

During glaciations the ice masses of the mountain systems and the continental ice sheets of the south and east effectively cut Alaska and the Yukon off from the rest of North America. Since periods of maximum glaciation were also periods of minimum sea level, Asia and North America were joined by the continental shelf — the Bering Land Bridge. Therefore, what is now the northwestern extremity of North America was then the easternmost extension of Asia. This certainly accounts for the distinct Asian influence seen in our flora. The topographic continuity of the North American mountain systems provides the necessary connections for the southern and northern alpine species that mingle here.

While glacierized, the St. Elias Mountains and

Artemesia rupestris   *Aster yukonensis*

the adjacent valleys could support no vegetation; if any of the floristic novelties are relics of pre-glacial conditions, it is necessary to assume persistence of these plants somewhere else while glaciers occupied the areas where we find them today. It is likely that conditions near the middle of the icefield today are a good approximation of conditions that prevailed over a much larger area during the last major glacial advance (20,000 to 14,000 years ago). Since plants survive on mid-icefield nunataks today, it is indeed possible that nunataks existed during a glacial period and provided *refugia* for plants at a number of sites in the Kluane Ranges. These sites, or former nunataks, form the highest vegetated areas in the Kluane Ranges today. Many rare and unusual plants are found in small populations quite isolated from each other on such mountain slopes and peaks. We can therefore propose that they survived successive glaciations in those sites or similar ones nearby, and remain as evidence of ranges that were once more widespread having been reduced by glaciations. These plants have failed to expand their ranges appreciably beyond their nunatak *refugia* because of biological systems so long constrained and adapted by those specific, harsh environments. This attractive explanation for disjunct distributions is, however, without solid evidence.

Although glaciers once covered so much of what is today Kluane National Park, large expanses of the Yukon plateau to the east, and

Agropyron yukonensis

interior Alaska to the north were unglaciated. Consequently, a diverse flora probably remained in these varied landscapes throughout the Pleistocene period. This *refugium* was likely the major source from which plant propagules were later dispersed onto the recently deglaciated surfaces. Much of the Kluane flora may be accounted for by migrations from the plateaus as the glaciers rapidly receded in the early post-glacial period. This leaves the isolated populations in the Kluane Ranges, many not known from the Yukon plateau, unexplained unless one presumes long-distance dispersal from distant sources. We are on uncertain ground with this hypothesis, since the agents of dispersal for the disjunct taxa are speculative.

Yet events, however unlikely they may seem when considered as single occurrences, become acceptable when repeated over a span of more than 10,000 years. Volcanic eruptions on the upper White River roughly 1,220 years ago left accumulations of ash that were buried in soil horizons in the valley, but remain as surface features in the northern St. Elias Mountains. On this ash we find *Rumex graminifolius*, otherwise restricted to coastal areas. The volcanic ash serves as the ecological equivalent to coastal sands and gravels, so it is possible that seeds were carried across the mountains by storm winds.

Another floristic problem concerns the unexplained absence of certain plants. Tree species common in the boreal forest and found on the north and south periphery of the park but not in the Kluane region are the black spruce and the larch. Two other species, the paper birch and the lodgepole pine, are represented by only a few specimens. Since there appear to be ample suitable habitats, one wonders whether these anomalies are evidence that the forest flora is still developing.

The flora of Kluane National Park and vicinity, although relatively unknown just a few years ago, has now been largely inventoried and described. The complicated but fascinating stories of plant origins and dynamics related to past climates and geological events allow the visitor to detect patterns and processes in the landscape, and enhance the enjoyment to be gained from these picturesque settings. Here we have an opportunity not only to study the present, but, by analogy, to learn something of past environments as well.

6. WINGS IN THE WIND

John B. Theberge

THE WINDS THAT sweep across Kluane's tundras carry fragments of plover whistles. Golden eagles ride the sky currents with set wings. Lesser yellow-legs sway on wiry willow branches beside the ponds, warning you away from their nests with shrill cries. Arctic terns dive-bomb unexpectedly as you pick your way along a lakeshore. At timber line, in the twilight hush of midnight, the plaintive three-note song of a golden-crowned sparrow drifts across a shadowed valley. Rock, wind, ice, and meltwater made the soil; seeds and seedlings formed the green mantle for the wild wings that fill Kluane with life for three months of the year.

At least 118 species of birds are believed to nest in the southwestern Yukon. This is a high count for a northern environment, probably the highest of any area north of the 60th parallel.

The explanation lies partly in the region's diversity of land forms and vegetation, providing varied bird habitats. Also, the Kluane region is geographically close to a number of major North American biomes—northern tundra, western montane, taiga boreal forests, northern prairie parkland. Species of birds commonly found in each of these biomes also live in the Kluane region. Nowhere else can you see rock ptarmigan and wandering tattlers (tundra) on the same day as mountain bluebirds (montane), hawk owls (boreal), and magpies (prairie).

The bird life of the Kluane Ranges was first studied in some detail in 1943, when the region became accessible from the new Alaska Highway. C. H. D. Clarke, a federal employee, compiled an annotated list of birds, which was added to in later years by a number of other ornithologists. Such lists tell you the degree of commonness of each species, but little about the ecological relationships. Interesting information and, indeed, evolutionary order begin to emerge only when you compare birds living in different habitats. Comparison is the key to ecological understanding for novice bird-watcher, naturalist, and scientist.

There are eight extensive and distinctly different bird habitats in the Kluane region. The tundra, predictably, is the most distinctive in terms of its bird life, followed by the sub-alpine. But, unexpectedly, the six lowland habitats that make up almost all of the valley floors and lower mountainsides have strikingly similar bird populations. This similarity is unexpected because the six habitats appear very different from each other: upland willow shrub (an early stage of forest succession after fire), lowland willow shrub (similar, but in poorly drained areas), spruce-poplar forest (a mid-successional stage after fire about 60 years previously), mature spruce forest, riparian (stream or river bank) poplar forest, and balsam poplar forest. These habitats provide not only diversity of forest structure (extent of low, mid, and upper layers of vegetation) but also a continuum of successional stages after fire. Yet the bird populations vary at most by only 40 percent among the six habitats.

Ecologists usually find that the number of species and the over-all abundance of birds increase as the variety in the structure of a forest increases. In Kluane's forests, however, three species of birds predominate, making up at least 50 percent of the bird population in each of the six habitats: dark-eyed junco, yellow-rumped warbler, and Swainson's thrush. An explanation may be found in two seemingly opposing evolutionary forces, one of which produces habitat specialists and the other habitat generalists. Birds, like most other animals, are under pressure of competition from other species. This competition, according to one theory, results in specialization as a means of reducing competition. At the same time, however, the environment is exerting pressure against specialization. Food specialists, for example, are more vulnerable to starvation than food generalists; populations of nest-habitat specialists (such as hole-nesters) are more easily limited than populations of nest-habitat generalists, which have a wider choice of acceptable sites. Of these two somewhat opposing evolutionary forces, competition resulting in ecological specializations appears to be less important in the north than it is farther south. This is probably because of the relative scarcity of species to compete with, and because of the greater variability in environmental conditions in the north, tending to make specialization a hazard to survival.

Yellow-rumped warbler

Swainson's thrush

The same three species have ranked among the most common in bird censuses in forest habitats outside the Kluane region, from the western Northwest Territories to northern British Columbia. All are cosmopolitan, with breeding ranges extending from Pacific to Atlantic. All eat both animal and vegetable matter. All nest in a variety of places—on the ground, in shrubs, and in the lower branches of trees. While all are generalists, each has distinct food habits, and this reduces competition between them: the thrush picks up invertebrates from the forest floor; the warbler eats invertebrates higher up in the vegetation; the junco concentrates on the seeds of ground herbs and grasses.

There are a few habitat specialists at Kluane. Brewer's sparrow is a nondescript brownish bird, more easily identified by its canary-like trills than by its appearance. In one patch of sub-alpine shrubs measuring perhaps 20 hectares (50 acres), above Sheep Creek, 10 or 12 male Brewer's sparrows stake out their territories each year. Great stretches of similar vegetation are available in the immediate vicinity, but these birds have grouped their territories together. A number of other sightings (or hearings) of Brewer's sparrows have been made, such as in the sub-alpine on the Chilkat Pass and elsewhere in the southern Yukon and very northern British Columbia, but otherwise these birds are far from their normal breeding range in southern Alberta and southwestern British Columbia down to southern California. Why they pick the sub-alpine as their nesting habitat, or what is special about the individual places they pick, is not known.

Similarly, rock ptarmigan and water pipits nest only on the tundra. The latter species is superabundant in the north, and during fall migrations is commonly seen in farmers' fields across Canada, especially in the west. Water pipits breed on the tundra from Labrador to Alaska and in high mountainous areas throughout British Columbia. Largely insectivorous, they poke around the ground vegetation on the tundra, typically flying a few feet, walking (not hopping) a short distance, then flying again.

Other species tend toward specific habits but are not found there exclusively: northern three-toed woodpeckers flick bark off spruce trees looking for insects in the cornices of the bark. They prefer mature spruce forests but will congregate in burned areas if timber is still standing. Varied thrushes, with their melancholy reedlike single note, also prefer the dark, mature forests but forage into mixed forests as well.

The lowland forests have their great charm: the evening fluting of thrushes, the crimson flash of white-winged crossbills skimming the tops of the spruces. But the tundra is especially interesting. This is where a brood of ptarmigan will fly up at your feet, and you can see an eagle a mile off. Both in the number of species occuring there and in the total over-all abundance of birds, the tundra ranks lowest; but most species found there are unusual. Birds classed as shorebirds nest in the wet places: golden plovers, yellow-legs, wandering tattlers. These three species migrate great distances, wintering from southern California to Argentina. The tattler, whose breeding range is confined to central Alaska and the Yukon, is one of the rarer gems of Kluane bird life. After wintering on islands in the Pacific, each bird finds its way back to exactly the same patch of dwarf willow along the same tundra ice-melt stream that it left eight months before.

Shorebirds exhibit a number of strategies that contribute to their success on northern breeding grounds. The majority of Canadian shorebirds nest in arctic or sub-arctic biomes. Shorebirds have "nidifugous" young, that is, young that are ready to leave the nest and forage for themselves within a few hours of hatching. Adults are thus free to maintain themselves and meet environmental contingencies, such as a summer snowstorm, without having to care for their young. Like almost all nidifugous species, shorebirds are adapted to running, nest on the ground, and have eggs that match their environment; and the adults use "injury feigning" or the "broken-wing act" when a human or other potential predator approaches. These are all adaptations to open environments such as the tundra.

On the rocky ramparts that rise above Kluane's tundra nest some of the more dramatic species. Golden eagles are more abundant here than they are on much of their range in North America; peregrine falcons and gyrfalcons are very rare. Golden eagles are by far the most abundant raptor in the St. Elias Mountains; they may be seen any day in summer, quartering low along steep sub-alpine slopes as they hunt arctic ground squirrels, or riding the thermal updrafts high in the sky. Occasionally one can watch these

Canyon-land habitat of golden eagles. (John Theberge)

huge birds with two-meter (six-foot) wingspans engage in aerial acrobatics, presumably with their nest-mates—steep vertical dives and rolls, not touching each other but displaying great flying skill. These performances are usually given above a nest, and they occur throughout the summer; their function is unknown.

The Slims River drainage area and vicinity (some 660 square kilometers—250 square miles) supported a breeding density of one golden eagle per 133 square kilometers (51 square miles) in 1978, a high density for this species—probably a result of the presence of abundant ground squirrels, a favorite prey.

Bald eagles nest in the tops of trees, usually close to water since this species relies primarily on fish. Nests have been observed in areas adjacent to the park, at Kluane, Dezadeash, and Pickhandle lakes.

The most common large hawk is one of the most widespread in North America, the red-tailed hawk, but in the northwest is a member of a distinctive color phase with a relatively confined breeding range. Red-tailed hawks in the St. Elias Mountains are melanistic, that is, with mainly black plumage. In contrast, the underparts of other subspecies are mainly white. This subspecies was once considered a true species, Harlan's hawk, but it has since been recorded as interbreeding with the red-tailed hawk despite differences in plumage. Only the tail is not black, and the colors vary between individuals; red is typical, but it may be white near the base and red near the tip, or all white with fine barring.

Great horned owls and hawk owls hunt the forest openings; short-eared owls in migration perch on tundra hillocks. The owls, hawks, and eagles take their toll of the smaller mammals, sometimes reducing the size of prey populations in combination with other causes of death such as starvation and disease, at other times living off a surplus beyond the capacity of the environment to support, and at all times providing ornithological highs for those who hike in the Kluane Ranges.

Few species can live year round in the north. Gone in winter are birds that feed on ground or aerial insects, leafy or aquatic vegetation—in other words, the majority of species. The only species that remain in Kluane's snow-clad mountains are those that feed on bark invertebrates (woodpeckers, nuthatches, chickadees), seeds of herbaceous plants (juncos, small

finches), cones of conifers (crossbills), or buds (grouse and ptarmigan); and carnivores and scavengers (hawks, owls, ravens, gray jays). During the summer the gray jays cache food to eat in the winter without which they would probably not survive. Ravens patrol the Alaska Highway looking for road-kills, or search interior valleys for wolf-kills. Hawks and owls watch for snowshoe hares prancing in the moonlight and for small rodents that have emerged from their ventilator shafts for an above-snow run.

Three species of ptarmigan live year round in the Kluane high country. They occupy three different habitats: white-tailed, on the rocky and talus slopes: rock, on the upland tundra; and willow, in the sub-alpine vegetation. All have evolved adaptations to cold, such as feathered feet, and all exhibit cycles of abundance characteristic of many permanent northern birds and

Great gray owl. (Manfred Hoefs)

Opposite: Golden eagle at its nest. (David Mossop)

mammals. Much research has been done on the cause of these cycles, and it is still not known whether they have survival value for the species or are merely evidence of incomplete adaptations in a relatively new and changeable environment. In rock ptarmigan, the species most studied, the peaks of the cycle occur approximately every 10 years. The cause of this appears to be related to changes in social behavior: when the population is large, aggressive individuals have an advantage and these individuals may claim large territories, which causes the population to drop to such an extent that nonaggressive birds that are content with smaller territories move in, and the population increases once again. This explanation is strictly tentative. Such a "strategy," whereby individuals with different behavioral characteristics are favored at different phases of a cycle, may allow a greater variability to exist in the gene pool of rock ptarmigan, making them better able to adjust to sudden changes in their own numbers, to the weather, or to environmental factors. One disturbing observation is that cycles of abundance may be disappearing in other species in more southerly environments. There may be a rough correlation between the extent of human disturbance and the disappearance of cycles. We do not know enough about population ecology to be sure.

The sub-alpine contains far more species of birds than the tundra, and is comparable in this regard to the lowland habitats. Many of the species, however, are not abundant. The large number of species in the sub-alpine is probably due to its position midway between lowland and tundra habitats. Representative species are found here, both from the lowland habitat, such as the dark-eyed junco, and from the tundra habitat, such as the rock ptarmigan, but the sub-alpine habitat is marginal for them both. The sub-alpine is the preferred habitat of only a few species, such as the tree sparrow. Townsend's solitaires are most common here, with an amplified thrush-like song that flutes in June days, and golden-crowned sparrows are confined almost exclusively to this habitat, for some ecological reason.

Grassland habitats are mostly patches on south-facing mountain slopes, too small for systematic censusing. Horned larks nest here as well as on the tundra. Say's phoebes and mountain bluebirds splash color along the edges of the forest openings. Black-billed magpies sail low over the bunch grasses, looking for dead arctic ground squirrels.

The bogs and marshes have not been systematically censused because of the nature of the terrain, but the greatest diversity and abundance of birds is found there. Such wetlands are not common in Kluane; they occur primarily behind beaver dams or at the edges of lakes that flood periodically. Some "puddle ducks" nest here: green-winged teal and mallards. In the larger ponds, diving ducks either nest or "stage" before migration: white-winged and surf scoters, harlequin ducks. Northern phalaropes dabble along the shallows. This species has perhaps the most unusual of northern adaptations. The roles of male and female are reversed, so that the male incubates the eggs, leaving the female free to find another mate and quickly nest again before the season is too far advanced.

Two swamp-edge species common all across North America south of the Yukon only just make it to the Kluane region: red-winged blackbird and song sparrow. It is unusual for an ornithologist to get excited about finding either of these species, but I once spent over an hour photographing a nesting song sparrow in a wet willow thicket, to document the second nesting record for the southwestern Yukon.

These wetland pockets of abundance are the bird "cities." The region, as a whole, taking in all the other habitats mentioned, has a lower density of birds than the more temperate regions

Dark-eyed junco

farther south. For example a typical hardwood forest in southern Ontario might contain 200 territorial males per 40 hectares (100 acres), and a west-coast coniferous forest might contain 250 males. In the Kluane region, densities are in the order of 30 (tundra) to 186 (lowland willow shrub) males per 40 hectares. (Precise comparisons with the results of other studies cannot be made unless the sizes of census plots are the same.)

There is a chain of reasons why both abundance and species diversity are lower in the north. Less sunlight means colder temperatures, permafrost at higher elevations, and a lower input of light energy. The result is lower plant productivity, which in turn results in lower animal productivity. Food chains are short. On top of that, sudden summer cold or snow can result in nesting failures. Many species of birds lay one egg a day and do not begin full-time incubation until the clutch is complete. An incomplete clutch and sudden cold can result in cracked eggs. Species whose young require brooding for many days after the eggs hatch may be caught between exposing their young to cold in order to obtain food for them or having them starve. Behavioral adaptations have evolved to reduce the risk, such as cooperative food-gathering for the young by the male; but time is short — in about 60 days the young must be of full adult size, complete with stored body fat and developed plumage, ready for often lengthy migrations.

It takes little to tip the scales between success and failure in the rearing of young in the north. Man can influence the balance in obvious ways, typified by an overzealous photographer keeping incubating birds off the nest for too long, and in less obvious but more far-reaching ways, such as the suspected but not fully understood manner in which we may be extinguishing natural cycles. Great care must be taken to maintain the north's avian ecological rhythms. We are only just beginning to understand them.

7. HORNS AND HOOVES

Manfred Hoefs

KLUANE NATIONAL PARK is one of the richest wildlife areas in the Canadian north. Both the diversity and the density of its large mammals are high for a northern region. The density of many of these populations is at the limit of the land's ability to support them, because of the unique climatic conditions, the diversity of land forms, and a ban on hunting in effect since 1942.

Mammals are found in the park that are associated with the boreal-sub-arctic biome (moose, black bear, caribou, red squirrel), with mountainous habitats (goat, sheep, cougar, grizzly, marmot, pika), and with the grassland-forest edge (mule deer, least chipmunk).

What follows is a brief description of the more obvious and spectacular mammals of the park, and of others that are known or assumed to occur.

Grizzly bears live in one of their last North American strongholds at Kluane. Much is known about them through the long-term studies of A. M. Pearson of the Canadian Wildlife Service. Good habitats (Dezadeash and Alsek valley, Klukshu River, and Sockeye Lake) support densities of one bear for every 26 square kilometers (10 square miles). Other ranges are less densely populated, but a reasonable estimate is that between 300 and 400 grizzlies live in Kluane National Park.

Kluane's grizzlies are relatively small. Mature males average 141 kilos (310 pounds) and sows 95 kilos (210 pounds); they lose 30 to 40 percent of their maximum fall weight while denned up between October and May. Sexual maturity is not reached until the sixth to eighth year, and successive sets of cubs (1.7 being the average) are at least three years apart. This makes the grizzly the slowest reproducing big-game animal in the Yukon. They reach a maximum life span of over 20 years.

Grizzlies have definite home ranges, those of males being considerably larger than those of females. Boars, particularly young ones, may travel considerable distances, and some move out of the protected park area. One bear that had been tagged near Haines Junction was shot near Carmacks after traveling at least 145 kilometers (90 miles).

Grizzlies at Kluane are primarily herbivorous animals. They may on occasion feed on carrion and catch arctic ground squirrels and marmots, but their diet consists largely of vegetable matter, primarily the roots of sweet vetch, willow catkins, sedges, and grasses, as well as soapberry and other berries if available. Bears living in the Klukshu and Tatshenshini valleys and around Sockeye Lake feed on salmon during spawning runs.

You may encounter a grizzly anywhere, but during the summer months they are most often observed at alpine elevations, or on wide river flats with an abundance of soapberry and sweet

Grizzly bear crossing Sheep-Bullion Plateau. (John Theberge)

vetch. Bears are potentially dangerous animals, particularly when accompanied by cubs, when feeding at a kill, or if approached too closely. To avoid unpleasant encounters, handle garbage properly and avoid carrying food items whose smell may attract them.

We must respect the prior occupancy of the land by bears, particularly in a national park. If proper precautions are taken and hiking trails are constructed to avoid prime bear habitat, there is no reason why grizzlies and man should not coexist harmoniously.

Black bears, unlike grizzlies, are found only in the forested areas of Kluane National Park. They are smaller than grizzlies, are usually black but sometimes cinnamon, and have less of a shoulder hump and shorter claws. Unlike grizzlies, they climb trees, and with amazing speed.

Black bears are more productive than grizzlies, for three reasons: they reach sexual maturity sooner, often after only four or five years; they have larger litters; and the time between successive sets of cubs is often only two years. Their maximum life span is similar to that of grizzlies.

Despite their higher productivity, there are probably fewer black bears than grizzlies in the park. Black bears may seem to be more numerous because they become accustomed to people quickly and are therefore more often encountered around campsites and garbage dumps. But their forest-only habitat is more confining. They do not get along with their stronger relatives; where grizzlies use lowland forested areas, black bears are usually absent.

In wilderness areas, most black bears run when they see a human. But they can be dangerous if approached too closely. Like grizzlies and all other forms of wildlife, black bears have prior rights in the park that deserve our respect.

Nowhere in the Yukon are there so many Dall sheep as in Kluane National Park. They are the most numerous large mammal in the park, estimated at a minimum of 4,000 year-round residents. They are found on suitable mountain ranges throughout the park, except for the southernmost areas (Alsek Range), where they are displaced by mountain goats. The most densely populated areas are the Slims River drainage and Donjek drainages.

Dall sheep are slightly smaller than bighorn sheep, which live farther south; rams may weigh from 82 kilos (180 pounds) to 113 kilos (250 pounds) during the fall and stand 91 centimeters (36 inches) high at the shoulders, while ewes may weigh from 45 kilos (100 pounds) to 59 kilos (130 pounds) at that time and stand about 76 centimeters (30 inches) high. Both sexes lose 20 to 30 percent of their maximum fall weight during the winter. In contrast to bighorn sheep, Dall sheep are white and their horns more slender and flaring. November is the rutting season, and lambs are born in May. Dall ewes usually have their first lambs when they are three years old, and only single lambs have been observed. They live a maximum of 12 to 13 years.

My recent studies of the sheep population on Sheep Mountain, overlooking Kluane Lake, have shown that they eat a great variety of plants in the span of a year—at least 110 different species. Only four, however, make up half of their forage: one species of sedge (*Carex filifolia*), one sage (*Artemesia frigida*), one grass (*Calamagrostis purpurascens*), and one willow (*Salix glauca*).

Dall sheep have many predators, including wolf, coyote, wolverine, lynx, eagle, and sometimes even bear. For this reason, their winter ranges, and particularly their lambing areas, are always close to escape terrain in the form of steep cliffs or canyon walls.

In my research I found that Dall sheep undergo distinct annual vertical migrations. During May and June they move uphill to spend the summer on alpine meadows. They move down in September and October and spend the winter months from November to May at relatively low elevations on exposed, wind-blown ridges, usually with a warm southern exposure. In winter the movements of sheep are greatly influenced by weather. Sheep feed whenever possible on areas with little or no snow. They avoid exposure to severe wind chills, and move to lowest elevations during periods of lowest temperatures. For most of the year sheep position themselves on mountain slopes to take advantage of the most readily available forage and the least severe weather conditions.

Dall sheep provide one of the wildlife spectacles of Kluane. To come around the shoulder of a mountain and encounter a big full-curl ram framed by blue sky is an experience possible only in Kluane and one other national park in Canada, Nahanni.

Mountain goats are the second most abundant large mammal in Kluane National Park, with approximately 700 to 800 year-round residents,

Sheep Mountain from across foot of Kluane Lake. (John Theberge)

while another 100 or so migrate annually back and forth across the southern and western borders.

Goats are most common in the southern portion of the park where, in certain areas, such as the Alsek Range and between Goatherd Mountain and Bates Lake, they have completely displaced sheep. In the northern portion of the park, only isolated, small populations are found in such places as the Slims River valley at the mouths of Bullion and Canada creeks, in the Cement Creek drainage of the Donjek River, and along certain glaciers (Chitina, Logan, Walsh) on the Alaska-Yukon boundary.

The distribution of both goats and sheep in the park may be correlated to snow conditions, although detailed research has not been conducted. It is known that goats can cope better than sheep with heavy snow, and areas of the park where goats replace or are more abundant than sheep are areas where snow conditions are most severe.

Goats resemble Dall sheep, not only in external characteristics such as size, weight, and color, but also in a number of biological traits such as age of sexual maturity, length of gestation period, season of rutting and giving birth to young, single births rather than twins, and

Moose in the Kluane high country. (Manfred Hoefs)

length of life. While goats are often confused with sheep, particularly female sheep, there are a number of important differences. Goats have longer hair, particularly along the center of the back, and the long hair continues down their legs to their ankles, giving the appearance of an animal wearing pants or knickers. Goats also have a pronounced dorsal hump similar to grizzlies and moose; they have a beard, and the tail is more pronounced than in sheep.

There is no evident distinction between ranges used in summer and in winter; goats are seen at similar altitudes the year round. In contrast to sheep, they utilize shrubs frequently and are also known to feed on coniferous species such as sub-alpine fir and juniper.

The best areas to observe goats in the park are the Kathleen Lake and Sockeye Lake drainages, as well as on Goatherd Mountain opposite the terminus of the Lowell Glacier.

The moose in Kluane National Park are members of North America's largest subspecies (*Alces alces gigas*), and bulls may reach fall weights of 725-817 kilos (1,500-1,800 pounds). Cows are about 20 to 30 percent lighter.

Because the topography of the Kluane region is very rugged, and most of the land is well above the tree line, few localities can be described as good moose habitat. The best areas are in the south, around Dezadeash, Kathleen, and Sockeye lakes, and in the valleys of the Klukshu and Tatshenshini rivers. About 400 to 500 moose live in the park, and since the best habitats are near the boundaries considerable movement into and out of the park takes place.

Moose also undergo annual vertical migrations, but these are less predictable than those of sheep, and not all moose take part in them. Most moose spend most of their time in the sub-alpine shrub zone, a vegetation belt near the tree line dominated by willows, dwarf birch, and alders. Some moose, however, stay in the valleys during the summer, especially where there are ponds, slow rivers, or shallow lakes with aquatic vegetation. Almost all moose stay in the valleys in late winter (January to March) when the snow at sub-alpine elevations becomes too deep or crusted for them to move easily there. On these winter ranges they can be very concentrated, and their density may reach two to three per square mile, which would be considered high anywhere but especially in a northern district such as the Yukon.

Moose are browsing animals. Willows, poplars, alders, and viburnums are their staple food items. During summer they also feed on submerged and emergent aquatic vegetation such as water lilies, horsetails, maretails, and pond weeds.

Moose may reach sexual maturity at 16 months of age, but in stable populations with a low annual productivity, such as Kluane's, they usually do not breed until 28 months of age. The rutting season is in late September and early October, and calves are born in late May and early June. Single calves are most common, although twins have been observed. Cows may have calves every year. Weaning is at four or five months. Moose may live for up to 20 years.

Wolves are the principal predators of moose, but occasional moose calves are killed by grizzlies, black bears, and even wolverines and lynx. The best place to observe moose during the summer is along the trail from Dezadeash Lake to Mush Lake. This valley has a high year-round density. Very striking complete and partial albino moose are occasionally observed there. While moose are normally afraid of man, cows occasionally defend their calves, and during the rutting season bulls have been reported to attack people, evidently having mistaken them for rivals.

Kluane National Park does not support caribou on a year-round basis. Two resident herds live near the park boundary: one in the Kluane Hills stretching from the southeastern corner of Kluane Lake to Kloo Lake more or less parallel to and east of the Alaska Highway; the other along the northern boundary of the park from the Burwash Uplands in the east, along Teepee Lake valley, to the White River basin in the west. Recent investigations indicate that the second of these areas supports several distinct populations, one of them consisting of 250 to 300 animals and more or less restricted to the Burwash Uplands directly adjacent to the park. Members of this herd occasionally cross into the park in midsummer in search of snow patches at high altitudes. A portion of the herd annually moves across the Alaska Highway, joining a small resident herd near the Brooks Arm of Kluane Lake. While en route they are especially vulnerable to hunting.

These caribou are members of a subspecies called "mountain" or "woodland." They are larger than the barren-ground caribou and do not undertake extensive annual migrations. Their movements are largely vertical in response to climatic conditions, primarily snow depth and type. They are usually at lowest elevations in midwinter (January and February), when they utilize open spruce forests. They ascend to highest altitudes during the hottest part of the summer (late July and August), seeking relief from heat and harassment by insects.

Caribou have a lower rate of annual recruitment of new animals of breeding age than most large herbivores in Canada — the birth rate is low and the death rate among fawns is high.

Consequently, caribou can withstand only moderate mortality if population numbers are to remain constant. Recent studies of the caribou of the Burwash Uplands showed that this herd has been experiencing an even lower than normal annual recruitment. In one year there appeared to be no young that lived to breeding age. Consequently, this herd cannot withstand very much hunting. Nor can it withstand within its range the kind of stress that is associated with the use of bulldozers and other activities of miners. These animals need protection.

Wolves are found throughout Kluane National

Woodland caribou on the Burwash Uplands. (Jeff Green)

Park, and observations indicate that the ranges of individual packs extend beyond the boundaries of this protected area. Since they are classified as predators in the remainder of the Yukon, they can be killed at any time and in any number outside the park and its adjacent sanctuary. Management of the "park wolves" therefore requires a cooperative effort between the National Parks Branch and the Yukon government.

At least three packs use the area, the largest of them being in the south around Dezadeash and Kathleen lakes. In late winter wolves appear to join up into larger packs, and up to 30 have been observed together in this region. A smaller pack of eight to 10 wolves hunts the central portion of the park around the Slims River and the southern end of Kluane Lake. Another, larger pack uses the northern portion of the park around the Donjek River basin, and north to the Teepee Lake valley. Approximately 50 to 60 wolves make use of Kluane National Park as part of their range.

Wolves prey primarily on moose, although other big game, and to a lesser extent small mammals, are taken as well. A recent study in the southern portion of the park, in which 450 wolf scats were analyzed, showed that moose provided more than 50 percent of the food of wolves. Surprisingly, smaller mammals including beaver, snowshoe hare, and arctic ground squirrel provided more food for the wolves in summer than did some of the larger mammals, such as Dall sheep and mountain goats.

At one time wolves went unprotected in national parks. Now they are understood as an important part of the fauna. As the demands for land and natural resources eat up more and more wilderness, national parks may become crucial to the survival of wide-ranging predators such as wolves.

The mule deer is a recent addition to the list of mammalian species (a northwestern range extension), but it is rare in the Kluane region. Also, there have been a few unconfirmed sightings of the coastal black-tailed deer, far north of its normal range. Other species that are more common close to Kluane National Park than right in it are the wolverine, especially in the vicinity of the Chilkat Pass south of the park, and the cougar, not yet officially confirmed in the Kluane region but found in small numbers in northern British Columbia.

The park has one non-native species that is unwanted — the horse. The open-range practice of the Yukon has resulted in wild horses, which enter the park's valleys and range far in the interior. These horses compete with native animals (sheep on Sheep Mountain and moose in the Dezadeash and Burwash areas) and must be removed before a condition develops similar to that witnessed in the southwestern United States, where burros that escaped during the gold-rush days displaced bighorn sheep. The competition between horses and sheep at Kluane has been carefully documented for the Sheep Mountain area, and is a cause for concern.

There is another very new species at Kluane, one with a great ability to become a dominant ecological force wherever it is found — man. Man's impact in Kluane will increase with anticipated development in the region — the proposed paving of the Alaska Highway with a resulting increase in tourism, and the proposed construction of a pipeline and related service centers, and also the promotion of Kluane National Park itself. However, the park is large, and the possibility lies in our hands to bring about, through proper planning, a harmonic coexistence of both outdoor recreation and education, on the one hand, and conservation of unique sub-arctic ecosystems, on the other.

8. MAMMALS BUILT CLOSE TO THE GROUND

Charles J. Krebs

S MALL MAMMALS ARE much less spectacular than large mammals, but what they lack in size, they make up for in numbers. A variety of small mammals live in Kluane National Park. I will discuss only the more common species; little is known of the rare ones.

Two small mammals abound in the boreal forest and tundra communities of Kluane National Park — the arctic ground squirrel and the snowshoe hare. The arctic ground squirrel, often incorrectly called the gopher, is one of nature's true hibernators. Adult squirrels emerge in April, just as the snow is melting, after seven or eight months of hibernation. The adult male fights for a breeding territory, encompassing a group of burrows spread over, at the most, a few acres of ground. By winning a territory, he earns the right to breed with the females living within

it. Young ground squirrels are born in the female's burrow and do not come above ground for three weeks, by which time they are weaned and ready to forage for themselves. Ground squirrels eat a variety of low-growing plants such as sage, dryas, and penstemmons, and also various seeds, seed pods, and berries. During the summer they acquire a thick layer of fat on which they will live during their hibernation.

The life of the ground squirrel is centered around its burrows. Here it finds protection from predators and from the weather, and here it spends the winter in hibernation. Burrow systems range from small ones with a single entrance to multi-chambered complexes with many entrances.

The arctic ground squirrel is one of the most important prey species of a large number of pre-

Dall sheep (46).

Mountain goat (47).

TOP: Moose (48). ABOVE: Woodland caribou in shrub tundra (49).

ABOVE: Grizzly bear (50).
TOP RIGHT: Red fox (51).
LOWER RIGHT: Collared pika in its rockslide habitat (52).
FAR RIGHT: Arctic ground squirrel (53).

Kluane Lake (54).

Mush Lake (55).

Sockeye Lake (56).

dators in the Kluane region. Fox, coyote, wolf, lynx, and grizzly bear are commonly seen hunting or digging for ground squirrels. In response, the arctic ground squirrel has evolved an intriguing system of warning vocalizations. When a predator is seen approaching on the ground, the threatened squirrel utters a sharp triple chatter, or "sik-sik-sik." Then, as the predator approaches, the squirrel increases the intensity and frequency of its call. So other squirrels are warned, not just of a predator's approach, but also of the direction from which the danger is coming. For aerial predators such as the golden eagle, marsh hawk, or falcon, the alarm call is quite different — a short, very high-pitched note. This call alerts other squirrels nearby but does not give away the location of the calling squirrel.

Snowshoe hares fluctuate dramatically in abundance in a 10-year cycle. In the Kluane region they were at peak abundance in 1971, and very scarce in 1976 and 1977. The next population high will be in 1981. They are well adapted to life in the boreal forest. They do not hibernate, but have enlarged hind feet for walking on the snow in winter and a thick fur for insulation. Snowshoe hares feed on a variety of small plants during the summer. In winter they depend on the buds of willow, birch, other shrubs, and spruce.

Snowshoe hares breed during the spring and summer months, producing two to four litters each year. Juvenile hares do not breed in their first summer. As the number of hares builds up, the reproductive rate begins to fall, and browsing during the winter months begins to damage more and more shrubs. The shortage of high-quality winter food stops the increase in numbers and starts a decline. Meanwhile, an abundance of predators is accumulating, and heavy predation forces the snowshoe hare population down to very low levels.

Many predators feed on snowshoe hares; lynx are their major predator in the Kluane region, but coyotes, red foxes, wolves, and several birds of prey also contribute to the annual loss. Many of these predators increase in numbers when snowshoe hares are on the increase, and thus the 10-year cycle of the snowshoe hare reverberates throughout the biological community.

Two tree squirrels are found in Kluane. The red squirrel is common in white spruce trees, and during the winter they feed on spruce seeds. During the other seasons they feed on a variety of fruits, seeds, and mushrooms. The chatter of the red squirrel is a common sound in the spruce forests of the park. You will also find their middens in the woods, under the spruce trees where they feed on cones. Squirrels nip off the scales one by one to get at the seeds, and great mounds of discarded cone scales are left on the ground at feeding sites. Red squirrels are preyed upon by pine martin, a rare member of the weasel family.

The northern flying squirrel is a rare tree squirrel that occurs in the southern part of the park. Little is known of its habits in the Yukon. It constructs nests of bark and twigs, 30-40 centimeters (12-16 inches) in diameter, normally in spruce trees.

The least chipmunk is another abundant small mammal in forested parts of Kluane. It may be seen darting about under shrubs and around logs, gathering berries and nuts. It stores a great deal of food in caches. During the winter, chipmunks hibernate in nests underground, but they do not sleep for the entire winter. They awake periodically to eat and then return to sleep. They have one litter a year, with about five young.

The porcupine is a common rodent of the boreal forest. It weighs up to 11 kilos (24 pounds) and next to the beaver is Kluane's largest rodent. Porcupines are solitary animals, active winter and summer. They feed on a variety of leaves in the summer and on the bark and buds of trees during the winter. In spite of their quills, they are killed and eaten by wolverines and fishers. Wolves and coyotes occasionally prey on them but are less adept at avoiding their quills.

Pikas are small guinea-pig-like mammals that live on rocky talus slopes in mountainous areas of western North America. In Kluane they are widely distributed and common wherever there are rock slides. Pikas are closely related to rabbits, and feed on a variety of green plants. They harvest food in the late summer and build haystacks for the winter. Little is known about their life history or populations in Kluane.

Mice are by far the most abundant mammals in the park, though they are seldom seen. Ten species of mouselike rodents may be found in the park, two of which are common and widespread, comprising about 80 percent of the mouse populations. One of these is the northern red-backed vole, which lives in a wide variety of habitats from the alpine tundra zone to the open shrub and forested communities; it is readily identified by the bright rufous stripe down its back. It eats

Porcupine. (Stephen Krasemann)

a variety of leaves, buds, and fruits, and is active under the snow during the winter. It breeds from May to September, and females can bear a litter of four to eight young every three or four weeks throughout this season. Young red-backed voles are weaned at three weeks of age, and some may begin breeding during their first year.

The deer mouse is the second very common mouse in the Kluane region. Except in the alpine tundra zone, it may be seen anywhere from gravel beach ridges to deep boreal forest. The deer mouse is nocturnal and hence rarely seen by visitors. It feeds on seeds and berries, supplemented by mushrooms and buds, and occasional insects in the summer months. Deer mice in the Kluane area often have only one litter a year,

with four to six young born in early June. The young emerge in the spring in very fat condition, and I suspect that they may save energy in winter by going into a torpor — a deep sleep like a short hibernation. The deer mouse is one of the most widespread species of North American mammals, and it reaches the northern limit of its range in the Kluane region.

Eight other species of mice live in Kluane National Park. Some, such as the brown lemming and the northern bog lemming, are very rare. Many of the voles fluctuate in abundance from year to year, so that some years are called "mouse years" by the local people. One of the more unusual voles is the singing vole, which was first described during the construction of the Alaska Highway in 1942, just north of Kluane Park. The singing vole is most common in tundra areas of the park, and it gets its name from its high-pitched trill. It makes hay piles in the late summer from a variety of leaves and twigs. Populations of this vole rise and fall from year to year for reasons no one yet understands.

Other nonmouse species of small mammals in the Kluane region add diversity but are rare; to the south they are typical boreal forest species: beaver, muskrat, otter, mink, pine marten, least weasel, and ermine. These species find only mar-ginal habitats in the Kluane region because there are few extensive wetlands or mature forested lowlands there.

Kluane National Park is especially rich in small mammals because an overlap occurs here of southern fauna species found commonly in the provinces, and the Alaska-Siberian fauna species that barely enter Canada from Alaska; hence the great number of species of small mammals, from mouse to beaver, that form part of the biological fabric of Kluane National Park.

Singing vole

9. LIVING WATERS

Roland D. Wickstrom

THE WATERS OF the Kluane region present a great diversity of aquatic environments: from cascading mountain streams to meandering valley brooks, from meltwaters of mountain snows and immense valley glaciers to broad rivers that find their way to the Pacific Ocean and the Bering Sea. Lakes, ponds, and wetlands are scattered throughout the region. The variety of aquatic plants and animals found in these habitats reflects the diversity of the environment. High alpine lakes and streams provide rigorous habitats for a sparse array of hardy aquatic species, while at lower elevations the lakes, ponds, marshes, and streams afford more moderate conditions and support a wider variety of living things.

The Kluane region is drained principally by two river systems, the legendary Yukon and little-known Alsek. All waters of the northern park slopes unite to form the White River, a major tributary of the Yukon River system, which ultimately empties into the Bering Sea, while the Alsek system drains the southern part of the park. The Alsek is noteworthy as the only major river of the Yukon discharging its waters into the Pacific Ocean.

Waterways provide the principal avenues of dispersal for aquatic plants and animals. But the drainage systems were not always as we find them now. Former water courses can be identified today by old beach lines, drowned forests, and ancient lake beds. Climatic shifts led to successive advances and retreats of ice masses, whose moraine gravels drastically changed the drainage patterns. Changes that were of greatest significance to aquatic life included the periodic

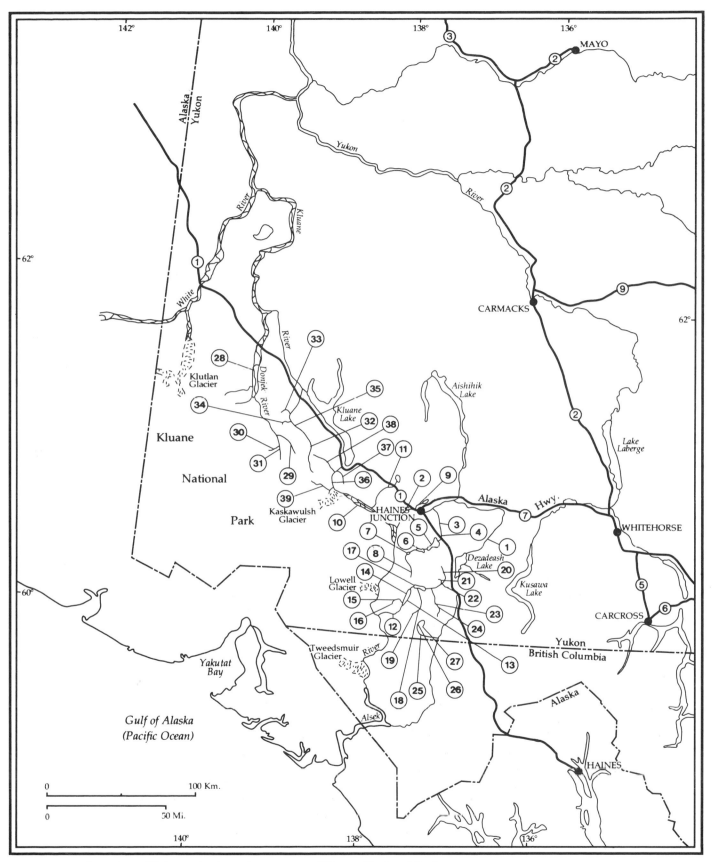

FIGURE 12. *Location of fish species in various waters of Kluane National Park.*

Tweedsmuir Glacier threatening to block Alsek River south of Kluane National Park, 1974. (Roland Wickstrom)

blocking of the Alsek River by both Pleistocene and recent glaciers. One of the Pleistocene blockings created Glacial Lake Champagne, which drained northeastward, so that all of the water of the upper Alsek River basin flowed into the Yukon system. Later the ice melted, allowing the water to flow straight down the Alsek to the Pacific as it does today. As recently as 130 years ago, ice again blocked the Alsek River, creating smaller lakes. Old beach lines with their windrows of driftwood are still visible, and the successive stages of vegetation reinvading the old lake basin provide interesting evidence of the previous water levels. In 1974 the foot of the Tweedsmuir Glacier threatened to block the Alsek River south of Kluane National Park, just as the Lowell Glacier did in past times.

Another significant change in drainage was brought about by advances of the Kaskawulsh Glacier, the most recent about 400 years ago.

The ice blocked the outlet of Kluane Lake, which at that time flowed south into the Alsek via the Kaskawulsh River. The level of the dammed lake apparently rose quickly and a new outlet was cut through at the northwestern end of Kluane Lake via the Kluane River, making Kluane Lake drain northward into the Yukon system as it does today. Significantly, this reversal of flow of Kluane Lake into the Yukon River permitted invasion by species from the Yukon River into the northern St. Elias-Kluane waters. Drowned forests, deep tributary estuaries, and other geological findings in Kluane Lake provide evidence for an interesting story. Natural events of this magnitude caused drastic alterations in the water levels, resulting in sudden changes in the habitat of the fish and other aquatic flora and fauna.

Dispersal of aquatic plants and animals follows the routes of drainage systems, but it also utilizes various other means such as wind and terrestrial animals. The actual establishment of aquatic species in new regions depends ultimately on the species finding suitable habitats. Ecological requirements and tolerances are large factors in determining distribution. Many species will tolerate wide ranges of habitat and physical and chemical attributes of the water, while others are more demanding; still others manage to adapt to the most forbidding of environments, where life seems impossible.

The rate of flow in a stream, the size and depth of a lake, the annual regime of water temperatures, and the chemical composition of the water are controlling factors for life in aquatic environments. Geological events and glaciation determine not only the shape and location of water basins and drainage systems but also the nature of surrounding rocks and soil, which give the water its basic chemical composition. Inflowing water dissolves inorganic and organic substances as it drains through surrounding soil and rock, and the water in the lake basin itself reacts with the sediments on its sides and bottom. The sun provides the energy that fuels the living system. Local climate, through its seasonal cycles, influences the solar input and modifies the habitat and surrounding water basins, thus playing a major role in determining the quantity and quality of the water.

Algae are the "grass" of the waters, the first link in the food chain. Invertebrate animals that graze on the algae are in turn consumed by the larger vertebrates. In the cold waters of the Kluane region, growth of living things is slow, and productivity is low in comparison with the waters of more temperate regions. In this northern latitude the primary energy source, solar radiation, is reduced by a shortened summer season, in turn reducing the ice-free period and lowering the mean summer temperatures. High alpine lakes and ponds experience the most severe conditions.

Streams in the Kluane area reflect the large and interesting range of flowing water habitats. Those of the high alpine zone that have ice, snow, and summer precipitation as their sources of water are almost devoid of aquatic life. Occasionally, blackfly larvae may be found clinging to the rocks. Short periods of flow and low and variable temperatures are the main factors causing this dearth of fauna. The upper reaches of most Kluane streams are like that.

As streams descend from the mountain slopes to the valley floor they pass through alpine, subalpine, and wooded montane vegetation zones, each with its particular type of habitat. Gentler gradients result in reduced silt loads and warmer water. Productivity and species diversity of aquatic flora and fauna are considerably greater. The lower reaches of Fraser Creek, southeast of Mush Lake, provide a typical example. At an altitude of 678 meters (2,224 feet), the stream gradient is less steep than higher up, and the surrounding tributaries drain the numerous warm wetlands and ponds. This input moderates the temperature and contributes algae-laden water. Fish are often present in these lower streams, chiefly the slimy sculpin although Dolly Varden char and Arctic grayling may also occur.

Heavy silt loads, so obvious in glacial melt streams and rivers in Kluane, usually prompt the question: "What can exist in these waters?" Some of the more turbid creeks, such as Vulcan and Canada in the Slims River basin, are very inhospitable to aquatic life. Only occasional larvae of blackflies and stoneflies are found. Other silted waters are similar. But, in streams less heavily silted, the diversity of species is greater and includes small fishes. Occasional specimens of the slimy sculpin and Arctic grayling have been taken from the silted waters of the Donjek River. Many flowing waters, such as the Duke River, become silty only after rain showers and then clear up considerably. The Duke's moderately silty water supports a broad range of algal species and aquatic insects, the latter represented chiefly by the blackfly, stonefly, mayfly, and caddisfly families.

Most lakes in Kluane are excellent examples of pristine alpine waters — clear, cold, and relatively unproductive. The lakes often resemble large pots, having steep rocky sides in some cases continuous with the surrounding slopes. The bottoms are relatively flat and regular and frequently filled with silt and sedimentation of glacial origin. Often somewhat elongated, they have low-lying land and sandy-gravel beaches at their ends, providing evidence of glacial scouring along the valleys. Upper Kathleen Lake is typical of this lake basin formation, as are Mush, Bates, and Onion lakes. Kathleen Lake, the deepest lake in Kluane (111 meters — 364 feet) is the only exception, having a broad, deep trench lying parallel to the southern shore, while the large expanse of the northeastern portion remains relatively shallow.

Lake depths present an interesting feature of Kluane waters. While Kathleen Lake is the deepest, one would expect from physical appearances of the terrain that Bates Lake would be just as deep. However, Bates Lake is only half as deep and is exceeded in depth by Upper Kathleen Lake (77 meters—253 feet), and Mush Lake (62 meters—204 feet), which from the surrounding terrain one would expect to be even shallower. Other lake depths are Onion Lake (29 meters–95 feet) and Sockeye Lake (27 meters—89 feet); all other lakes in Kluane are less than 20 meters (66 feet) deep.

Within the Kluane Ranges, the diversity of fish species is strikingly low compared with that in adjacent waters. Only a dozen species are scattered throughout the various lakes and streams (see Table 6 and Figure 12). The small number of species probably reflects the recentness of the lakes' emergence from their glacial coverings, their inaccessibility, and the unsuitability of some of their habitats, particularly the silty conditions of some waters in the northern region of the park.

Lake trout are probably the most widely distributed game fish of Kluane National Park. They occur in all major lakes drained by the Alsek River and its tributaries. Several lakes of the higher alpine and sub-alpine zone, not expected to contain fish because of their altitude and impassible outflow cataracts, have been found to contain lake trout. Climbing Lake, a small cirque lake at 1,158 meters (3,798 feet) near Onion Lake in the southern region, supports lake trout only. The trout appear to subsist on invertebrate animals such as snails and midge larvae of the bottom and shallows. Jutland Lake (1,189 meters—3,900 feet) is similar. Lake trout from these high lakes are small. None caught to date exceed 1.6 kilograms (3.5 pounds), which reflects the scarcity of food organisms and the very cold July water temperatures (5°C—40°F at the surface). By comparison, trout taken from Kathleen, Mush, and Bates lakes (Bates Lake 18°C—66°F at the surface), lying at lower altitudes of approximately 700 meters (2,300 feet), feed predaciously on other fish species and invertebrate animals and can grow to about 13 kilos (29 pounds).

In northern Kluane National Park, in the watersheds drained by the Slims, Duke, and Donjek rivers, no lakes occur that are larger than

Silt-filled waters of Slims River. (John Theberge)

Table 6 / *Distribution of Fish Species in Various Waters of Kluane National Park*

Waters	Map location[1]	lake trout	Dolly Varden	rainbow trout	chinook salmon	kokanee	sockeye salmon	round whitefish	pygmy whitefish	Arctic grayling	burbot	northern pike	slimy sculpin
Alsek River Drainage:		+	+	+	+	+	+	+	+	+	+	+	+
Dezadeash River	1	.	.	.	.	.	.	.	.	.	.	.	.
Lynx Lake*	2	−	−	−	−	−	−	−	−	+	−	+	−
Kathleen River	3	+	.	+	−	.	−	+	.	.	.	.	.
Rainbow Lakes	4	.	.	−	−	.	−	.	.	.	.	.	.
Kathleen Lake	5	+	+	+	−	+	−	+	+	+	.	−	+
Upper Kathleen Lake	6	+	−	−	−	+	−	+	−	+	.	−	+
Sockeye Lake	7	+	−	−	−	+	−	+	+	+	+	−	+
Cottonwood Lake*	8	+	−	−	−	−	−	−	−	+	−	−	−
Pine Creek	9	.	.	.	−	.	−	+	.	+	.	.	+
Kaskawulsh River	10	.	.	.	.	.	.	.	.	.	.	.	.
Jarvis River	11	.	+	.	−	.	−	.	.	+	.	.	+
Bates River	12	.	.	.	.	.	.	.	.	.	.	.	.
Bates Lake	13	+	+	−	−	+	−	+	−	+	−	−	+
Cranberry Lake*	14	−	−	−	−	−	−	−	−	−	−	−	−
Field Creek	15	−	−	−	−	−	−	−	−	−	−	−	+
Field Lake*	16	−	−	−	−	−	−	−	−	−	−	−	−
Mush Lake	17	+	+	−	−	+	−	+	−	+	−	−	+
Mush Creek	18	.	.	.	.	.	.	.	.	.	.	.	+
Jutland Lake*	19	+	−	−	−	−	−	−	−	−	−	−	−
Alder Creek	20	.	+	.	−	.	.	.	.	.	.	.	+
Cyclops Lake*	21	−	+	−	−	−	−	−	−	−	−	−	+
St. Elias Lake	22	.	+	.	−	.	.	.	.	.	.	.	.
Fraser Creek	23	.	+	.	−	.	.	.	.	.	.	.	+
Missing Lake*	24	−	+	−	−	−	−	−	−	−	−	−	−
Tatshenshini River	40	.	+	.	+	.	+	.	.	.	.	.	.
Bridge River	25	.	.	.	.	.	.	.	.	.	.	.	.
Onion Lake	26	+	−	−	−	−	−	+	−	−	−	−	+
Climbing Lake	27	+	−	−	−	−	−	−	−	−	−	−	−
Yukon River Drainage (Kluane region):		+	+	−	+	−	+	+	+	+	+	+	+
Donjek River	28	.	.	.	.	.	.	.	.	+	.	.	+
Bighorn Creek	29	.	.	.	.	.	.	.	.	.	.	.	.
Slipping Creek*	30	−	−	−	−	−	−	−	−	−	−	−	−
Snipe Lake*	31	−	−	−	−	−	−	−	−	−	−	−	−
Kluane River		.	.	.	.	.	.	.	.	.	.	.	.
Duke River	32	.	.	.	.	.	.	.	.	+	.	.	+
Granite Creek	33	−	−	−	−	−	−	−	−	−	−	−	−
Knob Creek*	34	−	−	−	−	−	−	−	−	−	−	−	−
Bone Lake*	35	−	−	−	−	−	−	−	−	−	−	−	−
Kluane Lake		+	−	−	−	−	−	+	−	+	+	+	+
Slims River	36	.	.	.	.	.	.	.	.	+	.	.	+
Vulcan Creek	37	−	−	−	−	−	−	−	−	−	−	−	−
Bullion Creek	38	−	−	−	−	−	−	−	−	+	−	−	+
Canada Creek	39	−	−	−	−	−	−	−	−	−	−	−	−

[1] location on Figure 12
+ present
− not found
. no data available
* unofficial name at present

20 hectares (50 acres) or deeper than 8 meters (26 feet). Except for two small lakes tributary to the Donjek River, the lakes here do not contain fish of any kind. However, in Kluane Lake adjacent to the park several species occur, including lake trout. Passable waterways connect Kluane Lake with northern park drainages, making them potentially available for exploitation by fish. Although fish will migrate upstream when silt and flow conditions permit, permanent residence in silty waters is undesirable for most fish.

One fish that is rare in North America is found in Sockeye Lake. The pygmy whitefish was captured in this lake by V. E. Wynne-Edwards in 1945 and not taken again until 1975. Apart from its small size and interesting habits, this fish is puzzling, because of its very scattered and discontinuous distribution in North America. Only recently (1952), it was discovered in Lake Superior, while all other occurrences are widely separated in drainages of British Columbia, western Alberta, Alaska, and the Yukon. The wide geographic gaps in its postglacial distribution present an enigma to biologists. Populations are known in western Alaska, and in the upper Yukon, Liard, and Peel rivers. Its presence in Sockeye Lake is one of only two known occurrences in the southwestern Yukon, the other being in Squanga Lake east of Whitehorse.

Pygmy whitefish coexist with round whitefish in Sockeye Lake. The difference in size between two mature specimens is striking: pygmy whitefish attain an average length of only 102-127 millimeters (4-5 inches), whereas round whitefish may reach more than twice that size. While pygmy whitefish have been found only in Sockeye Lake, round whitefish occur in most of the deeper lakes of Kluane National Park. The presence of round whitefish in Kluane Lake, and the connection of this lake with the northern park drainages, would enable them to enter the northern lakes, although none has yet been found there.

The Arctic grayling, an impressively colored species with a huge dorsal fin, is common throughout the Yukon. It appears to be present in all the larger lakes of the St. Elias-Kluane ranges, including the Sockeye-Kathleen and Mush-Bates chains. Grayling occur in Kluane Lake and tributaries that connect with drainages of the northern Kluane region. Even many of the silty tributaries of the Slims, Donjek, and

Duke river drainages have grayling when silt and flow conditions permit.

Throughout the waters of Kluane, an inconspicuous yet almost ubiquitous fish is found, one that usually escapes detection by the angler. The slimy sculpin is a small fish, reaching a maximum length of only about 140 millimeters (5.5 inches). It inhabits shallow waters adjacent to lake shores and areas of reduced flow in streams and rivers. Its food consists of insects and other small invertebrate animals, and in turn the sculpin is consumed by larger fish predators. However, because of its shallow-water and bottom-dwelling habits, the sculpin is eaten infrequently by other fish. This is the only species of sculpin occurring in Kluane National Park, and it lives in all waters from Onion, Mush, and Bates lakes in the southern region to the Slims, Duke, and Donjek rivers draining the northern area.

Burbot, or freshwater cod, inhabits many of the waters surrounding the St. Elias-Kluane region. Dezadeash Lake and Kluane Lake both support populations, but within Kluane National Park only Sockeye Lake has yielded this species. Since Sockeye Lake is uppermost in the Kathleen-Sockeye chain, burbot should be present in the lower waters. During recent investigations on Mush and Bates lakes, no burbot were captured. Although there have been no reports of it in these two lakes, its presence may be suspected.

Dolly Varden, a member of the char group in the salmon family, has a scattered occurrence only in the southern region of Kluane National Park, in drainages tributary to the Alsek River. Occasional specimens have been caught in Mush Lake and Bates Lake and specimens have been reported from Kathleen Lake, but the largest populations of this species apparently occur in the Alder-Fraser Creek drainages. Dolly Varden prefer to spawn in streams, and they use the waters of Alder and Fraser creeks for this. Cyclops, St. Elias, and Missing lakes contain the largest lake populations. These lakes have obstructions at their outlets, preventing movement of fish into their waters; therefore Dolly Varden are captive residents and must reproduce within the lakes. Cyclops Lake is only 5 meters (16 feet) deep at most, while Missing Lake is uniformly 2 meters (6.5 feet) deep, making fish survival over the winter problematical

Mature pygmy whitefish (below ruler) from Sockeye Lake, compared with round whitefish. (Roland Wickstrom)

since ice depths reach about one meter, and a long winter period should cause a "winter kill." Concentrations of dissolved oxygen become depleted during the ice-cover months as a result of oxygen-demanding decay of bottom organic material. Both lakes present an enigma with regard to winter fish survival.

Rainbow trout, or steelheads as they are called when anadromous (sea-running), occur only in the Kathleen River and in the Rainbow Lakes immediately below Kathleen Lake, except that a few have been reported from Kathleen Lake itself. Although rainbow trout occur along the west coast, those residing in the Alsek drainage apparently represent the only naturally occurring population native to the Yukon. Introductions have been made in several Yukon lakes near Whitehorse, Dawson, and Mayo.

The Alsek River and Yukon River drainages support populations of northern pike, but these do not seem to have become established in lakes of the Kluane ranges, except for Lynx Lake, a small riverside pond adjacent to the Dezadeash River a few miles above its confluence with the Kaskawulsh River. However, Pine, Dezadeash, and Kluane lakes around the periphery of the park support populations of northern pike.

The chinook, or king salmon is the largest of the sea-running salmon in the region. While not a member of the fish fauna within Kluane National Park, it is found in the Tatshenshini River, which drains the area just southeast of Kluane National Park and empties into the lower Alsek. Each summer, mature fish return from the sea and battle their way up the Alsek and the turbulent Tatshenshini to spawn in their quiet headwaters.

Sockeye salmon also migrate up the Tatshenshini River to spawn. The anadromous form of the sockeye is absent from the waters of the park, where only the kokanee, or landlocked form, occurs.

Kokanee occur in the Sockeye-Kathleen chain. The anadromous form seems to have lived in the upper Alsek drainage into Kathleen and Dezadeash lakes in the past, but recent advances of the Lowell Glacier blocked the Alsek River, possibly stopping sea migrations and forcing the landlocked existence. This ice obstruction of the Alsek is estimated to have cleared about 130 years ago, again permitting access to the sea. But the anadromous behavior has not returned, nor have sea-run strays re-exploited this waterway. At present this isolated population retains its landlocked behavior in the Kathleen-Sockeye chain and migrates to gravel reaches of the Sockeye River just below Sockeye Lake for late summer spawning. It is a population whose origin continues to invite investigation.

Further study is essential to illuminate the many unexplored features of life in the waters of this region. Because production is so slow, fish populations could soon be in danger from overangling unless monitoring and proper management are applied. Maintaining the natural balance in these sensitive aquatic communities will ensure perpetual excitement to the angler and wonder to the visitor who views these alpine waters for esthetic appreciation.

At the toe of the Kluane Glacier. (Wayne Neily)

Part Three
MAN

INTRODUCTION

THE HISTORY OF man in the St. Elias Mountains is a series of exciting events punctuating the solitude of an unpeopled land. It is as if the poverty of events caused by the scarcity of people has periodically erupted into the unusual, even the heroic. But the land brings out heroism; those people who won whatever challenge brought them into the St. Elias Mountains had to be heroes, sometimes just to stay alive.

The earliest people met the challenge of survival with primitive weapons. Despite the greater abundance of wildlife in prehistoric times, life, as glimpsed from the archaeological record, was tenuous. Then came the first white man, to explore and map an unknown region, and to find gold. Wherever the miners went in the north, the North West Mounted Police soon followed, to keep the peace. After them came the geological surveyors to identify mineral potentials, and the early entrepreneurs seeking to get rich by providing pack animals and supplies. To the highest peaks came the mountain climbers, facing some of the greatest challenges of their sport. And the wealthy big-game hunters.

Whether they triumphed or failed, few of these people stayed in the St. Elias Mountains. Only the Indians and a few whites — mountain men — chose to make their livelihood in this land and were capable of doing so. That was true until the Alaska Highway, built in 1942, brought a new era of easy access to the perimeter of the region.

Since then more people have come: the scientists, the gasoline-station owners, and the tourists with "Alaska or Bust" fingered in the dirt on the back windows of their cars.

The land is still "unpeopled and still," at least for eight months of each year; most of its history is being written in the summers by the park visitors and the scientists, by people supported with two-way radios, emergency aircraft, freeze-dried food, and lightweight camping gear.

"Things sure ain't like they used to be!"

10. PREHISTORIC MAN IN THE SOUTHWEST YUKON

Richard E. Morlan & William B. Workman

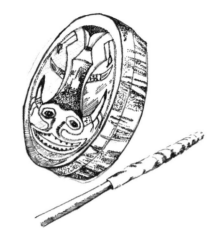

NO ONE IS certain when man first arrived in the Kluane region. Presumably, human settlement could have existed at the foot of the St. Elias Mountains just as early as recent evidence indicates for the Old Crow region of the northern Yukon. There, in and around Old Crow Flats, many fossilized bones have been found, and these bones have enabled paleontologists and archaeologists to reconstruct a picture of animal and human life predating the last major advance of the glaciers. This evidence is still only fragmentary, but it is enough to show that man entered the Yukon at least 30,000 years ago. It is possible that the first people of the Kluane area date from this time, but all evidence of any such occupation would have been erased when the glaciers advanced, around 20,000 years ago, and scoured the land of nearly all early deposits.

Unraveling the prehistory of early man depends upon understanding the geological, glaciological, and resultant soil history that influenced the region. Past events not only changed the hospitality of the land for occupation but erased or exposed the artefacts of earlier ages, and left clues to their dating. As the glaciers retreated, between 12,000 and 10,000 years ago, a blanket of loess was deposited in the valleys. During the following approximately 7,000 years of relative warmth, soils were laid down on top of the loess. The soils were largely a result of plant growth and decay on the nutrient-rich loess. The reddish-brown colors of the Slims soil are a common sight in the Kluane Valley, and a similar soil layer may also be seen in many parts of the nearby Aishihik Valley. Beneath the red layer is a pale yellow layer, which is also part of the Slims soil but has not been so strongly oxidized as the reddish layer above it. Deeper still in the loess profile, one can often find a gray layer that is probably similar in appearance to the original loess blanket before the Slims soil began to form.

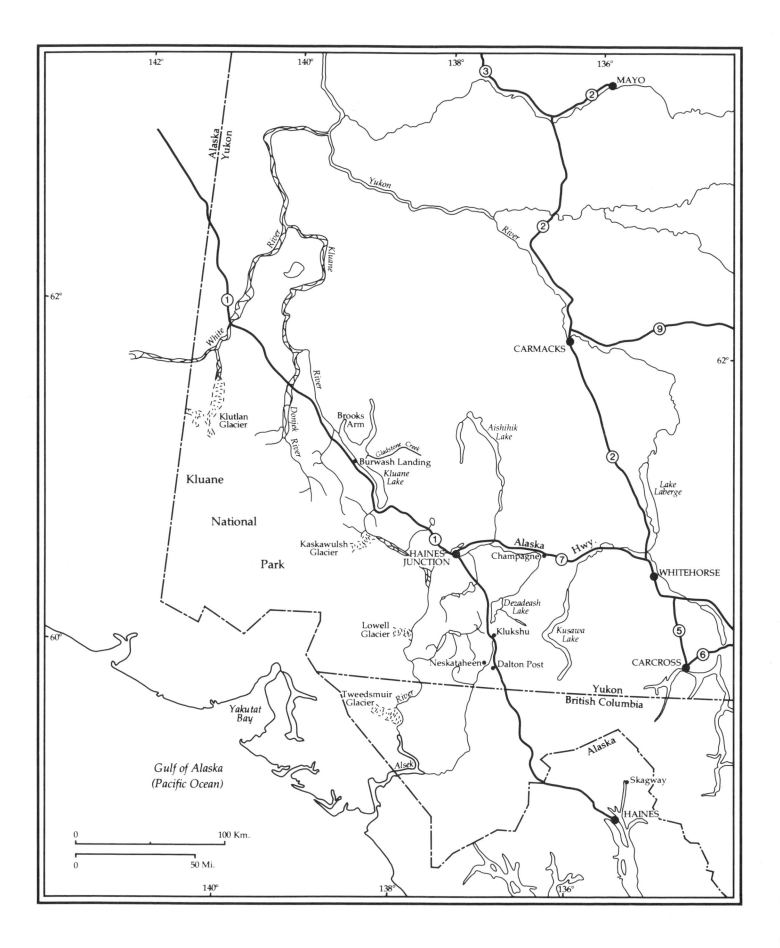

During the last 2,800 years, glaciers have advanced and retreated, churning up the soil in places or laying down new loess deposits on top of the old Slims soil. Thus, the soil layer in which artefacts are found reflects their age and the environmental conditions of the day.

Other kinds of sedimentary sequences are of equal importance for stratigraphic studies. In the Aishihik and Dezadeash valleys, stratigraphic profiles result from material laid down in the bottoms of the large lakes that formed in front of glacial advances. The volcanic ash-fall of 1,220 years ago provides another important stratigraphic marker.

The First Inhabitants: The Little Arm Culture (8,000-4,000 years ago)

Archaeologists have as yet recovered few traces of the people who occupied the Kluane and Aishihik areas in early postglacial times. The oldest known remains are those of a small group of hunters who camped briefly between 7,000 and 8,000 years ago on the bluff north of the former Canyon Creek roadhouse where the Alaska Highway crosses the Aishihik River. Here, more than 2 meters (6.5 feet) below the modern ground surface, we excavated a small hearth around which ancient bison hunters had camped. When they moved on, they left behind them two (broken) well-made spear points with rounded bases, a crude, unfinished, flaked implement, a (now badly decayed) slender bone tool, a handful of stone chips (by-products of a stone implement repair and manufacture), and two bones from a very large bison. We believe this was a hunter's camp overlooking the lush grasslands that flourished in the former bed of Glacial Lake Champagne.

Four other sites have yielded information on these pioneer occupants of southwestern Yukon.

Soil profile at Gladstone site. Neoglacial loess on top, followed by a dark band representing the White River ash, followed by Slims soil developed prior to 1,220 years ago, then loess, and, at the bottom, glacial till. (Richard Morlan)

All of these material remains we have grouped together under the term "Little Arm Culture," named after a fairly rich site on the Brooks (Little) Arm of Kluane Lake. Characteristic of the Little Arm technology was the production of small, slender, parallel-sided, sharp-edged, stone flakes called microblades, which were detached from specially prepared pieces of glassy stone that had been shaped to form micro-cores. Several kinds of burins were also in use; these are specialized stone tools that have had one or more edges removed by carefully directed blows to create a tough, thick cutting or scraping edge.

The spear points and knives of the Little Arm people were often quite thin and well made, with rounded bases but without notches to aid in attaching (hafting) the tip to a shaft. The bow and arrow were not to appear in the area for thousands of years, but Little Arm hunters probably were equipped with a throwing board to allow them to cast their light spears or darts with greater force than could be achieved by the unaided human arm. The Little Arm people used large stone tools flaked at one end on one side only (unifacially) for scraping and shaping

Tools from Little Arm site near Otter Falls. Three views of microblade cores, natural size: end where force is applied (left); side view (right); faceted end where microblades are detached (lower center). (Richard Morlan)

wood, bone, and other moderately hard organic substances, but they did not have the large bifacial knives (flaked on both sides) or the thick scrapers, flaked unifacially along one or more long margins, that were used by later occupants of the area. Also rare in Little Arm inventories are the various crude pebble tools that were used in later times for smashing and battering.

Little Arm spear point (left), scrapers (center), engraving tool (top right), and notched cobble (lower right). (Richard Morlan)

The Little Arm people also had thin flake tools worked into multiple sharp, delicate points. These were probably for delicate tasks in working bone and antler—for example, in the preparation of the bone needles or piercing tools (awls) that were necessary for sewing warm winter clothing and footgear, without which humans could not have survived the long, cold, sub-arctic winters. Almost certainly, these people used a variety of sophisticated bone and antler tools, but the erosion of time has spared few of them.

The daily life of the people of the Little Arm culture (which we believe, on the basis of radiocarbon dating of a few hearths, to have lasted over 4,000 years in the Kluane area) can be but dimly glimpsed at present. Upon entering the area in early postglacial times, these people found extensive grasslands where today there is spruce forest (although spruce had perhaps already begun to colonize the watercourses at the time of their coming). Scanty food remains that have been recovered from their camps indicate that they hunted bison, caribou, and moose. The bison they hunted were probably larger than the bison known in historic times elsewhere in North America.

Temperatures during the early part of the Little Arm people's long tenure on the land would have been cooler than those of today but rose steadily toward a peak, starting about 6,000 years ago, to a period of greater warmth than is now found in the area. Known Little Arm campsites are small, suggesting the leavings of small, constantly moving groups. One small site near Otter Falls in the Aishihik Valley, dated late in Little Arm times, yielded evidence suggesting the presence of a pole-and-brush shelter next to a large hearth; this shelter may have been similar to the brush lean-tos used in their youth by some of today's elderly inhabitants of the area.

We know little of the origin of these people. Their spear points and delicate engraving tools recall widespread cold grassland hunting technologies of early postglacial times to the south and east, while the diagnostic microblades and burins, although ultimately of Asiatic origin, probably were inspired by postglacial Alaskan technologies to the north and west. Technologies similar to the Little Arm seem to have flourished in the western part of the District of Mackenzie, in the central Yukon, and possibly in the Tanana Valley of Alaska.

The Taye Lake Culture (4,500-1,300 years ago)

Between 5,000 and 4,500 years ago, the Little Arm technology appears to have been abruptly replaced in the Kluane and Aishihik area by a new one, the Taye Lake culture, which intruded into the area from the north and west. Although many questions remain to be answered, the technologies of the Little Arm and Taye Lake cultures appear to be so different that the former can scarcely be said to be the ancestor of the latter. Therefore, we suggest, actual movements of new peoples brought the Taye Lake culture to the Kluane area, and the Little Arm people were displaced or absorbed by them. This event marks the only time in the 8,000-year prehistory of the area, other than the first appearance of the Little Arm people, when an intrusion or migration of alien peoples appears to be the best explanation for cultural changes deduced from the archaeological sites of the southwestern Yukon.

The immigrant groups were doubtless small, and we cannot specify at present why their ways were superior. Later cultures in the area, up to and including that of the modern Tutchone Athapaskan inhabitants, appear to be rooted in Taye Lake. Quite possibly, the Taye Lake peoples were speakers of an ancestral Athapaskan language.

A technology quite similar to the Taye Lake appeared without local antecedents on the southern flanks of the Brooks Range in northern Alaska between 7,000 and 6,000 years ago, that is, 1,000-2,000 years before the first Taye Lake peoples appeared in the southwestern Yukon. It seems likely that ancestral bearers of the Taye Lake culture moved south from northern Alaska, staying west of the Alaska Range and the Tanana Valley, and filtered by this somewhat circuitous route into the southwestern Yukon between 4,500 and 5,000 years ago.

A similar replacement of a culture like the Little Arm by a culture like the Taye Lake occurred at about the same time in the western part of the District of Mackenzie, to the east. The Taye Lake culture does not appear to have flourished in the central Yukon to the north or in the Tanana Valley of Alaska, to the northwest, and there is some reason to believe that a way of life rooted in the Little Arm culture persisted there into the Christian Era.

Although future work will doubtless lead to

Site of Little Arm culture and its succeeding Taye Lake culture near Gladstone Creek. In the excavation on the right, the White River ash forms a visible thin white band. (Richard Morlan)

further internal subdivision of the time periods, Taye Lake is at present the best documented of the prehistoric cultures in the Kluane and Aishihik areas. There are five major and a number of minor collections at specific sites that are thought to represent the Taye Lake culture. Present evidence suggests that human groups reoccupied certain favorable localities on a seasonal basis over many human generations during Taye Lake times. Moose, caribou, smaller mammals, and fish were exploited throughout, while early Taye Lake hunters also took bison. Permanent houses apparently were lacking. One important Taye Lake site at the head of Aishihik Lake yielded a rough circle of large stones that presumably weighted the edges of a skin tent; otherwise we have little information on Taye Lake architecture.

The Taye Lake people lived in the southern Yukon during a period of significant environmental change. They entered the area early in the postglacial period of maximum warmth, and they persisted there through the climatic change, between 3,000 and 2,500 years ago, that brought cooler and wetter conditions to the area and rejuvenated long-dormant mountain glaciers, to usher in the Neoglacial climatic episode. This late postglacial cold spell culminated in a very severe cold snap—the "Little Ice Age" of the 15th-19th centuries A.D. Early Neoglacial ice advances dammed the Alsek River, backing flood water up over the lush grasslands that occupied the bed of earlier Glacial Lake Champagne, and created Lake Alsek. The spruce forest continued to expand at the expense of grassland during Taye Lake times. Human hunting pressure on bison herds, increasingly restricted by forest expansion and by the formation of large Neoglacial lakes, may have exterminated this valuable grazer, probably at least 3,000 years ago. These environmental changes must have required major adjustments in Taye Lake culture, but we cannot document them with certainty at present.

The technology of the Taye Lake people differed in a number of significant details from that of the earlier Little Arm peoples. Taye Lake spear points have straight or concave rather than rounded bases, or they are notched to aid in hafting on a wooden shaft. Taye Lake people made abundant use of large, blunt-ended knives flaked on both surface (bifaces) and thick scrapers unifacially flaked along one or more long edges. End-scrapers (scrapers with a thick working edge on one end) occurred in a variety of forms, and a few of them were prepared for hafting rather than holding by hand. Blunt skin-dressing tools of schist or other coarse stone, with rounded outlines, a kind of tool still used today for hide-working, appeared in the Kluane area during Taye Lake times, as did a number of crude stone tools made from intentionally broken water-smoothed cobbles. Not common, but significant in Taye Lake collections, are large,

flat, notched cobbles that may have been hafted clubs for dispatching wounded game. Significantly, microblades and microcores are not found in Taye Lake collections, and burins, while present in low frequencies, differ in important details from those of the Little Arm culture.

Bone and antler tools are again poorly represented, due to problems of preservation, but we have a sophisticated curved fish spear point with numerous small barbs cut in one edge, bone awls for sewing skin or working in bark, several slotted handles of uncertain function, and a number of well-made fragments attesting to a sophisticated and important hard organic technology.

The Taye Lake technology, while competent, appears to have been utilitarian, with the emphasis more on function than on esthetics. Tools are undecorated and as yet no ornaments have been found, although red pigment (ochre)

Tools from Taye Lake site near Gladstone Creek: spear point (top left); end scrapers (top right); side scraper (lower left); biface tools possibly knives (lower right). (Richard Morlan)

found at one site may have been used for cosmetic purposes as well as in the processing of animal skins.

Around A.D. 700, an enormous volcanic eruption, centered in a vent under what is now the Klutlan Glacier in the St. Elias Mountains, deposited 3-15 centimeters (2-6 inches) of white volcanic ash over the Kluane area. The effects of this catastrophic volcanism on the vegetation, food animals, and human inhabitants may have been severe for a few years thereafter, although we cannot as yet document this impact in the archaeological record. We use this widespread "White River ash" somewhat arbitrarily as a stratigraphic marker to separate the Taye Lake phase of culture from the descendent Aishihik culture, although it is our interpretation that the Taye Lake peoples were the ancestors of the Aishihik folk.

The Aishihik Culture (A.D. 700-1,800)

Nine small sites occurring stratigraphically above the volcanic ash but lacking European trade goods constitute our evidence for the Aishihik culture. As might be expected, the Aishihik culture contains a number of traits that were also present during Taye Lake times, such as particular styles of stone and bone weapon heads and end-scrapers. Schist hide-working tools and stone wedges, although known to the Taye Lake people, attained their maximum popularity in the Aishihik culture, while large bifacial knives and thick scrapers diminished in popularity; Aishihik end-scrapers and side-scrapers tend to have thin rather than thick edges. Native copper arrowheads and perforators were a significant addition to the technological inventory of the Aishihik people. These metal tools were manufactured locally from copper nuggets obtained in the White River country; similar forms were being made at about the same time by interior Alaskan peoples to the west. Small notched and stemmed stone projectile heads strongly suggest that the Aishihik people used the bow and arrow. Tools of ground stone, including abraders and the ground stone adze, constitute a small but significant portion of the inventory. Crude heavy cobble tools also seem to have been fairly popular.

People of the Aishihik culture had to cope with several severe environmental challenges. Early in Aishihik times the spruce forest appears to have expanded to roughly its present extent at the expense of the grasslands, and the last few centuries of the tenure of the Aishihik culture witnessed the severe cold of the Little Ice Age, when the climate became colder than it had been at any time during the previous 10,000 years. Renewed glacial expansion inundated a portion of the area and produced two successive ice-dammed lakes of moderate size, the last of which drained only late in the 19th century. The first Euro-Canadians entering the area in the late 19th century encountered Indians whose immediate ancestors had been coping with the area in its most demanding condition for four centuries.

The Bennett Lake Culture (A.D. 1,800-1,900)

Bennett Lake is the culture of the indigenous population called Southern Tutchone, which lived in the Kluane area during the 19th century and was characterized by increasing involvement in the fur trade. The hallmark of this culture is the appearance of Euro-Canadian trade goods, such as metal tools, rifles, and glass beads. These exotic items were added to an Aishihik culture base of locally manufactured tools, but the indirect connections with the outside world implied by these trade goods justify the creation of a cultural boundary here.

Although people of the Kluane area had hardly any direct contact with Euro-Canadians until late in the 19th century, this century was a period of rapid culture change in the area. Tlingit traders from the coast served as middlemen in the fur trade and imported many coastal ideas and practices along with their more tangible wares. Locally felt needs for these exotic trade goods, and the increased emphasis on the trapping of fur-bearing animals whose pelts were necessary to obtain the goods, brought fundamental changes in aboriginal life. Meanwhile the European-derived diseases and intergroup hostilities fueled by the fur trade may have drastically affected the size and distribution of the sparse population.

Only two archaeological sites, a season camp at Taye Lake and a log cabin village at the head of Aishihik Lake, document this dynamic period, but memories of living Tutchone Athapaskan Indians and limited written records reach back into the late 19th century. In 1898, hordes of gold-seekers traversed the margins of the Kluane area on their way to the Klondike, initiating the modern era and effectively ending the story told here.

During Bennett Lake times, solid log-cabin villages came to be built and occupied seasonally, in certain favored localities such as Neskatahin near Dalton Post on the Tatshenshini River, Klukshu on the Klukshu River, and Old Aishihik Village at the head of Aishihik Lake. Access to metal axes for ambitious timbering operations, and perhaps the need for permanent base villages from which to pursue intensified winter trapping, probably led to the partial abandonment of age-old mobility with its attendant use of easily constructed and ephemeral shelters.

Also during the 19th century, the trade musket came increasingly to replace the bow and arrow, the snare, and certain communal hunting techniques for large game animals, with a corresponding loss of some of the finer points of the stalker's art. Locally manufactured containers of wood, bark, and skin for boiling stones were increasingly supplanted by metal containers that could be exposed directly to the fire, and tools of native copper, heretofore a valuable trade item, gave way to imported metal tools. Tlingit middlemen jealously guarded their privileged position in the trade network linking interior peoples with the outside world. The power and appeal of the Tlingit cultural pattern, based on the rich resources of the North Pacific coast and enhanced by the new wealth of the fur trade, enormously impressed the interior natives who were in closest contact with these coastal overlords and added a Tlingit veneer to the social and economic life of some of them.

According to anthropologist Dr. C. McClellan, "In the 19th century, a very sparse population was spread over a vast area, making a loosely linked social network with very few sharply defined linguistic or cultural boundaries. Everybody shared roughly the same pattern of subsistence and technology. Cohesive political units did not exist   just widely scattered clusters of living groups whose composition and size changed throughout the year as people constantly moved about in quest of food." In the recent past, and to a lesser extent at present, the Southern Tutchone exploited the food resources of the Kluane region, based on generations of knowledge.

(The following descriptions are abstracted from the publication *My Old People Say* by Dr. C. McClellan (National Museum of Canada, Publication in Ethnology No. 6(2), 1975, and are used with the permission of the Canadian Ethnological Service of the National Museum of Man.)

The old pattern, as mentioned, was for families to move about ceaselessly in summer and fall, storing food in caches and taking advantage of the abundance of local big game, fish runs, and berry crops, and in the winter to move from cache to cache or from one kill to another. Caribou were much more abundant before 1900; after that, moose replaced them as a major food item. Moose and caribou were killed in a variety of ways. Fences of brush, sometimes more than a mile long, were constructed at strategic locations, and snares were hung in openings through which the animals were forced to run. The snares were made of "babiche," connective sinew from the neck or back of a moose or caribou. Fences were erected across well-used game trails, around salt licks, and along mountain slopes frequented by caribou herds.

These large animals were also killed by crude bows and arrows; this normally meant hours or days of tracking a wounded animal while the arrowhead worked its way into the body. During the rut in the fall, moose were "called" by rubbing a moose scapula (shoulder blade) on a tree trunk or on some brush, and in more recent times by grunting into a rolled-bark trumpet. In one of the more bizarre methods of capturing caribou, the hunter would place the head and antlers of a caribou over his own head and advance close enough to the herd for a shot. Another method was to light up a spruce burl; caribou allegedly will come towards smoke.

Sheep and goats were also important to the Southern Tutchone. These animals, living high in the mountains and often in or near rugged escape terrain, were perhaps more difficult to capture. Again, snares were used; several men would drive the animals down into them (although there is some question about how easily sheep can be driven downhill). The great curved horns of Dall rams were often fashioned into ladles and dishes. Mountain goat fleece and hide were sought after, for making into winter trousers that were worn with the hair inside.

Some smaller mammals were important sources of food, especially in late winter and early spring when meat in caches was running low. Snowshoe hares were trapped by the women by felling spruce trees to attract the hares with a fresh supply of food; snares were set in gaps between the butt ends. Arctic ground squirrels were also caught, after they emerged from hibernation; a snare was set in the mouth of a burrow, and when the animal triggered a spring pole nearby it was pinned to the roof of the burrow. The fur of ground squirrels and hares was used for robes, parkas, and hats.

The fur trade led to the hunting of a number of species of mammals that in earlier times had been largely ignored: lynx, fox, and even red squirrel. Beaver were a major species for trade, but had already been a food item. Beaver were caught near their lodges, either by spearing through a hole in the ice and baiting with poplar or willow, or by a net made of babiche, set with a spring pole that resulted in the captured animal being suspended high in the air. Steel traps later replaced snares, spears, and nets.

Wolves and bears were considered symbolic, and accepted and treated on a par with humans, or even as superhumans. Both species, however, were killed at times, formerly with snares or deadfalls and later with steel traps. Wolves were not considered dangerous, although a few accounts have been recorded of alleged attacks on humans; bears were viewed as dangerous, and taboos existed against saying anything offensive about them for fear of retribution. High-powered rifles, a demand for bearskin rugs, and a government bounty on wolves resulted in an increased kill of these species.

Among birds, only grouse and ptarmigan were at times important sources of food for the Southern Tutchone. They were often snared with a simple loop of babiche on the end of a long pole. Spruce grouse, very trusting of humans, were sometimes caught by hand, or stoned. Ptarmigan were netted in the fall and winter with a woven babiche net strung in the willows, into which flocks of birds were herded.

Waterfowl were not the important source of food for the Southern Tutchone that they were for the Indians to the north and east along the Yukon River. Ducks and geese were occasionally shot with bows and arrows, or snared along their grass trails leading to water.

Eagles were sometimes killed for their wing feathers, which were used for ceremonial headdresses and other dancing paraphernalia. In times of dire need, gray jays and snow buntings were caught by being baited under a propped-up snowshoe to which a long pull-cord had been attached.

Some species of birds, rarely or never killed, were important because of their spirit powers — notably the raven, the owl, and the loon. Indian shamen considered ravens and loons as "spirit-helpers."

Fish may have been as important as animal flesh to the Southern Tutchone living around Klukshu and Neskatahin. Alsek River salmon find their way into spawning streams at these locations, and have been, and still are, exploited. Efficient fish traps, with funnel-shaped openings facing downstream, have been the principal method of capturing salmon. In the past, salmon were also gaffed with wooden hooks. Some whitefish and lake trout were speared through holes in the ice on Dezadeash and Kluane lakes.

Plants were of only minor significance for food. Berries were picked, mostly by parties of women and children who played and sang at their work. Blueberry, strawberry, highbush cranberry, lowbush cranberry, bearberry, soapberry, and rose hips were most favoured.

The most important root vegetable was "bear root" (*Hedysarum alpinum*). Like the grizzly bears, the people dug these out in the spring when they are sweet, before the leaves appear. Bearberry leaves were smoked as a tobacco. Some plants were valued for medicinal reasons: crowberry, sage, and Labrador tea were boiled to make a tea, the former good for curing diarrhea, the other two for curing colds.

The 20th century has seen a series of major technological advances by man, and some of these have made a significant impact on the Kluane area: a major permanent highway, a series of telephone lines, and a rusting pipeline. For these facilities, a swath nearly a mile wide was carved out by bulldozers and other heavy equipment in some areas. Extending from the main highway are numerous mining roads, which are often visible from great distances as long scars along hillsides. One such road is located on the northeastern shore of Kluane Lake, where it runs northwestward to Gladstone Creek; it was used only briefly and has now been made useless by erosion. The eroding road cuts may be seen from the other side of the lake by travelers using the Alaska Highway.

Some of the natural resources of the Kluane area could be directly threatened by future developments, and we should take any necessary steps to safeguard them. One resource so threatened lies buried in archaeological sites. The remains of former inhabitants of the area constitute our only means of learning about early man's life in the Kluane region. We can recover these remains and learn about the past only through the careful excavation of archaeo-logical sites. Bulldozers and backhoes can destroy this record forever. The proposed pipeline near the Alaska Highway is currently routed through archaeological site concentrations at Burwash and Champagne, and its right-of-way lies directly on the Canyon Creek site, from which our earliest evidence has been obtained. In planning our future development needs, we must safeguard such resources. The beauty of this land comes not only from seeing it today but understanding what it once was.

11. THE WHITE MAN AND MOUNTAINS

John B. Theberge

Men of the High North, you who have known it;
You in whose hearts its splendors have abode;
Can you renounce it, can you disown it?
Can you forget it, its glory and its goad?

R. W. SERVICE

THERE WERE FAMOUS men, like J. B. Tyrrell and Alfred Brooks, whose names survive in geography books, and forgotten men like Charles Towl, who thought he would get rich but didn't, and Constable Sam, an Indian hired by the North West Mounted Police, who tried to cross the icy Kaskawulsh River and never made it. Everyone who has paraded through Kluane's history has touched the land in some way, and been touched by it. To the mountains, whose snowy slopes have poured 10 million spring freshets into Kluane's rivers, man toiling up through its passes must have seemed just a new evolutionary contrivance — he cut a few trees, built a few cabins, shot some caribou, dug out some river banks for gold, but never did enough to disrupt the region's life processes. Most of them left, some broken by the harshness of the land, others uplifted by its beauty.

The First Map

The whole Indian band, close to 400 people, stood on the bank of the Chilkat River in early August 1869 as the American surveyor George Davidson stepped out of his boat. They had shot at him, down river a few miles, before they realized that their own chief, Kohklux, was in the boat with him. Now he was welcome.

Davidson had traveled up the coast of British

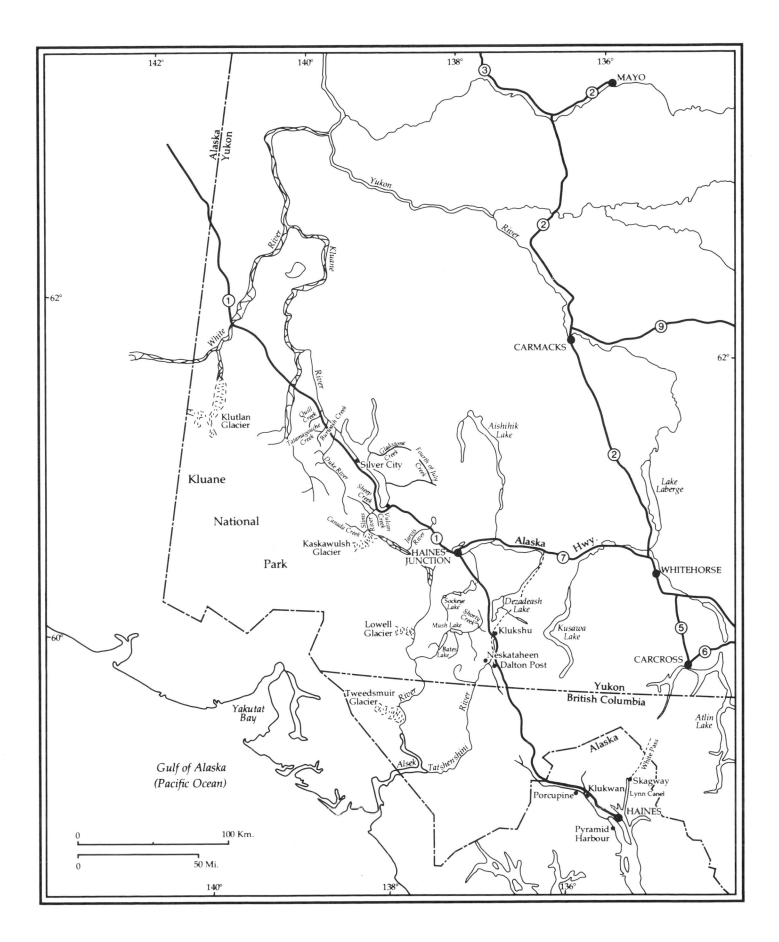

Klukwan Chilkat Indian village in 1898. (Yukon Archives 3652)

Columbia and Alaska to observe a total eclipse of the sun from a northern vantage point. After a brief stop at Sitka he pushed on to the head of the Lynn Canal, and then 15 miles (24 kilometers) up river to the Indian village of Klukwan. He had met Kohklux, chief of the Chilkat nation, at Sitka where Kohklux had been in jail for a petty offense and was returning with him to his tribe. Davidson described him as "a man of commanding presence, nearly six feet high, broad chest, and a well-formed head that measured 24 inches in circumference. He carried a bullet-hole in his cheek. He was held to be the greatest warrior and diplomat of all the tribes north and west of the Stak-heen [Stikine River in northern British Columbia]."

Kohklux was not at war with the whites when he met Davidson, but he had been. In 1854 he had traveled 200 miles (320 kilometers) inland, through the Kluane country, to the Hudson's Bay Company post of Fort Selkirk and burned it to the ground. This crime was committed to extricate his nation from a play of historic events.

For many years the Pacific northwest coast of North America was Russian territory. Vitus Bering recorded the first visit, and in 1741 he named the peak he thought was the highest Mount St. Elias, after a Russian saint. Subsequently, in 1783, the Russians started up a fur empire, trading with the Chilkats and other coastal Indians. The Chilkats, in turn, traded with the interior

"Stick" Indians (from the land of little sticks—trees), including those of the Kluane country. For years the Sticks (Tutchone) were held in semi-subjugation, denied direct access to the coast and to the Russians. The Chilkats traveled inland to trade with the Sticks, and occasionally fought with them, near the villages of Neskataheen and Kluksu (both within five miles of the boundary of the present park).

The British, however, complicated this trading arrangement. They, too, had a claim on the northwest coast. In 1776 James Cook took possession of much of the same coast for Britain. Captain George Vancouver followed in 1792. Hostilities were avoided by a Russian-British boundary treaty in 1825 that gave the coast to the Russians. However, the Hudson's Bay Company continued to invade the interior fringes of the Russian territory. Their Fort Selkirk on the Yukon River, built in 1848, was close enough to the Kluane country to offer the Stick Indians an alternative trading post by traveling east about 150 miles (240 kilometers). That is what incensed Kohklux and provoked his attack.

Kohklux was apparently grateful to Davidson for returning him to his village, so much so that he and his two wives labored "two or three days" to draw on a large sheet the first map of the interior of the southwestern Yukon Territory. While distances on it were inaccurate, the large lakes and rivers were there, with the Indian names they still bear. Davidson did not publish the map until 1901, when the Alaska-Canadian boundary was in dispute. By then, miners had discovered gold in large amounts at Dawson and in small amounts in Kluane's creeks, and the mountain climbers had discovered the challenges of the St. Elias peaks. The land was becoming known.

Kluane King Jack Dalton

In the late spring of 1891 Jack Dalton, the most famous man in the history of the region, dismounted from his horse at the Stick village of Neskataheen. Most of the Indians who gathered around him had never seen a white man or a horse before. "Everyone was certain that the man and his white companion were sick, and perhaps carrying that sickness to their village," recounted Jimmy Cane, a long-time resident who was there as a boy of 14.

Dalton was not a stranger to the southwestern Yukon. In 1886 he had accompanied an American, Lieutenant Frederick Schwatka, in an unsuccessful attempt to climb Mount St. Elias from the coast. Schwatka later became famous for his raft journey down the Yukon River. Then, in 1890, Dalton and E. J. Glave, exploring for an American publication, *Frank Leslie's Illustrated Newspaper,* were the second white men recorded to cross the Chilkat Pass, reaching Neskataheen, but the Sticks were 60 miles (96 kilometers) down river on the Alsek, fishing for salmon. They were met instead by a visiting band of Chilkat Indians. Eight years previously, the German anthropologist Arthur Krause had crossed the pass about 50 miles (80 kilometers) east of Neskataheen, reaching Kusawa Lake.

This was Dalton's third trip. He and Glave persuaded the Sticks that they were not sick and were allowed to stay. For the next few days Glave made voluminous notes on their way of life. He wrote: "At the time of our visit to Neskataheen there was already a crowd of people there, all busy plying the gaff among the salmon. The land abounds in wild berries; and the native hunter, who knows the haunt of every beast, can rely on finding game."

Dalton and Glave left Neskataheen a few days later and continued on to the northwest to become the first white men to travel into the interior of what is now Kluane National Park—via Sockeye Lake to the Alsek River, which they followed upstream to the Jarvis River and thence eastward beyond the Kluane region on the Yukon plateau. On their return trip they reached Kluane Lake (Lake Tloo Arny, at that time), the first white men to record doing so. Here they almost drowned. Hidden in the bushes was a dugout canoe in which they tried to cross the southern end of the lake. Kluane Lake is treacherous; winds and waves come up suddenly. In the middle of the lake they hit a squall and foundered. Thewater was ice cold, but they clung to their boat until it drifted to shore, only minutes before they would certainly have perished.

Glave did not return to the Yukon after this trip. He joined the explorer Henry Morton Stanley and died while with him in the Congo a few years later. But Dalton came back. In 1896 he began clearing out the old Chilkat trail to Neskataheen (now followed, in part, by the Haines Highway), later extending it to the Yukon River via two branches, one of them following old Chief Kohklux's route to the ruins of Fort Selkirk. He built his own trading post at Neskataheen and, when gold was discovered at Dawson, capitalized on this by charging miners $2.50 a horse to cross the Alaskan portion of his trail — allegedly patrolling the trail with a gun to keep out parties that had not paid. Because of a demand for beef at Dawson, he drove cattle over the trail to the Yukon River in the spring of 1897 — 42 oxen, two cows, and 60 Herefords. He slaughtered half and rafted the rest live to Dawson where the meat sold for up to $2.50 a pound. The following year, 2,000 cattle were driven across the pass, along with some sheep.

The Dalton Pony Express Company was another of his enterprises, set up to carry passengers from the Five Fingers Rapids on the Yukon

Jack Dalton (second from left, with pistol on hip) and Inspector A. M. Jarvis (third from left) at Dalton House, summer 1898. (Yukon Archives 3635)

Logan high mountain camp (57).

Cabin in historic Silver City at south end of Kluane Lake (58).

Bullion Creek canyon (59).

RIGHT: Mount Hoge from Burwash Uplands (60).
BELOW: Summit of Vulcan Mountain (61).

Mount Steele above the surging Steele Glacier (62).

ABOVE: Kluane Lake (63).
TOP RIGHT: *Primula sibirica*, a rare North American plant (64).
LOWER RIGHT: Woodland caribou with recently lost antler velvet (65).

Mount Kennedy (66).

River across his trail to the coast. He bought 250 horses and saddles, but the company failed after steamers began to navigate the upper Yukon, successfully shooting the Five Fingers Rapids.

When the North West Mounted Police established a detachment on his trail, Dalton contracted to pack all their provisions. He won their respect; Colonel Sam B. Steele, commander of the Yukon forces, wrote: "Dalton's adventures would fill several volumes of romance ...he proved a good contractor, always giving the men more than their allowance."

Today the coastal town of Haines, Alaska, celebrates "Dalton Days" — partly a tourist gimmick, partly a tribute to the man. Dalton was a strange mixture of mountain-man and entrepreneur, one of a kind in the history of the region. Fluent in the Chilkat tongue, respected by all, he paved the way for others to follow. The mountains were his challenge, adventure his reward.

The Claim-Stakers

Charles Towl and his partner crossed the Chilkat Pass in the spring of 1901. They thought they would find gold and go home rich. They may have heard of the secret "strike" made two summers before by the "mysterious 36" at Shorty Creek in the Kluane Ranges, about 10 miles (16 kilometers) from Dalton's post. The "strike" had been made by a former U.S. Cavalry lieutenant named Adair and 36 men sworn to secrecy as to their destination and doings. Adair even brought in a mining expert from California, and built a bunkhouse and dining hall. But Towl and his partner were not as well funded as Adair. They pushed west across a divide from the normal trail to Shorty Creek and staked a claim on a creek of "good promise." They conferred the name of "Mush Creek" on the site of their bonanza, because after they had located pay dirt in the initial stages of their prospecting their larder was reduced to oatmeal and they had to go on a diet of "mush," as porridge is universally called in the north.

When word of Towl's discovery got out, a stampede occurred from a "diggings," at nearby Porcupine. But Towl and his partner never got rich. Nothing is known of where they came from, how long they stayed, or where they went. In this regard they are typical of the early miners. Towl

Fred Colburn, member of the "mysterious 36," on Dalton Trail, August 7, 1898. (Yukon Archives 3657)

is only a name in a brief North West Mounted Police report describing the Mush Creek strike. His name never showed up again. (Mush Creek flows north into Mush Lake, which was called Bates Lake until it was discovered a few years later that there are two large lakes close to each other — one of which was then named Mush Lake.)

Members of the "mysterious 36" whipsawing lumber near Mush Creek, 1898. (Yukon Archives 3737)

The Mush Creek stampede fizzled out within a year or two, to be replaced by stampedes to Fourth-of-July Creek, just east of Kluane Lake, where a discovery claim was staked on July 4, 1903. Two days later another claim was staked at Ruby Creek. When these creeks had been fully staked, miners looked elsewhere. One party of four staked claims on Bullion Creek in August, and on nearby Sheep Creek in October — both on the west side of Kluane Lake, now in the park. The next spring, the same party of miners staked farther north in Burwash Creek, which proved

the most productive of Kluane's creeks. While these creeks yielded the most gold, many others were staked, at Vulcan, Canada, and Gladstone.

All this activity on the east side of the region led to the establishment of Silver City on the south shore of Kluane Lake. It was primarily a tent city, with a mining recorder and a police detachment, and by 1904 was complete with a wagon road from Whitehorse (now part of the Alaska Highway). A sign has been erected on the highway marking the site. From Silver City the miners drifted north along the west side of

Kluane Lake to copper prospects, discovered on the White River in 1905 and on Tatamagouche and Quill creeks in 1908.

For some men the search for gold or other placer minerals was compulsive. They drifted from strike to strike, always listening for rumors around the mining recorder's office, always ready to pack their kits and move on to try again. Of them, poet R. W. Service wrote: "It isn't the gold that they're wanting, so much as just finding the gold." A few years later a major gold strike was made at Chisana, Alaska, and miners moved even farther north, staking more claims in the upper White River district, on both sides of the border. But by about 1917 it was just about over.

There are no records that anyone got rich. In all the creeks named, the value of the gold produced totaled $70,000 at the most, according to a geological report by D. D. Cairnes. The Bullion Hydraulic Company, which operated from 1904 until 1906, spent about $300,000 in buildings and equipment, and it got only $1,000 in gold in return.

Long-abandoned miner's food cache, an elevated platform on which to store food out of reach of wildlife. (John Theberge)

The Law—July 1898

Inspector A. M. Jarvis reined up his horse on the bank of the churning, milky Tatshenshini River. On the other side stood the freshly cut log buildings of Dalton's Post and beyond them the Indian encampment of Neskataheen. Three months earlier, Inspector Jarvis had taken charge of the North West Mounted Police's new Dalton Trail Detachment. He had traveled from Vancouver to Skagway with 18 men and 21 horses, and then across the Lynn Canal to the abandoned Haines Mission, where the Dalton Trail began. In those three months he built a customs house and fenced 11 acres and sowed them in timothy. (The post was 4½ miles, or 7 kilometers, from the Chilkat Village of Klukwan, mentioned earlier.) Because of the mining near Dalton's Post, he had decided to build a barracks there as well, before snowfall.

Jarvis was already a well-known officer of the Force. He had served on the prairies and led one of Canada's most famous manhunts, for the murderer Charcoal, and he had served in British Columbia at the time when the Canadian Pacific Railway was being built.

When Jarvis crossed the Tatshenshini River on that July day in 1898, he met the new chief of the

Overgrown graveyard at Neskataheen. "Soul house" in center. (John Theberge)

Chilkat nation, who was visiting the Sticks. The chief was the son of Kohklux. The meeting was friendly and the new chief invited the inspector to a potlach back at Klukwan village. The potlach was made memorable by the showing of the British flag that the chief's father had taken when he pillaged Fort Selkirk.

Jarvis was the first of several men to command the Dalton Trail Detachment between 1898 and 1905; Assistant Surgeon Frazer and Inspector McDonell also had the command at different times. They acted as mining recorders, justices of the peace, tax collectors, Indian agents, doctors, and lawyers, and did search-and-rescue work in many acts of humanity. Their task of maintaining harmony between the miners and the Indians was often difficult. The Indians shared what they had, by custom, and were therefore often accused by the miners of robbery. One miner remarked: "If I ever catch anyone robbing my cache, I will mistake him for a ptarmigan and blow his head off." The police stepped up their patrols in places of conflict and succeeded in preventing any violence.

Jarvis left the force in the spring of 1900 to serve in South Africa in the Lord Strathcona Rangers with his long-time fellow officer and commander, Colonel Sam Steele. But the Yukon must have held a strong appeal for Jarvis because he was back in charge of the Dalton Trail Detachment in May 1901. In October he was reposted to the Dawson Detachment, and then he was lost sight of. The Dalton Trail fell into disuse by 1905 when local mining fizzled out. Dawson was no longer a lure, and in any case the best route to the interior of the Yukon, now, was the new White Pass and Yukon Railway from tidewater to Whitehorse and wagon road to Silver City. Dalton Post was abandoned in September 1905.

Neither Dalton Post nor the graveyard at Neskataheen, which is the only remaining evidence of the Indian village, is in Kluane National Park or receiving any form of protection. They are only five miles (8 kilometers) from the park's boundary. They were excluded because of present-day mining speculation—no proven reserves, no operating mine, just speculation. Some of the historic buildings are occupied in the summer by miners. Others are falling down or being used as firewood. Soon they will be gone.

Surveyors and Geologists

D. D. Cairnes of the Geological Survey of Canada looked down at the five-ounce nugget of gold in his hand. It was worth about $75. It was August 1914 and he stood between the high walls of the Burwash Creek canyon at claim Number 65. The nugget was the largest to have come from the creek. Most of the gold was characteristically very fine, and what could be dug out with a pick and shovel was already gone. Cairnes estimated that $30,000 to $40,000 had come from the creek, but now the best sites yielded only about $3 per day per shovel—less than the wage rate of the district.

Cairnes's task was to assess and describe the bedrock geology and mineral occurrences of the Kluane region west and north of Kluane Lake. He had come from Whitehorse on the wagon road to the largely deserted site of Silver City, and after one side trip to the east had followed the western shore of Kluane Lake, along the present Alaska Highway and park boundary. He was not the first geological surveyor in the region. R. G. McConnell, later Deputy Minister of Mines, had been at the same place in 1904 and 1905 when mining in Kluane's creeks was at a peak. McConnell remarked that when he visited Burwash Creek most of the miners were spending the short season doing "useless assessment work on several claims," trying to find the big payload instead of working one claim; consequently, little gold was being recovered.

While McConnell was the first surveyor around Kluane Lake, the very earliest surveyors in the region predated Silver City and gained access to the country on the Dalton Trail. A dispute over the location of the Alaska-Yukon boundary focused attention on the southwestern corner, where the Dalton Trail began. While the United States and Canada agreed on the 141st meridian as the western boundary of the Yukon, a problem arose near tidewater in the south as to whether the boundary should run along the peaks of the coast range or "ten marine leagues limit from the shore" at the head of inlets such as the Chilkat. While most of the debate took place in formal chambers of joint commissions far to the south, surveyors tramped the Dalton Trail.

In 1898 a San Francisco engineer surveyed the whole trail for a railway, but Canadian permission for the bulk of the route was never given because of the boundary dispute. If it had, undoubtedly the White Pass and Yukon Railway would not have been built, nor Whitehorse located where it is. In 1899 Alfred Brooks, the famous Alaskan geologist whose name now stretches across the most northerly mountain range on maps of Alaska, crossed the Dalton Trail, but he was interested in mapping and geology and paid no attention to the boundary dispute. From Dalton Post he traveled through the interior of what is now the park, following the route taken by Dalton and Glave eight years earlier: to the Alsek River via Sockeye Lake. But then he continued up the Alsek to the Kaskawulsh Glacier (then called the O'Connor Glacier) and followed the Slims River to Kluane Lake. In the same year Canadian geologist J. B. Tyrrell also crossed the Dalton Trail, filling in detail on bedrock geology collected in very preliminary form the year before by J. J. McArthur, who had helped Dalton to finish his trail. Tyrrell had written some exciting pages of history five years earlier when with his brother he traveled and mapped a route across the arctic tundra between Lake Athabasca and Hudson Bay.

Like the police, all these men had missions to perform. Their reports are dry—almost devoid of description. If they were impressed by the beauty of the land, they never let it slip into government documents. Perhaps it was considered unprofessional to be moved by beauty.

After 1915 no more surveyors came until the AlaskaHighway was built in 1942. Then it wasn't pioneering any more—it was the age of air photographs and easy access.

The Hunters

"It was the meat we wanted, and that badly. The Chief used his 30-40 Winchester rifle, and the two of us started shooting. With the first two bullets two of the rams fell, the others running up the side of the mountain as fast as if they were on level ground. They dodged backwards and forwards, now behind a rock and again above it, until another one fell. The ram that was running the fastest seemed to bear a charmed life for a while, but a bullet from my Mannlicher dropped him, and he rolled over, and down the side of the mountain."

So wrote Thomas Martindale in an account of his hunting safari in Kluane in 1912. He had climbed to the tundra on the upper Slims River, within sight of the huge Kaskawulsh Glacier. He was one of many (primarily) American hunters eager for frontier experience and rich enough to pay for it—providing a new source of gold for some of the miners who had stayed on. Martindale's hunt had been organiized for him by Louis and Eugene Jacquot, who had settled eight years earlier on Kluane Lake at the present site of Burwash on the Alaska Highway (close to the Burwash Creek diggings). They had stayed. A settlement had grown up of mountain men with independent spirits who panned a little, trapped a little, lived off the land, and now guided. They included Thomas Dickson, a chief guide, and Jack Haydon, who in 1906 had traveled with Charles Sheldon, a founder of Mount McKinley National Park in Alaska. Haydon had "mucked and delved in the Klondike" before his travels with Sheldon, but he had come back to the Yukon "with twenty dollars in my ragged trousers, a gun, a smile, and a one-eyed dog." Most of the mountain men of Burwash married native girls and the settlement became Indian and white.

The client got the best of treatment from these men, and some of the best hunting in North America. He was met in Whitehorse and taken by wagon and four-horse team to the foot of Kluane Lake, then by boat up the western shore of the lake to Burwash. In the meantime horses and provisions were ferried across the Slims River and taken to Burwash by a trail along the edge of the lake that is now the Alaska Highway. From Burwash the client traveled by pack train up the Duke River and across the Burwash Uplands into the caribou country, going north to the White River on the Alaska border. Sheep, grizzlies, moose, and caribou were the main fare, and the occasional book that was written by one of these hunters is full of pictures of dead animals, piles of antlers, and hunters with rifle in hand and one foot on the kill. On their return they often took a side trip up the Slims River for mountain goats.

They were trophy hunters, recreational killers, with an ethic more and more in question today. Yet, paradoxically, they were the only people until very recently to leave evidence in their writing of being inspired by Kluane's beauty. But it is difficult to reconcile the frontispiece in

Martindale's *Hunting in the Upper Yukon* of a huge caribou standing on a tundra hummock and the caption inscribed "His majesty the Osburni Caribou Bull" with the picture near the end of the book of Martindale standing beside a boatload of caribou antlers.

To Harry Auer, who hunted in Kluane in 1914, goes the credit for the first lyrical writing. Just before reaching Whitehorse on his return trip he wrote: "There was nothing of cheerfulness as we drove ahead along the sunlit wagon road with the oppressive realization that behind us lay the God-given mighty wilderness of majesty, freedom and peace, while each succeeding mile brought us nearer the man-made rattle, constrictions and pettiness of a complex civilization. In sullen silence we topped the last pine-clad hill and rolled down the slope to the affronting railway and telegraph station."

The hunters' day ended in 1943 when the whole southwestern corner of the Yukon was made a game sanctuary to protect the wildlife from their guns.

Men and Machines

When the Japanese attacked Pearl Harbor, Robert H. Bowe was studying business administration in Minneapolis. He changed his plan to enter the wholesale grocery business and enlisted

First truck convoy on Alaska Highway, November 20, 1942. (Yukon Archives 1501)

U.S. soldiers building Alaska Highway, 1942. (Public Archives Canada C-25739)

in the U.S. Army in January 1942. He was to make history, but not as a military hero. He was destined to be the first man to drive a truck over the Alaska Highway.

The United States feared a Japanese invasion from the north. The defense was to be a road to Alaska, 1,600 miles (2,600 kilometers) across muskeg and mountain from Dawson Creek to Fairbanks. On March 9, 1942, the army pulled into Dawson Creek; on November 20, 1942, only nine months later, the Alaska Highway was officially opened at the Slims River bridge at Kluane. Robert Bowe was at the ceremony with his truck companion, Corporal Otto Gronke. Bowe had worked since April 1942 on the south-

ern part of the highway near Fort St. John, not in the Kluane region which had been the responsibility of the 18th Regiment. The highway had been built in sections, with the 18th rushing north toward the Alaska boundary to meet the 97th rushing south. It was a joint venture of the United States, which built the road, and Canada, which built airfield and support facilities. Major glacial rivers had been bridged, a major mountain range crossed, hundreds of miles of wet northern spruce forests traversed—all in nine months.

The opening ceremony was austere. The day was bitterly cold − 15°F (− 25°C). A red, white, and blue ceremonial ribbon crossed the gravel

Alaska Highway construction camp at south end of Kluane Lake, 1942. (Yukon Archives 1533)

Bridging the Donjek River, 1942. (Yukon Archives 3554)

road. Canadian Broadcasting Corporation microphones recorded the dignitaries' speeches. A military band played and a great bonfire nearby provided some warmth for the 250 people attending.

Bowe and Gronke drove their truck on north after the ceremony. They reached Fairbanks a few days later, and the northwest was never the same again. The army left its mark at Kluane, and you can still see fallen-down barracks there. A spur road was built to Haines, Alaska, following much of Dalton's old trail. Along that road and then north along the Alaska Highway, the U.S. Army strung a pipeline for petroleum products. It was used until 1968, and is still very visible, along with its pumping stations.

Opening ceremony for Alaska Highway, near Kluane Lake, November 20, 1942. (Public Archives Canada C-80775)

Kluane was now accessible to a new batch of gold miners, some using abandoned cranes and bulldozers from the highway construction. And the scientists came to study. And the tourists came to travel North America's last romantic frontier road.

The Life Scientists and Park Planners

Mammalogist C. H. D. Clarke and ornithologist T. M. Shortt bent over an enormous bear track in the shoulder mud of the newly completed Haines Highway. Here, about 45 miles (72 kilometers) south of the Yukon-British Columbia boundary, the highway runs exactly on the old Dalton Trail where Indians and miners and police once toiled on foot. It was 1944; Clarke and Shortt, the first biologists to record any observations in the region, had traveled by truck all the way from Edmonton.

The bear track was the largest they had ever seen; hind foot 12½ inches (32 centimeters) long, including a 1½-inch (4-centimeter) claw. "Alaskan Brown Bear," Clarke concluded. This was one of its few records on Canadian soil. In 1934, a German sportsman had shot a 900-pound (400-kilo) bear near present-day Haines Junction, where the Alaska and Haines highways meet, and an Indian had seen a bear "as big as a moose" near Dezadeash Lake.

Clarke was on his second visit to the Kluane region, to continue a description of the birds and mammals he had begun the year before for the National Parks Bureau. In December 1942 the whole southwestern Yukon, over 10,000 square miles, had become a national park reserve, the Canadian government having acted on a suggestion by United States Secretary of the Interior Harold Ikes for a common effort between the countries to protect wildlife along the soon-to-be-built Alaska Highway. On his first trip Clarke and his party had followed the old hunting trail from Burwash Landing to the upper White River. They had also traveled up the south side of the Slims River to the Kaskawulsh Glacier. On his second trip he examined the Chilkat Pass along the Haines Highway for a possible extension of the park reserve.

Soon other government agencies were staking scientific claims in the newly opened region. The National Museum of Canada, with its mandate to describe and classify Canada's living resources, sent botanists, ornithologists, and mammalogists in the late 1940s. These were the days of annotated lists—species-by-species descriptions of abundance, distribution, and taxonomic characteristics. Soon after that the Canadian Wildlife Service, with a mandate to manage wildlife resources, instituted specific studies, such as waterfowl breeding habitat surveys, in 1950, and a study of the impact of native peoples trapping in the northern part of thesanctuary, in 1951.

The Icefield Ranges Research Station of the Arctic Institute of North America and the American Geographical Society was founded in 1961 with a base camp near the former Silver City at the southern end of Kluane Lake. Its objective was and is to obtain fundamental knowledge about the high mountains and associated ranges from a multitude of disciplines. From this station, founded largely through the effort of Dr. Walter A. Wood, most of the contributors to this book have worked, with many others, building up the store of information that exists today.

The national park reserve of 1942 did not establish a park but merely prevented private land holdings. Game sanctuary status, which was added in 1943, prevented hunting, but mining interests were still free to operate, unrestricted by any measures to protect the land. Establishment of the park was opposed by mining interests inside and outside of government. Plans to create a national park surfaced again in 1955, after a study of the suitability of the Kluane region, compared with other areas in the southern Yukon, ranked the region highest by far. But then the park idea, still opposed by mining interests, waned.

Hopes for the park reawakened in the late 1960s, however, due to two events: the appointment of a cabinet minister with a resolve to establish new parks, the Honourable Jean Chrétien, and a concerted attempt by citizen conservation organizations, led by the National and Provincial Parks Association, to push park plans to completion. The result: the announcement of Kluane National Park in February 1972.

Park status has brought wardens to oversee the wildlife, planners to prevent the land from the potential damage of too many visitors, and interpreters to help people understand the beauty they see. But, most important, it has given hope that in the future the land will be governed by the principal mandate of Parks Canada, to "protect for all time."

12. MOUNTAINEERING IN THE ST. ELIAS MOUNTAINS

Walter A. Wood

WHEN THE MATTERHORN was first climbed in 1865, what now constitutes Alaska and the Yukon Territory was a vast unexplored region save for the coastal waterways and the major valleys of the interior. The high fastnesses of the St. Elias Mountains remained unexplored until the late 1890s, but many of their high peaks had been seen, both from the Gulf of Alaska and from the Yukon plateau of the continental interior, and names had been placed on most of them by the advent of the 20th century.

The first name to appear was, of course, Mount St. Elias whose 5,489-meter (18,008-foot) stature closely dominating the coastline gave Vitus Bering his first glimpse of the North American continent on July 16, 1741. Fifty years were to pass before such navigators as Cook, Vancouver, and Malaspina sailed the Alaskan coastline, mapping as they went, and their names, in time, found their way onto the resulting charts.

On the landward side of the mountains, J. J. McArthur gave the names of Steele, Walsh, and Wood to three great peaks that he sighted in 1900 from the hills to the east of Kluane Lake. Names used by the native people also found their way into official usage, including Kluane, Kaskawulsh, Donjek, and Natazhat. Then, from 1909-13, the surveyors of the International Boundary Commission, delineating the Yukon-Alaska boundary, fostered many names that have found official acceptance, for example, Brooks, Lambert, Riggs, and McArthur. But by far the largest number of place names came from mountaineering sponsors, all of them complying fully with conditions laid down by the government agencies concerned with the propriety of the proposed name. Still, 230 years after the naming of Mount St. Elias, fully 90 percent of the physical features of the St. Elias Mountains that might reasonably be named can be identified only by geographical coordinates.

Since the topography in and around the park is of very high relief, it is natural that mountaineers should have played a major role in raising the curtain of knowledge of its peaks, passes, glaciers, and valleys. Some, too modest to call themselves explorers, have told us much in their journals that the recreational climbers had neither the time nor the inclination to record. However, the chronology of human impact on virgin country depends on the existence of a literature from which to trace events. Where voids exist in the written records, we have only human memory from which to piece history together. Fortunately, the story of exploration of the St. Elias Mountains is reasonably complete in

mountaineering journals and scientific reports; and the time span of the story is short enough — less than a century — that word of mouth can fill the gaps.

The story begins in 1886 with the first reconnaissance aimed at an ascent of Mount St. Elias. An American party consisting of F. Schwatka, W. Libbey, H. Seton-Karr, and J. Dalton landed on the beach along the perimeter of the great Malaspina Glacier. From there they traveled over the surface of the Tyndall Glacier for some 26 kilometers (16 miles), and they reached an elevation of about 2,100 meters (7,000 feet) before returning to the coast. Two years later a British-American party of four followed much the same approach but attempted to follow first the Libby Glacier and then the Agassiz. They reached an elevation of about 3,300 meters (11,000 feet) on the southern flank of Mount St. Elias before turning back.

Near the head of the Hubbard Glacier, the hydrologic divide of the icefield. (David Murray)

In 1890 the distinguished mountaineer-scientist I. C. Russell entered the scene. Toward the end of a field season that took him across the southern slopes of Mount Cook and up the Seward Glacier nearly to the international boundary, Russell crossed the Dome Pass into Canada and onto the Newton Glacier. With M. B. Kerr he reached the 2,100-meter (7,000-foot) contour but, of greater importance, he found the route by which Mount St. Elias would later be climbed. This he all but confirmed in 1891 by again following the Newton Glacier to a 3,660-meter (12,000-foot) col on the crest of the main range, and by climbing to more than 4,300 meters (14,000 feet) on the northeastern ridge of Mount St. Elias. From this perch he became the first to see the full southern exposure of Mount Logan, which he named for the Surveyor General of Canada, and the great snow and ice reservoir of the upper Seward Glacier.

The way had now been found, but it was only in 1897 that it was followed to the summit, by one of the great European high-mountain explorers, the Duke of Abruzzi. In what was probably the most highly organized and elaborate expedition of its time, Abruzzi, with five experienced companions, four Italian professional guides, and a team of Alaskan packers, moved easily across the Malaspina Glacier and joined Russell's route at Dome Pass. From a high camp at 3,660 meters (12,000 feet) near Russell Col, the entire Italian team reached the summit on July 31, 1897. To the north, Abruzzi recognized the great mass of Mount Logan and Mount Bear, both named by Russell. He added two names of his own for two major peaks, Bona and Lucania. Fifty-four years were to pass before the last of these four would be climbed.

Although Great Britain and Russia signed a convention in 1825 that defined the boundary between their respective possessions in North America as, in part, the 141st meridian of west longitude, a similar agreement between the United States and the United Kingdom was not reached until 1906. The U.S.-U.K. agreement called for the immediate surveying and marking of the boundary. The work began at the Arctic Sea coast in 1907 and by 1912 it had reached the White River. Between that stream and Mount St. Elias, the boundary passes over "a land of desolation," as it is referred to in field reports. For nearly 128 kilometers (80 miles) it crosses the

structural grain of the most rugged and extensively glacierized terrain in North America. Most of that distance was virtually unexplored in 1912. In that year and in 1913 the surveying work necessary to demarcate the boundary went forward, and mountaineering skill as well as highly professional field organization, logistics, technical skill, and endurance were required before the southern turning point, Mount St. Elias, was reached.

Necessarily, the progress of such a survey is accelerated by establishing observing stations on prominent features at high elevations. In the St. Elias Mountains, the surveying teams occupied more than 100 stations. These varied in elevation from about 1,500 meters to 4,100 meters (5,000 feet to 13,000 feet). The highest peak to be climbed during the course of the boundary survey was Mount Natazhat (4,095 meters — 13,435 feet), and it is singled out in the report of the International Boundary Commission for special mention, probably because of its prominence. Not so the scores of stations on ridges, spurs, and summits that were established in 1912 and 1913. Still less is published on the hundreds of miles of high-mountain and glacier travel performed in those years, almost all of it original exploration. With the anonymity with which government agencies are inclined to shroud the deeds of their members, the official account includes only a few names of men who helped to accomplish one of the greatest feats of high-mountain exploration in history.

Despite this, two episodes did take place that left their mark on future mountaineering history. In 1913 T. C. Dennis led a survey party up the Chitina River and Logan Glacier to a point some 27 kilometers (17 miles) into what is now Kluane National Park. From this journey came the first description and photographs of the northern slopes of Mount Logan. These greatly aided not only the eventual ascent of Canada's highest mountain but also the selection of objectives for the 1967 Centennial year.

The second episode was the classic journey of exploration carried out by a joint Canadian-United States survey team led by A. C. Baldwin in the late spring of 1913. This group traveled south from the Chitina River, followed the Baldwin Glacier to the topographic divide, and continued on to the base of the northern shoulder of Mount St. Elias. With the objective of establishing a survey station on the summit of

The true summit of Mount Logan (center). (Walter Wood)

Mount St. Elias, the party was able to establish a high camp at 4,120 meters (13,500 feet) below the west face. On June 30, 1913, they set out for the summit, but, at over 4,900 meters (16,000 feet) and a short distance below the northwestern shoulder, a sudden storm dispelled their hopes and dictated an immediate retreat to their high camp and, food being in short supply, to the Chitina Valley. They had accomplished a round-trip journey of 112 kilometers (70 miles) in four weeks through totally unexplored country and had almost succeeded in making the second ascent of Mount St. Elias. Strange to tell, although this great mountain has now been climbed at least fourteen times, it was not until 1978 that complete ascent of the "boundary route" was made.

One of the results of the work of the boundary survey parties was the determination that

Mount Logan (5,951 meters — 19,525 feet) is the highest mountain in Canada and second only to Mount McKinley in North America. Mount Logan is also one of the world's most massive mountains. Rising in the heart of Kluane National Park, 96 kilometers (60 miles) from the coast and nearly 112 kilometers (70 miles) from the nearest point of the Alaska Highway, it is one of the world's most elusive mountains. Its summit is visible from only a few miles of coastline near Yakutat, Alaska, and from no point at all on the Alaska Highway. Indeed, so shy is this great mountain that beyond the boundaries of the St. Elias Mountains in the Yukon Territory it can be seen only from prominent points on the Yukon Plateau nearly 160 kilometers (100 miles) away.

In the aftermath of World War One, mountaineering, especially in western Canada, took a fresh spurt. Many peaks of the Rocky Mountains along the Alberta-British Columbia border were still unexplored, let alone unclimbed, and the mountains of the Coast Range were still a land of mystery. Mount Logan, however, thanks to the International Boundary Commission, had been fairly well reconnoitered, and Russell and Abruzzi had reported on the southern exposure. Thus Mount Logan had been seen from the south, west, and north, and the photopanoramas of the boundary survey parties seemed to show that an approach from the northwest might lead to the high slopes of the mountain.

In 1923 W. W. Foster, president of the Alpine Club of Canada, and his climbing partner, A. H. MacCarthy, proposed a joint Canadian-United States expedition to attempt Mount Logan. A strong party was recruited from both countries and in the early spring of 1925 MacCarthy and Andrew Taylor freighted by dog team the bulk of equipment and supplies that would be needed to a site near the threshold of Mount Logan at 1,800 meters (6,000 feet). This left about 4,100 meters (13,500 feet) to go. In May the remaining members of the expedition set out from McCarthy, Alaska, for the 128-kilometer (80-mile) journey over the route that had been worked out, with caches, by MacCarthy and Taylor. The base camp was set up by May on the surface of Ogilvie Glacier. Now began the process, not only to work out a route, but to stock each successive camp with food and equipment. This required repeated relays until more than 900 kilos (2,000 pounds) of necessities had beenput in place. To do this involved both technical climbing and straightforward progress, and, up to King Col at the 4,100-meter (13,500-foot) level, the route was somewhat protected by the high slopes of Mount Logan from foul weather driving over the mountain from the Pacific. From King Col the party was exposed to the full fury of a series of storms that were to continue until long after the summit had been won. Advances were made and retreats followed. Exposure to the elements brought frostbite to one member and forced his descent to the base camp, accompanied by a selfless volunteer to see him safely down. The remaining six climbers eventually succeeded in establishing a secure camp at about 5,500 meters (18,000 feet) on the high roof of Canada, and, following a new onslaught of blizzard, they were rewarded by a fine day on June 23. They set out at 10 A.M. and at 4:30 P.M. reached their goal—or was it their goal? From their summit they suffered the dismay of seeing a higher summit about 2.5 kilo-

meters (1.5 miles) to the east; it had been hidden from their view up to that time. On they went as another storm engulfed them, and at 8:30 in the evening the six reached the summit of Mount Logan.

The descent was a nightmare. The two parties of three men each became separated in the storm, and one of these parties was forced to bivouac twice before courage and sheer determination enabled it to reach the high camp. They had been without shelter or hot food for 44 hours.

Such, in brief, was the epic first ascent of Mount Logan. In assessing the expedition's triumph more than half a century later, it is well to remember a number of factors that make the climb remarkable. In 1925 the topographical details of the mountain, especially above 4,000 meters (13,000 feet), were unknown and could be only vaguely inferred. Then, equipment and clothing, while reasonably protective, were heavy and cumbersome; footgear was styled to alpine needs in civilized ranges. Tents, too, were heavy and barely effective in the severe arctic environment. This was high-mountain exploration at its most severe.

By 1976 the summit of Mount Logan had been reached more than 20 times, and high prominences of the mountain other than the summit had been visited on more than 30 occasions. Weather, good or bad, smiled or frowned on these parties, but in terms of low temperatures, high winds, and white-out conditions no parties have been subjected to circumstances so inhospitable to human existence as those of 1925.

As the decade of the 1930s dawned, so, too, did the modern period of exploration and mountaineering in the St. Elias Mountains. The airplane had much to do with it, and by the end of the period enough had been learned of the topography—especially that of the Icefield Ranges—to meet mountaineering needs until detailed maps appeared in 1961.

The first great peak to fall in the modern period, and only the third major summit to have been reached, was Mount Bona (5,005 meters—16,420 feet). It was climbed by Terris Moore, Allen Carpé, and Andrew Taylor. Setting out, as had the Mount Logan party, from McCarthy in the Chitina Valley, the party followed the well-traveled trail that connects the Copper River drainage with that of the Yukon. From Skolai Pass on the watershed, they traveled up the Russell Glacier and established a camp at 2,650 meters (8,700 feet) at the base of the broad cascade of snow and ice that is the north face of Mount Bona.

Their objective then became a high saddle at about 4,000 meters (13,000 feet) that forms a dip in the northwestern ridge. This they reached, and after an attempt that was frustrated by storm they reached the summit on July 2, 1930. In the long twilight of midsummer they easily retraced their steps to their high camp, and a week later they reached McCarthy.

Five years passed before the St. Elias Mountains were visited again. In the spring of 1935 a party under the leadership of Bradford Washburn explored the core of the Icefield Ranges (Mount Hubbard and Mount Alverstone, adjacent to the Lowell Glacier), and for the first time aircraft played a part in the exploration of these mountains. Much topographical survey work was done, and Washburn produced the first comprehensive aerial photographic coverage of the region. As break-up approached, the party split, one element to make the first traverse of the range to tidewater in Nunatak Fiord, the other to travel overland eastward to Whitehorse. Both journeys were accomplished, and the expedition was a classic of high-mountain exploration.

Later that summer, as Robert Bates and Ome Daiber of Washburn's party walked into Whitehorse, they encountered an expedition on the point of leaving for the high mountains west of Kluane Lake, and for a compelling reason. Since the days of the gold rush, two Alsatian brothers, Jean and Louis Jacquot, had staked their fortunes, not on gold, but on fur. The local Indians were skilled trappers, and a feudal community sprang up in which the Jacquots staked the trappers to their needs in return for pelts. The Jaquots also bred and raised a string of pack and saddle horses, which, by 1935, had reached a population of 75. From these were formed the pack trains that were used by hunters who came from all over the world in quest of the wildlife that abounds below the snow-line of the St. Elias Mountains. I saw these horses as the key to summer exploration in the high ranges, and during five field seasons between 1935 and 1947 I conducted scientific programs throughout the northeastern flank of the mountains, until the airplane supplanted the pack train in 1948.

In 1935 my target was a valley locally called Wolf Creek, but which today appears on maps as Steele Creek. To reach it the pack train had to contend with soggy tundra, racing glacier-fed rivers, and, finally, the trailless lateral moraines of Steele Glacier. Mountaineering played an important role in the summer work, and the ascent of Mount Gibson (2,990 meters — 9,810 feet) was made in early July. The advance of the pack train to a point above the bend of Steele Glacier disclosed that two great mountains connected by a high ridge stood on the divide between the drainage to the Copper River and that flowing into the Yukon River. These peaks were Mount Wood (4,839 meters — 15,875 feet) and Mount Steele (5,069 meters — 16,630 feet). They were named, along with Mount Walsh (4,493 meters — 14,740 feet), by J. J. McArthur, who sighted them from the Yukon Plateau east of Kluane Lake in 1900. The names are those of commanders of the North West Mounted Police in the Yukon Territory during the gold rush. My goal became the summit of Mount Steele.

From a base camp at 1,800 meters (6,000 feet) in the highest meadow that provided fodder for the horses, the advance on Mount Steele began. An intervening ridge blocked the view of the lower slopes of the mountain, but it appeared that, barring unlikely difficulties, the eastern ridge would provide a straightforward route to the conical summit. A week of relaying equipment and supplies to the foot of the eastern ridge at 2,600 meters (8,500 feet) still left 2,400 meters (8,000 feet) to be climbed.

The weather of August had been poor and it was decided to attempt the entire ridge from a secure camp rather than to relay further supplies to higher elevations. At 1 A.M., by the light of the full moon, the climbing party set out for the summit. All went well and at 6 A.M. a 3,650-meter (12,000-foot) prominence had been reached. At this point high lenticular clouds over Mount Logan and an opalescent sky over Mount Walsh and Mount Vancouver prompted a conference. Snow plumes on the ridge above sealed the matter, and the party descended. En route, we were overtaken by very high winds that blew one member of the party right off the crest, and a full storm had developed by the time camp was reached. Any hope of another attempt seemed dim.

On August 14, I decided to establish a survey station as high as possible on the eastern ridge. My brother Harrison and I climbed to 3,000 meters (10,000 feet), and to our delight we found the ridge to be one of hard-packed, wind-blown snow, ideal for climbing and for rapid progress.

Mount Steele at head of Steele Glacier. (Walter Wood)

Hurrying down to camp, we made plans for another attempt on the summit, and the party set out again at 1 A.M. on August 15. This time the weather was benign and difficulties were few, and at 3 P.M. the summit was reached. Not a breath of air stirred and the Icefield Ranges stood out sharp and clear, even at the distance of Mount Fairweather nearly 320 kilometers (200 miles) away. As we descended to our snug base camp on Steele Glacier, little did we think that

this was to be the last ascent of a major peak of the St. Elias Mountains in which aircraft played no part.

In 1937 Washburn persuaded Alaska's famous pioneer bush pilot, Robert Reeve, to take off on skis from the slick tidal flats of Valdez, Alaska, and establish his climbing party on the Walsh Glacier at the base of Mount Lucania (5,226 meters — 17,147 feet). The take-off was successful, but all sorts of problems developed after

Washburn and Robert Bates were landed on the glacier. First, Reeve's plane had to be extricated from a crevasse into which one ski had made its way. Then a severe thaw developed, which left Reeve almost no runway from which to take off, much less to land on when the time came to pick up the two mountaineers after their attempt on Mount Lucania. Reeve declined to attempt a take-off with Washburn and Bates aboard, but managed to get the plane up himself. Washburn and Bates found themselves on the horns of a dilemma: whether to return to civilization by descending the Walsh Glacier and Chitina Valley to McCarthy, a 144-kilometer (90-mile) journey, or to escape over the summit of Mount Steele and follow my 1935 route to Burwash Landing. They chose the latter.

In the days that followed, the two mountaineers made their way toward the broad saddle between Mount Lucania and Mount Steele. A snow-and-ice buttress provided a natural route to the saddle at 4,300 meters (14,000 feet), and from a camp at that point they reached the summit of Mount Lucania on July 9. From the same camp they made the second ascent of Mount Steele two days later. Now they were on known ground, and when they reached the base of Mount Steele they discarded all butthe absolute essentials for reaching Burwash Landing. The Donjek River was in full July flood, and they were unable to ford it. However, a 32-kilometer (20-mile) detour over the terminal ice of the Donjek Glacier put their last obstacle behind them. Now fate smiled, for they met up with a string of pack horses that had been rounded up for a fall hunt. They covered the last 32 kilometers (20 miles) on pack saddles, and entered Burwash Landing in well-earned triumph on July 2.

As the war intensified, I made one more visit to the St. Elias Mountains, in 1941. The Steele watershed was again the objective, but this time the airplane completely supplanted the pack train. A party of seven led by myself combined scientific investigations with the application of air-ground logistics techniques and the testing of personal high-mountain equipment that might have military applications. In early July two tons of food, equipment, and supplies were parachuted to base camp near the bend of Steele Glacier. Eight more loads, each containing the total requirements of four persons for varying periods of time, were dropped along two routes to be followed during late July and August. The first led from the base camp to the high slopes of Mount Wood; the other followed 40 kilometers (25 miles) of glacier and crossed two divides to reach the base of Mount Walsh (4,505 meters — 14,780 feet).

Following these ladders of camps, first to Mount Wood, then to Mount Walsh, was a team of mountaineers composed of Robert Bates, Anderson Bakewell, Albert Jackman, and myself. We reached our first objective on July 25 and our second on August 17. All the loads that had been dropped in advance were recovered. Thus, a happy relationship was achieved between lightly burdened ground parties and effective air support.

After World War Two mountaineering gained widespread acceptance. High-mountain exploration found its share of devotees, largely in the little-known coastal ranges of British Columbia, in Alaska, and in the St. Elias Mountains. In Kluane National Park a number of great peaks fell for the first time to members of the mountaineering fraternity: Mount St. Elias (5,489 meters — 18,008 feet), this time by a new route from the southwest in 1946, Mount Vancouver (4,834 meters — 15,860 feet) in 1949, and Mount Hubbard (4,576 meters — 15,013 feet) and Mount Alverstone (4,439 meters — 14,565 feet) in 1951. By 1953 Mount Logan had been climbed three times, King Peak (5,173 meters — 16,970 feet) twice, and Mount Augusta (4,289 — 14,070 feet) and Mount Cook (4,195 meters — 13,760 feet) both for the first time.

There is a natural tendency in exploring new country to select objectives that are challenging enough to inspire pride of conquest if the goal is attained. So it was with the peaks of the Icefield Ranges of Kluane National Park. The named peaks, being the most prominent, were the first to be approached and climbed. After what have been called "the years of an enthusiastic few" (1930-49), the enthusiastic many followed them into the mountains, and in the ensuing 25 years more than 300 individual ascents or journeys were undertaken in the St. Elias Mountains. The vast majority of these forays were made by teams of from four to a dozen climbers. The remainder were by members of four institutionally organized groups, three of which sought scientific information while the fourth was devoted exclusively to mountaineering.

In 1954 and 1956 the Geological Survey of

Canada dispatched a team to the St. Elias Mountains to carry out reconnaissance surveys of the geology of certain areas of the Kaskawulsh watershed and the Kluane Ranges. Those studies were directed by a seasoned mountaineer, John O. Wheeler, and, as with the International Boundary Survey, almost total anonymity shrouds the exploration and mountaineering done by Wheeler and his associates during the course of this scientific work. Their contribution was the geographical coordinates for no fewer than 40 summits which they were the first to reach, and they did this in two field seasons—a remarkable scientific achievement.

The first interdisciplinary scientific program in the Icefield Ranges was sponsored by the Arctic Institute of North America and was given the name Project Snow Cornice. During 1948 and the next three field seasons the watershed of the Seward Glacier became a natural laboratory in the physical and biological sciences. Senior investigators and graduate students were transported from Yakutat to a nunatak projecting from the snows of the glacier, on which a semi-permanent facility was erected. This building was a hub for activities across the broad expanse of the Seward "reservoir" and onto the Malaspina Glacier. Studies were carried on in glaciology, geophysics, meteorology and climatology, topographic mapping, and botany.

An essential element of the project was a team of mountaineers responsible for the safety of scientific personnel not completely at home in a high-mountain environment, and for the logistic support of field parties. These groups traveled widely over the gently rolling surface of Seward Glacier, ascended numerous rocky prominences suitable for survey stations, and, at the end of each season, were rewarded by complete ground and air support for an attempt on a mountaineering objective of their choice. Thus it was that Mount Vancouver was reconnoitered in 1948 and successfully climbed on July 5, 1949, by a highly experienced team composed of R. McCarter, W. Hainsworth, A. Bruce-Robertson, and the veteran hero of the British Mount Everest Expedition of 1924, Noël Odell.

Project Snow Cornice came to an end in 1951 and it was not until 1961 that the mountains of Kluane National Park again served as a national scientific laboratory. The Icefield Ranges Research Project, like its predecessor, is sponsored by the Arctic Institute of North America,

with the American Geographical Society adding its prestige through the publication of scientific results of the field work. Like Snow Cornice, the new project promotes field studies leading to increased understanding of a high-mountain environment. Also like its forerunner, it was conceived and directed by myself. Unlike Snow Cornice, it is based on the continental side of the range where weather conditions and communications are more favorable than those prevailing on the Pacific Ocean coast, and logistical needs more easily met.

In 1979, the Icefield Ranges Research Project completed its 18th field season. During these years its members traveled and worked throughout the St. Elias Mountains, from Skolai Pass in Alaska to the southern boundary of the park; from surging Steele Glacier to the waters of Disenchantment Bay. Numerous ascents were recorded by project members, but of greater importance was the advice, assistance, and surveillance freely given by experienced senior members and especially by the chief pilot, Philip Upton, who has logged more than 5,000 hours of flying and the same number of landings and take-offs on glaciers and other unprepared surfaces. Light aircraft modified to land on either ground or ice have proven their worth many times over. But for this innovation in the late 1940s, high-mountain science in North America would have advanced little indeed.

The fourth and last departure from small-team mountain exploration came in 1967. In that year Canada celebrated her centennial while neighboring Alaska paused to review its first hundred years as a possession of the United States. As its part in the celebration of the centennial, the government of the Yukon Territory proposed a mountain-climbing expedition. Meanwhile the Alpine Club of Canada was thinking in complete harmony with the Yukon proposal. The meeting of minds resulted in agreement that the Yukon Territory would supply the mountains and the club would furnish the climbers. This very simple solution ultimately led to the Yukon Alpine Centennial Expedition. When the planning had been completed—and it was a giant task—the participants numbered nearly 300. Three fixed-wing aircraft and two helicopters played primary logistic roles, and 30 summits were attempted, most of them successfully. Mount

Steele and Mount Walsh, among others, were climbed several times.

The major thrust was in the direction of 14 high summits, all unclimbed, all unexplored. In an international gesture the joint Canadian-United States team successfully climbed the south summit of Mount Vancouver (4,792 meters—15,720 feet), a point on the international boundary, and named it Good Neighbour Peak. Then came a major effort to airlift 12 teams of four climbers each into position to attempt 12 peaks, each to be named for one of the provinces or territories of Canada, and one additional team to attempt a mountain named Centennial Peak. The Centennial Range in which these peaks rise forms part of the divide between the Chitina and Walsh glaciers in Canada. It is as remote from conventional supply points as any

group of peaks in the St. Elias Mountains. Finally, to round out the program, the Alpine Club chose the Steele Glacier valley as the site of its annual climbing camp. This was to involve 200 members, who would be accommodated during two successive 15-day periods. It is not hard to see that this was to be the largest and most complex mountaineering expedition ever undertaken in North America, and probably in global history.

The Yukon Alpine Centennial Expedition got under way in mid-June with the airlift of the Canadian-American eight-man team to the base of Good Neighbour Peak. All went well and camps were established up the southeastern buttress and on the summit ridge. On June 25 the entire party reached its goal. So strong was the team that, not content with their prize, three of

Peaks in the Centennial Range: Centennial peak at left, Mount Quebec in center. (Walter Wood)

the members continued along the two-mile cor-
niced ridge to the high summit of Mount Vancouver. It was an auspicious start for the expedition.

The peaks of the Centennial Range, though all
somewhat lower in elevation than Good
Neighbour Peak, nevertheless presented logistical problems that only thoroughness, patience,
and good humor could solve. These qualities
were amply provided by David Fisher, soon to
become president of the Alpine Club of Canada.

By July 8 the first of three base camps, each
serving as a springboard for several objectives,
was stocked and occupied by climbing teams.
Two more followed as rapidly as the helicopters
could operate in the fickle weather. During the
ensuing 16 days the climbers attacked,
retreated, bivouacked, and advanced again. The
weather was generally poor, with temperatures
that fostered dangerous snow conditions.
Despite these obstacles, almost all the chosen
summits were reached; and in the few cases of
disappointment the climbers were wise to turn
back even though the summits rose only a few
feet above their heads. On July 24 the final party
was evacuated.

Meanwhile Steele Valley was being invaded
by the Alpine Club troops. In 48 hours 100 people
were whisked 64 kilometers (40 miles) from a
staging area on Kluane Lake by bus to a helicopter pad at the end of an obscure mining trail, and
from there they were taken another 64 kilometers by helicopter to a prepared camp at 1,737
meters (5,700 feet) on the inside of the great bend
of Steele Glacier. Some stalwarts even trekked
from the helicopter into the Donjek Valley, to be
picked up later by passing helicopters. For the
following month Steele Valley and its tributaries
were busy places indeed. Climbing parties made
early starts from the base camp and returned
late into the twilight of sub-arctic July and

August. Some found worthy objectives that
needed no helicopter assistance. Others sought
summits that could only be won between dawn
and sunset if the parties could be set down at the
base of their chosen climb. This was particularly
true of peaks rising above the left bank of Steele
Glacier which, at that time, was in the state
known as "catastrophic surge." Such was the
chaos of the moving ice that to cross it on foot
would have been next to impossible. Finally, the
more experienced and venturesome mountaineers were given opportunities to attempt the
three giants that are accessible from the Steele
Valley: Mount Steele itself, Mount Wood, and
Mount Walsh. For these peaks, satellite camps
were air-lifted to convenient jumping-off points,
usually above 3,000 meters (10,000 feet). By the
time the second group of 100 climbers had had
its fill, 18 summits had been reached, 13 of them
for the first time. Mount Steele and Mount
Walsh were climbed four times and Mount Wood
once. Many of the lesser peaks were also
ascended several times. This was an extremely
well-organized expedition, and perhaps the
proof lies in the fact that not a single accident or
illness occurred that deprived any member of
more than a day of exercise.

My objective here has been to present vignettes
of episodes that are typical of the many that
brought about the unveiling of the St. Elias
Mountains. Since the ascent of Mount St. Elias
in 1897, there is documentary evidence for more
than 400 individual mountaineering successes or
failures in the St. Elias Mountains — more than
70 of these have been on the huge mass of Mount
Logan. Yet for every one of these forays there
remain hundreds of summits as yet untrodden,
beckoning to all who would savor a high-
mountain environment matched by few, and second to none.

13. FLYING IN THE ST. ELIAS MOUNTAINS

Philip Upton

THE ST. ELIAS Mountains, seen from the window of an aircraft on a bright sunny day, present a composite picture of blue sky, jagged peaks, and dazzling white snow-covered glaciers. The changing vistas of snow, ice, rock, and sky are spectacular. Except for intrepid mountaineers, the only people to see these magnificent mountains, locked in their frozen world, are in aircraft. Even since the building of the Alaska Highway, few travelers have become aware of the grandeur behind the lesser mountains along the road.

Mountains manufacture their own weather, and the imposing scenery can quickly disappear into a white nothingness; the smooth air can suddenly become extremely rough. In the early days of flying, engines were not quite as dependable or powerful as today's, airframes were not quite so rugged, and sophisticated instruments were not found in light aircraft. Pilots flew in mountainous areas out of necessity and not for pleasure. Even today the wise pilot treats mountain flying with caution and respect.

In 1935 the first pilot known to have ventured into the St. Elias Mountains flew a Fokker Super Universal (CF-AAM) to the Lowell Glacier and landed there on skis. Bob Randall, later to become chief pilot for Canadian Pacific, had leased the aircraft to Northern Airways, owned by George Simmons and Everett Wasson at Carcross, Yukon Territory. They, in turn, had a charter with Bradford Washburn, director of the Boston Museum of Science, for a mapping expedition sponsored by the National Geographic Society. Washburn planned a traverse from a base camp on the Lowell Glacier across

Fokker Super Universal taking off from Kluane Lake, September 1935. (Walter Wood)

Fairchild 71 at Burwash Landing, Kluane Lake, 1935. (Walter Wood)

the range to Yakutat, Alaska, supported by aircraft. Randall made several trips to establish the base camp, landing on the glacier, but he was unable to set out caches for resupply along the route because of poor weather conditions and difficulties in finding suitable landing areas.

Randall also flew a Fairchild 71 on floats, based at Burwash Landing on Kluane Lake, for aerial photography of the area being surveyed by Washburn; he made several flights in this aircraft, without oxygen supplies, to between 12,000 and 18,000 feet (3,600 and 5,500 meters). Both the Fokker and the Fairchild were used later in the same year for photographic mapping flights for Walter A. Wood, working mainly on the Steele Glacier.

The next year a Stinson SR-5A on floats, piloted by John D. Kay, was used to support Wood's survey parties from Tepee Lake, and to supply a climbing party on Mount Equinox at the head of Wolverine Creek. This was the first party to depend completely on air support, including transport into and out of base camp.

In the following years aircraft were used by both Washburn—a Fairchild 52, flown by Bob Reeve of "Glacier Pilot" fame, which landed the climbing party on the Walsh Glacier in 1937— and Wood—the Fairchild, a Ford Trimotor, flown by Everett Wasson, and two U.S. Army Air Force Douglas B-18 medium bombers for air

photos and the latter also to drop equipment and supplies for a number of climbs in 1941. In the space of a few years aircraft had become the key to the exploration of the icefields.

Project Snow Cornice, based on the Seward Glacier in 1948 to study glaciology, meteorology, and geophysics, was serviced by a Norseman equipped with one of the first sets of ski-wheels. All early aircraft employed skis, which were exchanged for wheels or floats after the winter season, leaving a period of uncertainty as to which to use in the fall before there was snow, or ice on the lakes, and in the spring while the thaw took place. Ski-wheels, with the wheel protruding a few inches through a slot in the fixed ski, enabled the aircraft to land on snow or ice or on a prepared runway. Maurice King, based out of Yakutat, flew Wood's party to a nunatak near Mount Vancouver, landing on the snow at about 6,000 feet (1,800 meters).

The ski-wheel combination enabled an aircraft to operate all summer long, from a snow-free airstrip to a snow-covered landing area. King's first attempt to use ski-wheels resulted in the Norseman's nosing over because the wheels protruded too far below the skis. The aircraft was salvaged by project members working under King's minute supervision, and then was flown out and largely rebuilt. The rebuilding included installation of hydraulically operated skis,

Stinson SR-5A, Teepee Lake, August 1936. (Walter Wood)

Norseman on ski wheels, Yakutat, Alaska, June 1949. (Walter Wood)

Ski wheel, for take-off from runway and landing on snow or ice. (Walter Wood)

which could be raised or lowered by the pilot, depending on the type of landing surface to be used. After that, the aircraft fully supplied the needs of the project until its conclusion in 1951. A remarkable amount of equipment was transported to make a comfortable base camp, including a Jamesway building that was cached at the end of each season. Various photographic flights were made, as well as an airdrop on Mount Vancouver to resupply a climbing team at 13,000 feet (4,000 meters).

In 1951 the RCAF began an aerial photographic mapping survey. This survey continued until the whole area had been covered, and in 1967 the first topographic map of the area was published.

After World War Two, the new developments in aircraft capabilities soon spurred ideas to conduct research in the area and make the mountains more accessible to climbing parties. During the 1950s, Wilson Air Service of Gulkana, Alaska, transported many groups into the St. Elias Mountains, using the Cessna 180 on ski-wheels, the new workhorse of the north. Before the development in 1949 of hydraulic controls for ski-wheels, some pilots used unusual techniques for landings and take-offs. Bob Reeve used his ski-equipped Fairchild throughout the sea-

son, taking off from and landing on the tidal mud flats at Valdez. There is also an account of a Grumman Goose (amphibian) landing on the snow of the Seward Glacier and taking off again, but using amphibians or floats for this purpose is not exactly recommended by either manufacturers or pilots.

In 1961 the vital contribution of aircraft as a tool for research was recognized by the Arctic Institute of North America when it established the base camp for the Icefield Ranges Research Project at an abandoned airstrip at the southern end of Kluane Lake. Glaciologist-pilot Richard H. Ragle, using a ski-wheel-equipped STOL Helio Courier, established a camp on a broad snowfield of the Icefield Ranges at the 8,000-foot (2,400-meter) level. From this main base, parties traversed the snowfields, surveying and gathering data in glaciology, meteorology, and geophysics.

The Helio Courier, with its rugged airframe and short-field landing and take-off capabilities on unprepared surfaces, was found to be an ideal vehicle to carry personnel and supplies safely into the Icefield Ranges. Working bases were established at various locations and altitudes throughout the ranges, including the Kaskawulsh, Hubbard, Seward, and Ogilvie glaciers, and as high as 12,000 feet (3,600 meters) at the head of the Donjek Glacier.

From 1965 on, the Bell G-2 helicopter gradually became extremely useful, particularly at the lower elevations in localities where even a rough landing strip could not be found (for example, the Steele Glacier, which began to surge at that time). From time to time a Beaver (deHavilland) aircraft, piloted by Lloyd Ryder and based in Whitehorse, was used to take in climbing parties, but with the exception of the Arctic Institute's Helio Courier no aircraft were using ski-wheels throughout the summer season.

By 1967 supercharged Bell G-3B1 helicopters had greatly increased the usefulness of helicopters at higher altitudes. The Arctic Institute initiated a study of high-altitude human physiology in that year, using a turbocharged Helio Courier, which I piloted. The basic difference between supercharging and turbocharging an engine is the method used to run the compressor that forces air into the carburetor to compensate for decreased atmospheric pressure at higher altitudes. A supercharger employs a gear-driven compressor, while a turbocharger uses exhaust

Bell Jet Ranger helicopter. (John Theberge)

Looking up the Hubbard Glacier at a panorama of mountains, from left to right, Mount Logan, Mount McArthur, Mount King George, and Mount Lucania in distant right. (Walter Wood)

gases to drive the compressor turbine. A landing site for high-altitude research was found at the 17,600-foot (5,350-meter) level on Mount Logan, and a camp was established that rapidly became a working laboratory. This lab has been used every season since.

Although the Helio Courier performed well, and made the trip to "Logan High" almost on a commuting basis, it was realized that to depend entirely on one aircraft was risky. The Bell G-3B1 was able to attain the altitude, but unable to carry the necessary loads, and therefore could not be considered for emergency back-up. Not until the Bell Jet Ranger made its appearance (in this area around 1969) was there an aircraft that could be called upon in an emergency. Several flights were made to Logan High by Trans North

Turbo Air Jet Ranger helicopters, to ensure this back-up capability. In 1973, when altitude limitations were placed on the Jet Ranger, the Arctic Institute acquired a second turbocharged Helio Courier as a back-up aircraft. These newer aircraft continue to be used to support scientific studies, transporting supplies, scientists, and sophisticated equipment and landing them at very high altitudes.

There have been many unrecorded overflights of the icefields, as private aircraft have come to perform at higher altitudes and over long distances. Some historic flights have even been recorded involuntarily, like the one by a poacher who flew his Piper Super Cub across the snow-fields from Alaska with a hunter aboard, landed on a gravel bar, shot a sheep, and flew back again. The plane was seen on the gravel bar and reported as an aircraft in trouble—and the pilot *was* in trouble, with the law!

Gradually, as experience in the snowfields accumulated, routes into the range were established. The main route is up the Kaskawulsh Glacier, over the broad accumulation area to the natural divide leading to the Hubbard Glacier, and thence to the Seward, Logan, and Walsh glaciers. Another route, across the Burwash Uplands to the Donjek River valley, leads into the Steele, Donjek, and Kluane glaciers and to a number of smaller glaciers. A third natural route starts from Haines Junction and heads down the Dezadeash River to the Alsek, up the Lowell Glacier or the Dusty Glacier to the Hubbard Glacier and the Alverstone-Hubbard-Kennedy massif, as well as to Mount Vancouver.

These broad valleys provide natural routes leading to large glaciers whose surfaces are gradual in slope, and which in turn lead to the high mountains and the broad snow accumulation areas of the St. Elias Mountains. Wildlife (sheep, goats, and the occasional grizzly) grazing on the high grassy benches are unconcerned by the passage of planes—unless the aircraft attempts to buzz them, a practice that is forbidden within the park boundaries. Fixed-wing aircraft are less noticed by wildlife than are helicopters, due to the peculiar sound helicopter rotors make as the aircraft passes overhead.

The high mountains of Kluane National Park will probably continue for the foreseeable future to be inaccessible except for mountaineers. From the window of aircraft, however, sightseers may view the beauty and grandeur of this unique land.

14. CLIMBING IN THE KLUANE RANGES

Monty E. Alford

THE INCLEMENT WEATHER that had suddenly blown in from the Gulf of Alaska deposited rain on the wide terminus of the Malaspina Glacier and, a little later, a layer of wet snow on the southern slopes of Mount St. Elias. It continued across the Seward Glacier and soon enveloped the huge massif, Mount Logan. Peak after peak of the St. Elias Mountains disappeared in cloud as the bad weather followed a northeasterly course. The high wind and falling snow seemed to lessen somewhat as the front approached the Hubbard-Kaskawulsh Divide. Then, leaving the snow behind, but obedient to the laws of gravity, the cold wind picked up speed again as it flowed down the Kaskawulsh Glacier toward the warm, dry valleys occupied by the Slims and Kaskawulsh rivers. Cutting through the Kluane Ranges, the valley of the

Slims served as a natural funnel for the wind: surging and eddying, it picked up the fine glacier silts from the banks and sandbars of the river and carried them in dense white clouds across the delta and far out over the green waters of Kluane Lake.

A party of six, camped at about 17,500 feet (5,300 meters) on the southern side of Mount Logan, was experiencing a fairly common event in the high mountains. They had carried their supplies to the 18,500-foot (5,600-meter) level the day before, to the site of what would be their fifth and final camp. Fourteen days earlier, a small ski plane landed them at the 9,000-foot (2,740-meter) level on the Quintino Sella Glacier. For those two weeks they had been staging themselves up the mountain, sometimes making three trips between camps, in such a

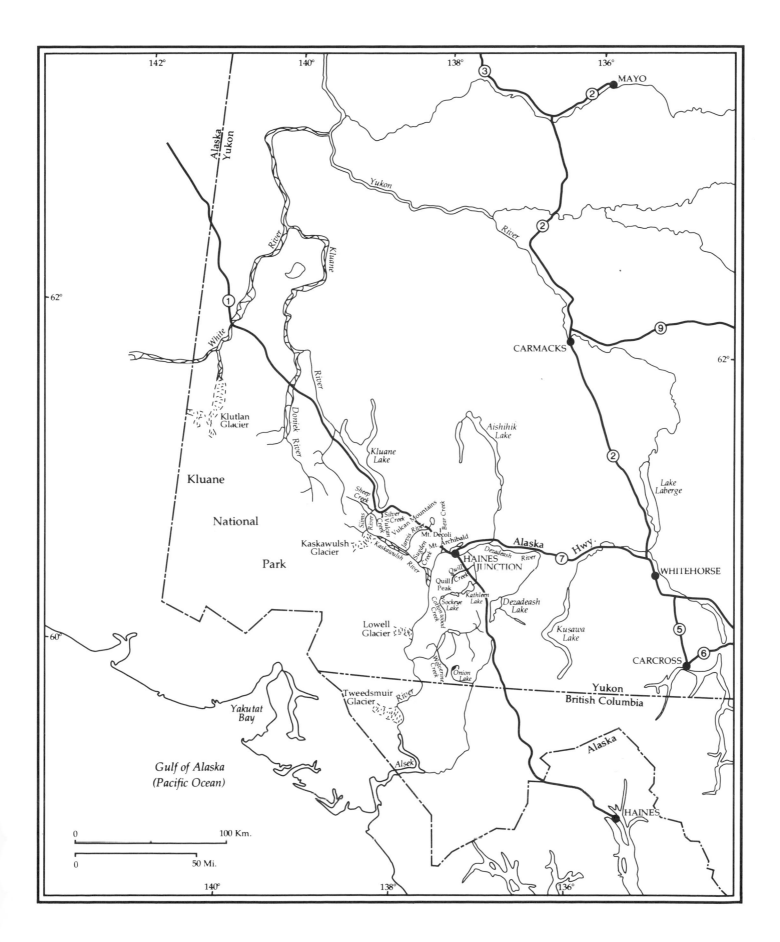

manner that, with ample supplies, a storm at any level could be waited out in safety.

They had hoped to move the tentage that day, but a storm had dictated otherwise. The enforced delay in moving up was of minor concern. More serious was their inability to escort one of their members, who was suffering from mountain sickness (a loose term covering the malaise brought about by oxygen deficiency), quickly back down to a camp site at the 13,000-foot (4,000-meter) level. Loss of appetite, headache, nausea, and a general disinterest in everything around him had been evidence enough: the diagnosis was easy. One climber had volunteered to serve as escort,which meant sacrificing his part in the summit attempt. But that is what expedition climbing is all about: a team effort demanding many sacrifices by individual members of the party.

The criteria governing the selection of climbers for an ascent of one of the high-mountain massifs, particularly when the mountain is remote, are quite different from those that may be used to choose a team for a high-angle climb that will take only a few days. The expedition climber, though bowed by a heavy load and breaking trail through fresh snow, must be as pleasant a person to meet between camps as he might be when relating his experiences in the Sourdough Tavern in Whitehorse. There is much drudgery in expedition mountaineering, so that a person who is tolerant, patient, and always cheerful is invariably a good choice. The technical difficulty of the route can be controlled, but the dangers of avalanches, ferocious winds and paralyzing storms, and the ever-increasing effect on the body of an ever-decreasing supply of oxygen are less predictable and may impose demands that will place all in jeopardy.

It was an anxious moment for the expedition. Fortunately, visibility improved a little during the night so that the sick man and his escort were able to leave early the next day to follow the marker wands that led down to the lower camp. The other four climbers moved up in spite of the marginal weather and reached the summit two days later. Lower down, the sick climber recovered in the more normal atmosphere, and when the party was reunited at base camp everyone shared in the triumph of the expedition.

But let us leave Mount Logan and follow the storm as it continued to move across the mountains. Lying in the lee of the vast precipitation barrier of the Icefield Ranges, the frontal Kluane Ranges have fewer storms, and it is not surprising that much of the Yukon has been classified as semi-arid. Extending from Dezadeash Lake on the Haines Road to the White River on the Alaska Highway, the Kluane Ranges are never far from the highway and the traveler is treated to a close-up view of the serrated ridges and sharp buttresses of the Dalton, Auriol, and Donjek ranges. These ranges, standing like a series of parallel ridges, offer the alpinist at least 6,000 feet (1,800 meters) of climbable relief.

Not only may the Kluane climber expect better weather, but he has a wide choice of mountains, some of them never climbed before, whose summits can be reached in two or three days. However, no region represents perfect mountaineering, and it is the fragmentary nature of the rock that dismays the climber here — a mixture of volcanics, sediments, and granite intrusives that often afford poor footing.

Between the Kluane Ranges and the high icefields and giant peaks of the Icefield Ranges lies a narrow belt of green that is a hiker's paradise. It is known as the Duke Depression, and its sparsely forested valleys and high, open grasslands offer little impediment. From aspen and spruce forest to patterned moraine to glacier ice to shattered rock and, finally, to the wind-packed summit snow, the climber's experience is a succession of discoveries that leaves an indelible impression. Tiny alpine flora, the flushed ptarmigan, and the Dall sheep on the hillside across the valley all add to the charm of these sub-arctic hills.

Of course, not all is outdoor bliss. The Kluane climber must be equipped for snow and ice, since most routes demand the traverse of glaciers or snow slopes, and virtually all summits have a perpetual snow cover; the patience and serenity of the traveler may be sorely tested should he run afoul of those devilish bushes that are a serious hindrance to man's progress. The "buck-brush," or dwarf birch, may grow just about anywhere, and the only advice I can give is to maintain control over your temper. Thick entwining branches that grow downhill are often so formidable that it is all you can do to force a passage, and then only by throwing yourself against them.

Free of brush, and on higher ground, we may be momentarily startled by the shrill whistle of a hoary marmot or the nasal bleat of a collared

Tundra camp. (Monty Alford)

pika; or perhaps the eye will be drawn to a circling eagle as it waits for the slightest movement below. Such sights and sounds remind us that we are not alone, that we are under surveillance, and that we are, in fact, intruders.

Despite the comfort of knowing that animal life is present, we feel the solitude, and because so few people have climbed in these ranges we also feel an excitement. Few, if any, have gone before us—we are pioneers.

There are a number of interesting routes requiring atleast one night out that may be taken by hikers and climbers in the Kluane Ranges, beginning at the highway.

Auriol Range

Quill Creek is an unobtrusive watercourse that drains the northeastern flank of the Auriol Range. Driving to Haines, Alaska, from Haines Junction, one crosses it seven miles (11 kilometers) out, without being aware that this is the key to an ascent of one of the most prominent peaks in the area. This summit is as yet unnamed. I always refer to it as Quill Peak.

Leaving the road, follow the left bank (right—looking upstream) of the creek as far as the 3,100-foot (750-meter) contour, a distance of about three miles (5 kilometers). A hike over washed gravels is a walk through a picture gallery. The luster of multi-colored rock and the patterns they form provide a mosaic that is often quite beautiful. The going is easy, though I recall having to enter timber in four or five places to skirt the channel.

To reach the top of the southeastern ridge, leave the creek at the upper end of the first high bank. A conveniently placed gully enables you to reach your first and only obstacle—a band of thick buck-brush. It is understandable that the mountain should exact some kind of toll, and it does so at the very beginning. This belt of vegetation is dense enough to promote audible protestation, but it is narrow and before you know it you are through the barrier; you have paid the admission.

There is something comforting about a long ridge, and the southeastern buttress of Quill Peak is no exception. You can gain elevation at a pace that is not only tireless but conducive to observation of such detail as the saxifrage and moss campion underfoot. Beyond the ridge is a wide vista: to the east, the Dezadeash range encircled by a meandering river of the same name; to the southeast, across a valley, the dominating bulk of a neighboring mountain, and, to the south, the high cirques and snowfields that provide the source of Quill Creek.

Two small clefts in the ridge, like V notches, offer wind-free rest stops. At its upper end the ridge turns abruptly to the southwest, and a satellite peak must be crossed before the way to the summit is clear.

Packs may be cached at the 7,500-foot (2,300-meter) level, where it is advisable to rope up for the last section. The ridge steepens and becomes knife-edged before it disappears under a mantle of permanent snow. The final ascent is on hard snow, and care must be taken in the negotiation of cornices; crampons could be used although they are not mandatory.

The view from Quill Peak (8,153 feet—2,485 meters) is a grand one. A peak of the frontal ranges invariably offers the viewer a glimpse of the lofty summits and huge massifs of the St. Elias Mountains. If the weather hides such a distant panorama, then the nearer peaks of the Auriol Range will surely provide satisfying mountain scenes. The climber is awed by the extent of the Shakwak valley, which runs from the far northwest to the distant southeast.

Returning to your pack, happy with photos taken, you may descend the ridge to a point where a traverse across a scree slope leads to a cirque glacier. This upper basin, at the 6,500-foot (2,000-meter) level, offers a good camp site.

Unless you are deterred by sharp ridges of badly shattered rock, you may continue west to other peaks of the range. I don't mind saying that we were quite content to return via the same route. For us, Quill Peak provided a most enjoyable two-day sortie.

Vulcan Mountain

As in the approach to Quill Peak, the first steps toward Vulcan Mountain are taken over the gravels of a mountain stream. This is another two- or three-day climb that may begin at the old highway crossing of Slims River. Vulcan Creek has been used by many climbers to reach one or another of the two glaciers that nourish its tumbling waters.

Upper Vulcan Creek with Vulcan Mountain on the right. (John Theberge)

The first ascent of Vulcan was made by two climbers in 1963, via the second tributary that enters from the east, about one mile (1.6 kilometers) above Jessie Creek. They traversed the glacier at the head of the creek in a semicircular direction in order to reach the eastern ridge, which they followed to the summit pyramid. Any route you take to attain this peak will not only give you a pleasant and not too severe physical challenge but will place you at another unique vantage point in the Kluane Ranges. From Vulcan you can get some idea of the size of the Kaskawulsh Glacier, a 45-mile (72-kilometer) river of ice that is visible to the south.

The return from Vulcan's 9,200-foot (2,804-meter) summit may be made by a speedy descent onto the north-draining glacier or by the less obvious but more interesting northeastern exit. The latter route involves descending the eastern ridge, crossing the glacier, and climbing over a rock rampart to a western tributary of Silver Creek. Following this drainage, you will be led to the comfort of Silver Creek Lodge, where you can toast your triumph, mug in hand.

Mount Archibald

Farther to the southeast along the Kluane Ranges there are numerous peaks inviting those who wish nothing more than a weekend sortie in the hills. Between Silver Creek and the Jarvis River the western horizon is dominated by Mount Cairnes and its satellite peaks. Reaching

Mount Archibald viewed up Sugden Creek. (John Theberge)

altitudes of over 9,000 feet (2,700 meters), the Cairnes group has been visited by several parties. The first ascent was made by members of the Geological Survey of Canada in 1954; the second was made by an Italian expedition in 1966.

On the eastern side of the Jarvis River, and visible from the town of Haines Junction as you look west, lies a prominent snow-covered peak with two summits of about the same elevation. It is Mount Archibald (8,400 feet —2,560 meters), first climbed in 1954 by a party of three. Starting from Bear Creek on the Alaska Highway, the climber may use the trail that leads to Sugden Creek in order to reach the stream that drains Archibald's eastern slopes. The route is interesting because you ascend the huge outwash plain as far as the canyon. You can see the well-defined beaches of recent Lake Alsek and evidence of a much larger creek than the one you are following. Passing through the canyon, to avoid much bush-whacking, you should stay with the creek for the next mile or so, at least as far as the first steep side-gulley, which will lead to the moraine of the east-facing glacier. From this point the route is an obvious one. Some climbers have made their approach from the northeast, starting at Bear Creek Summit.

Whatever route is taken, a profusion of alpine flora and a very good chance of seeing Dall sheep make Archibald a pleasant mountain to climb. From the summit you can see the full magnitude of the Shakwak valley with the Alaska Highway and Haines Road, ribbons of white extending as far as you can see. To the south you can identify the Kaskawulsh River and see where it joins the Dezadeash River to make the Alsek River.

Mount Archibald and its smaller neighbor peak, Mount Decoeli, are the high points of a massif that is separated from the rest of the range by the Dezadeash River on the east and the Jarvis River on the west. This isolation gives it a distinctive prominence, particularly when viewed from the direction of Kluane Lake. This same geographical independence is shared by the Auriol Range, which you can see to the southeast in its entirety. Named after President Vincent Auriol of France to honor his visit to Canada in 1952, this group of peaks provides an inspiring backdrop to the settlement of Haines Junction.

No discussion of the Kluane Ranges would be complete without mention of their great possibilities for the hiker. The beauty of Cottonwood Creek is within easy reach of the campground at Kathleen Lake. Onion Lake and Wolverine Creek may be reached from Dalton Post, and there can be no more impressive region than this, with the spires and sharp-crested ridges of the Alsek Ranges providing a unique vertical perspective. From the shores of Kluane Lake, you can reach the pass at the head of Sheep Creek, cross over into Dickson Creek, and return to the highway via the Duke River and Ptarmigan Creek.

Compared to the majestic, almost overpowering Icefield Ranges, the Kluane Ranges are mere hills, but like the former they offer a rare virginity, for relatively few people have traveled within them. Whether you are a hiker or climber you can find in these ranges and in the valleys that surround them the pleasure of wilderness travel, including an opportunity to view arctic alpine wildlife and plants.

15. WHAT THE MOUNTAINS SAY

John B. Theberge

IN THE ST. ELIAS Mountains, wind, water, gravity, heat, and pressure have folded, twisted, gouged, and uplifted the land for 500 million years to make what is there today. While the land writhed, biological evolution cloaked and recloaked it with green tapestries and throbbing life. The landscape has changed, and is still changing. Change has been the dominant theme throughout this book.

All landscapes change, but change is especially obvious in the St. Elias Mountains. Even a small difference in one of the many climatic features may reverberate through the ecosystems, altering the patterns of erosion and run-off, soil nutrients and stability, plant growth and the feeding habits of herbivores and predators. They must all adjust. With time they may revert to an earlier norm, or they may not. Fundamental

change, evolution, will then creep ahead. The Kluane of a million or even 100,000 years hence will be very different from the Kluane of today.

Some of the possibilities for change are bizarre. The various crustal blocks of the St. Elias Mountains may continue their northward migrations—in effect, leave. Or the huge mountains may be worn into a flat or rolling landscape similar to much of the interior of the Yukon and Alaska. Or, if vertical uplift exceeds erosion, the mountains may someday tower even higher than they do today.

We know that the mountains will not remain as they are now. Whatever they do will profoundly affect not only local and regional but perhaps even western continental climates, particularly if onshore Pacific wind patterns are changed. If the mountains rise higher, there will

be an increase in the interior rain-shadow effect in the Kluane Ranges, with more of the moisture falling instead on the high icefields. Perhaps the steppe-like vegetation that predominated during much of the Pleistocene Era will dominate the region again. Mammoths, giant bison, and mastodons will not graze on it; they are gone forever. Instead, pronghorns and sheep may increase while browsers such as moose disappear. However, if erosion exceeds uplift, the rain-shadow effect will someday disappear. Boreal forests will invade the area, and elements of the wet coastal forests will penetrate into the river valleys. The range of tundra-loving birds, such as rock ptarmigan, will shrink, while that of their boreal counterparts, such as spruce grouse, will expand.

Not so far down the millennia, the present global cooling, which has been documented by glaciologists, may thrust Kluane's valley glaciers forward. Glacial Lake Champagne may come again, and then the town of Haines Junction will be visited only by skin divers. Then the pygmy whitefish of Sockeye Lake will no longer be confined, because Sockeye Lake will itself be drowned. The Kaskawulsh River may disappear (it carried no flow during much of the summers of 1975 and 1978); the gravels at the terminus of the Kaskawulsh Glacier may divert all its meltwaters into the Slims River.

Living things adapt to altering circumstances through physical or genetic changes, or variations in behavior. Animal populations may move into more favorable areas, or modify their

Mount Augusta across Seward Glacier. (Walter Wood)

(Monty Alford)

Mush Lake. (Roland Wickstrom)

food selection to better match the foods that are available, or, if they can, increase their reproductive output to offset losses. But these are limited adjustments. If the changing environment requires living things to make too many changes too rapidly, some will become extinct, leaving ecological niches unoccupied, perhaps to be filled someday by new evolutionary forms selected by new environments, or perhaps to remain vacant forever.

Man has a duty in all this, and it is to recog-

nize himself as a force with a proven capacity to cause environmental change that is "too much too fast."

The land and the living things it supports are continuously evolving. We do not see mountains rising or eroding away before our eyes, or new species coming into being, because our time frame is not nature's. We operate in decades, or hundreds of years at most; major evolutionary changes operate in millennia. We simply cannot grasp the meaning of millennia, but attempting to grasp it is worth while. At Kluane, you may come close to doing so. The rocks of ancient sea beds, the ash of extinct volcanoes, the sculpture of former glaciers, the floral features of a different age, the artefacts of human cultures long gone—all these reveal the past. And they reveal more than the past: in aggregate, they make up the present landscape. Our "moment in the sun," when viewed against the natural historic backdrop, takes on a proper time perspective. An appreciation of this perspective can generate a profound respect for the natural forces that have shaped and continue to shape our world, and us with it. These are the forces that determine the constraints within which we must live. Floodplain and fault zone are not man's to build upon, at Kluane or anywhere else. Renewable resources—trees, crops, fish, and wildlife—are only renewable if we allow nutrient cycles to continue to function as they always have. Air

and water are the underpinnings of life; to tamper with their quality is like climbing up the base of an avalanche chute in the St. Elias Mountains daring the snows to slide down.

Another theme that has run throughout the book is that, in the words of the naturalist John Muir, "everything in the universe is hitched to everything else." The periodic formation and disintegration of glacial dams on the Alsek River, and the consequent appearance and disappearance of lakes, were significant events in many chapters of this book: they influenced the quality of the soil, the distribution of plants, fish, birds, and mammals, and the fate of the men who lived near the now-extinct shorelines. Similarly, the great loess storms of wind-blown sand are part of the geological and glaciological history of the region, but are also significant in any study of the archaeology of man, the formation of steppe vegetation, or the history of birds and mammals

Moose antler. (John Theberge)

of the region. Similarly, again, the pattern of Pleistocene glaciation affected the distribution of plants, the types of animals that lived in the region of old, the distribution of fish, and possibly the distribution of early man. For practical reasons, we tend to pigeonhole knowledge according to established disciplines, but by doing so we may miss the complexity of interrelationships that are the essence of nature's ecosystems. A phosphorus atom moving from rock to soil to plant to animal to soil, and so on, knows nothing of the pedologist, the climatologist, the botanist, the ornithologist.

Because of nature's interrelationships, man has another obligation: to identify and fully consider the ecological implications of his actions before initiating any changes in any environment. All ecosystems are, in different ways, both threatened by and resilient to the activities of man. If we are to live successfully with the land, we must understand this and act accordingly. It is ironic that, even where so many natural forces beyond his control operate to change the land, man has the ability to destroy. But if archaeologists of today can tell us where a party of Little Arm hunters camped 8,000 years ago, then archaeologists in another 8,000 years will have no trouble knowing where we built mines, roads, pipelines, and towns, or where our bulldozers drove, even only once across the tundra.

Information that has come from studies in the St. Elias Mountains and other northern areas clearly suggests some restraints that we should put on our actions in northern lands that have been designated for protection, such as Kluane, and throughout the north, if the land is to be allowed to bear gracefully the impact of our technology.

We should take infinite care not to disrupt the vegetation where it provides insulation to keep the underlying permafrost from melting. To ignore this means "thermokarst erosion," which is often an unending washing away of the soil, eventually of whole hillsides. And we should recognize the slow regenerative power of plants in a cold environment, where bacterial action and decay are slow and soil nitrogen is consequently low in upland places that are not periodically flooded. And the low productivity of cold lakes, where fish growth and reproduction are both retarded. And the vulnerability of plant communities growing on thin organic soils, or on the gravel bars of rivers. And the normal ebb and flow of species—plants, predators, and prey—which must all be free to interact and seek their own dynamic relationships. And the importance of natural fire in cycling nutrients and establishing early successional forests, vital to many species, from flycatchers to moose. These are processes of nature that must remain intact.

Many northern species depend for their existence on special places. We must not disturb in any way the critical nesting sites of the peregrine falcon or other endangered wildlife species, or the denning sites of grizzlies, wolves, coyotes, and foxes. Nor the south-facing bunchgrass communities so vital to wintering herds of Dall sheep. Nor the caribou calving grounds. Nor the pockets of great abundance and variety of birds. Nor the relic northern steppe communities, so uncommon in North America, with their rare plant species. The land is whole and complete because all its parts are there.

Kluane is a national park. This means that it hopefully will receive the highest level of stewardship. It ensures that the land will remain forever wild. National parks like Kluane are of inestimable value as laboratories out of which the vital understanding of man-land relationships can come. Ultimately, and with proper policies acknowledging this value, national parks will contribute even more to man in this way than through their great potential for recreation. They are reservoirs of new knowledge.

National parks are not only living laboratories but living museums of nature, displaying samples of the best nature can offer. They are for our enjoyment, but their value for both enjoyment and science depends upon the preservation of their wildness. Otherwise, their very essence will be eroded away. They will become like land everywhere else. If enjoyment requires air-conditioned, centrally heated, windshield-gazing comfort, the land will suffer and the laboratory and the museum will be threatened. The more technology man brings to Kluane, the less Kluane will have to teach him.

Go to Kluane, then, ready to feel the stiff wind off the glaciers in your face, and to smell the sweet odor of balsam poplar leaves in the warm summer sun, and to hear a gray-cheeked thrush singing its flute-like song at dusk. Go to see a caribou crashing off the trail into the willows ahead of you. Go to sense man's place in nature.

Climb the mountains, get their glad tidings.
Nature's peace will flow into you as sunshine
    flows into trees.
The winds will blow their freshness into you
    and the storms their energy, while cares will
    drop off like autumn leaves.

JOHN MUIR

APPENDIX A / Common and Scientific Names of Flora, Birds, Mammals, Fish and Invertebrates Mentioned in the Text

Flora

aspen, quaking   *Populus tremuloides*
baneberry   *Actaea rubra*
bearberry   *Arctostaphylos uva-ursi*
bear root (sweetvetch)   *Hedysarum* spp.
birch, dwarf   *Betula glandulosa*
birch, paper   *Betula papyrifera*
blueberry   *Vaccinium ulginosum*
bluejoint, Canada   *Calamagrostis canadensis*
camus, death   *Zigadenus elegans*
cranberry, high bush   *Viburnum edule*
cranberry, lowbush   *Oxycoccus* spp.
crowberry   *Empetrum nigrum*
fern, bladder   *Cystopteris fragilis*
fern, grape   *Botrychium lunaria*
fireweed   *Epilobium angustifolium*
fir, sub-alpine   *Abies lasiocarpa*
hawk's beard   *Crepis nana*
hellebore, false   *Veratrum eschscholtzii*

Jacob's ladder   *Polemonium pulcherrimum*
juniper   *Juniperus* spp.
larch   *Larix laricina*
monkshood   *Aconitum delphinifolium*
pine, lodgepole   *Pinus contorta*
poplar, balsam   *Populus balsamifera*
poppy, arctic   *Papaver radicatum*
rose   *Rosa acicularis*
saxifrage, purple mountain   *Saxifraga oppositifolia*
soapberry   *Shepherdia canadensis*
sorrel, mountain   *Oxyria digyna*
spruce, black   *Picea mariana*
spruce, white   *Picea glauca*
strawberry   *Fragaria virginiana*
tea, labrador   *Ledum* spp.
valerian, Sitka   *Valeriana sitchensis*
willow, greyleaf   *Salix glauca*
willow, Scouler's   *Salix Scouleriana*
yarrow   *Achillea millefolium*

Birds

blackbird, red-winged *Agelaius phoeniceus*
bluebird, mountain *Sialia currucoides*
bunting, snow *Plectrophenax nivalis*
crossbill, white-winged *Loxia leucoptera*
duck, harlequin *Histrionicus histrionicus*
eagle, bald *Haliaectus leucocephalus*
eagle, golden *Aquila chrysaetos*
falcon, peregrine *Falco peregrinus*
grouse, spruce *Canachites canadensis*
gyrfalcon *Falco rusticolus*
hawk, marsh *Circus cyaneus*
hawk, red-tailed *Buteo jamaicensis*
jay, gray *Perisoreus canadensis*
junco, dark-eyed *Junco hyemalis*
lark, horned *Eremophila alpestris*
magpie, black-billed *Pica pica*
mallard *Anas platyrhynchos*
owl, great horned *Bubo virginianus*
owl, hawk *Surnia ulula*
phalarope, northern *Lobipes lobatus*
phoebe, Say's *Sayornis saya*
pipit, water *Anthus spinoletta*
plover, golden *Pluvialis dominica*
ptarmigan, rock *Lagopus mutus*
ptarmigan, white-tailed *Lagopus leucurus*
ptarmigan, willow *Lagopus lagopus*
raven *Cervus corax*
scoter, surf *Melanitta perspicillata*
scoter, white-winged *Melanitta deglandi*
solitaire, Townsend's *Myadestes townsendi*
sparrow, Brewer's *Spizella breweri*
sparrow, golden-crowned *Zonotrichia atricapilla*
sparrow, song *Melospiza melodia*
tattler, wandering *Heteroscelus incanum*
teal, green-winged *Anas carolinensis*
tern, arctic *Sterna paradisaea*
thrush, Swainson's *Hylocichla ustulata*
thrush, varied *Ixoreus naevius*
warbler, yellow-rumped *Dendroica coronata*
woodpecker, northern three-toed *Piciodes tridactylus*
yellow-legs, lesser *Totanus flavipes*

Mammals

bear, black *Ursus americana*
bear, grizzly *Ursus horribilus*
beaver *Castor canadensis*
bison *Bison* sp.
caribou *Rangifer tarandus*
chipmunk, least *Eutamias minimus*
cougar *Felis concolor*
coyote *Canis latrans*

deer, coastal black-tailed *Odocoileus hemionus sitkensis*
deer, mule *Odocoileus hemionus hemionus*
ermine *Mustela erminea*
fisher *Martes pennanti*
flying squirrel, northern *Glaucomys sabrinus*
fox, red *Vulpes vulpes*
goat, mountain (ibex) *Oreamnos americanus*
ground squirrel, arctic *Citellus parryii*
hare, snowshoe *Lepus americanus*
lemming, brown *Lemmus sibiricus*
lemming, northern bog *Synaptomys borealis*
lynx *Lynx canadensis*
marmot, hoary *Marmota caligata*
marten, pine *Martes americana*
mink *Mustela vison*
moose *Alces alces*
mouse, deer *Peromyscus maniculatus*
muskrat *Ondatra zibethica*
otter *Lutra canadensis*
pika, collared *Ochotona collaris*
porcupine *Erethizon dorsatum*
sheep, Dall *Ovis dalli*
squirrel, red *Tamiasciurus hudsonicus*
vole, northern red-backed *Clethrionomys rutilus*
vole, singing *Microtus miurus*
wapiti *Cervus elaphus*
weasel, least *Mustela nivalis*
wolf, timber *Canis lupus*
wolverine *Gulo gulo*

Fish

burbot *Lota lota*
grayling, Arctic *Thymallus arcticus*
pike, northern *Esox lucius*
salmon, chinook (king) *Oncorhynchus tshawytscha*
salmon, sockeye *Oncorhynchus nerka*
sculpin, slimy *Cottus cognatus*
trout, Dolly Varden *Salvelinus malma*
trout, lake *Salvelinus namaycush*
trout, rainbow *Salmo gairdneri*
whitefish, pigmy *Prosopium coulteri*
whitefish, round *Prosopium cylindraceum*

Invertebrates

blackfly *Family Simuliidae*
caddisfly *Order Trichoptera*
mayfly *Order Ephemeroptera*
midge *Family Chironomidae*
snail *Family Gastropoda*
stonefly *Order Plecoptera*

APPENDIX B / Information for Visitors

The Kluane Ranges can be reached in two ways, providing the possibility of a round trip: drive to Haines Junction (km 1,633 or mile 1,015 on the Alaska Highway) via either the Alaska Highway or Stewart-Cassiar Highway; or take the automobile ferry system either from Seattle (Alaska Ferry System) or from Port Hardy on Vancouver Island (British Columbia Ferry System plus Alaska Ferry System) to Haines, Alaska. Both ferry systems require early booking; they travel the scenic "Inside Passage" among coastal islands and fiords. From Haines, the Haines Highway runs 265 kilometers (165 miles) across the Chilkat Pass to Haines Junction.

Besides private vehicles, tour buses regularly travel the round trip in the summer, originating at a variety of western North American cities. Information can be obtained from travel agents.

More than 160 kilometers (100 miles) of the Alaska and Haines highways follow the eastern boundary of Kluane National Park. Park headquarters is at Haines Junction, and information can be obtained there about backpacking or climbing trips (the latter must be registered in advance).

The address for information is:

> Superintendent, Kluane National Park
> Haines Junction,
> Yukon Territory.

The Icefield Ranges and the highest peaks are not visible from the highways. Vista points can be reached by hiking, but require at least one night out. Limited food and camping supplies are available at Haines Junction; more are available at Whitehorse, 157 kilometers (98 miles) southeast of Haines Junction.

NOTES ON CONTRIBUTORS

Monty Alford was a member of two scientific expeditions to the Antarctic, has contributed to several outdoor and geographical magazines, and is a recipient of the Order of Canada. A Yukoner for thirty years, he went from the design board of an aeronautical firm in England to the stern seat of a canoe, paddling 4,000 miles from British Columbia to the Gulf of Mexico. He finally settled in the Yukon as a hydrometric surveyor and has participated in nine major and several minor mountaineering expeditions. Traveling throughout the Yukon and Alaska, he enjoys most of all to hike in the peripheral ranges of the St. Elias.

Richard B. Campbell first worked with the Geological Survey of Canada in 1946 as a summer field assistant in central British Columbia. During and following his education in geology at the University of British Columbia and the California Institute of Technology, he spent most summers with the Survey studying the geology of the mountains of British Columbia and the Yukon. This work led to the publication of over forty scientific reports, papers, guidebooks, and maps. He later became the first Survey resident geologist in the Yukon and has recently had the opportunity to work in the last large, geographically unknown region of the mountains of western Canada.

George W. Douglas received his undergraduate degrees in forestry from the University of Washington and completed his Ph.D at the University of Alberta in Edmonton. He owns and manages Douglas Ecological Consultants Ltd. in Victoria, B.C., a firm that specializes in plant ecology and conducts both basic and applied research. Much of Douglas's work has been carried out in the alpine regions of the Pacific Northwest, and during the last six years he has personally conducted research into the flora and vegetation of Kluane National Park.

Valerius Geist is Professor of Environmental Science in the Faculty of Environmental Design at the

University of Calgary, Alberta. His research has dealt largely with the behavior and ecology of large northern mammals. A particular interest has been the evolution of ice-age mammals, including modern man. In 1965 he did research on Dall sheep in the St. Elias Range, and visited the range repeatedly during a search for ecological reserves under the International Biological Programme. He has published two books on mountain sheep, and a recent book on human origins. He is also a regular contributor to scientific and popular publications.

Manfred Hoefs is a wildlife biologist specializing in ungulates and habitat matters. He has been employed by the Yukon Game Branch since 1972 and before that time worked in Kluane National Park for four years with the University of British Columbia and the Canadian Wildlife Service. He has to his credit some twenty publications, many of them dealing with the wildlife and vegetation of the Kluane area. His early personal involvement in this area helped to establish Kluane National Park in 1972.

Charles J. Krebs is employed by the Institute of Animal Resource Ecology at Vancouver, B.C. He has studied extensively in the north from the Pribilof Islands and Bristol Bay to the Mackenzie Delta and Baker Lake, N.W.T. For six years he has worked out of the Arctic Institute Base at Kluane Lake, where he is currently researching the causes of the ten-year cycle in snowshoe hares. His publications include forty ecological papers and a standard textbook for introductory ecological courses.

Melvin G. Marcus is Professor and Chairman at the Department of Geography, Arizona State University, Tempe, where he earlier served a four-year term as Director of the Centre for Environmental Studies. He is also a member of the Governor's Commission on Arizona Environment and is immediate past president of the Association of American Geographers. The primary focus of his research activities is alpine environments, with particular emphasis on climatology and glaciology. His experience in Alaska and the Yukon spans some thirty years; he has also worked in Turkey, Mexico, New Zealand, and the American Rockies and served as director or project scientist on several expeditionary research projects.

Richard E. Morlan is the Yukon Archaeologist with the Archeological Survey of Canada, National Museum of Man. His interests include all aspects of prehistoric environmental change, and he has done research in fossil insect and bone analysis as well as in archaeology. His current research focuses primarily on the earliest evidence for human occupation in the New World, evidence that has been discovered in the northern Yukon region. This research has helped to prove that the first men in the St. Elias region entered the Yukon more than 50,000 years ago.

David F. Murray is Professor of Botany and Curator of the Herbarium at the University of Alaska, Fairbanks. He began his work in the Kluane and Icefield Ranges in 1965 with the Icefield Ranges Research Project. His studies there followed experience with alpine tundra in Alaska and Colorado, where he obtained his M.Sc. and Ph.D. His principal interests are the taxonomy and ecology of arctic and alpine plants and the biogeographic relationships of the flora in Alaska and Yukon with alpine and steppe floras of the southern Rocky Mountains and northeastern Siberia.

Richard H. Ragle has been involved in polar research since 1952 and has a broad knowledge of sea and lake ice, of glaciers, and of the polar environment. He received degrees in geology from Dartmouth College and Middlebury College and studied glaciology and glacial climatology at the Norsk Polarinstitutt and the University of Oslo, Norway. He has been geologist/glaciologist with the U.S. Army Cold Regions Research and Engineering Laboratory and The Arctic Institute of North America and was Assistant Director for Operations at the Naval Arctic Research Laboratory, Point Barrow, Alaska. He is a pilot with long experience in alpine and arctic flying, and he has conducted field studies on the Greenland Ice Sheet, in the Canadian Arctic Islands, Antarctica, Labrador, and the St. Elias Mountains, Yukon Territory. He has authored and co-authored many professional papers. From 1961 through 1969 he helped direct the Icefield Ranges Research Project and from 1970 until 1972 was Project Director. He is now a consultant in cold regions research and resides in Anchorage, Alaska.

Vern N. Rampton received a B.Sc. Eng. (Geol.) from the University of Manitoba in 1962 and a Ph.D. from the University of Minnesota in 1969. Prior to 1974, he was employed with the Geological Survey of Canada as a research scientist and was engaged in studies of quaternary stratigraphy and geomorphic processes in the Yukon and the District of Mackenzie. He now has his own consulting firm, Terrain Analysis and Mapping Services Ltd., which specializes in mapping of surficial materials, permafrost studies, and land-use planning for industry and government in northern Canada.

John B. Theberge is a wildlife ecologist in the Faculty of Environmental Studies and Department of Biology, University of Waterloo, Ontario. His research focuses on wolves and other canids and their prey, but he maintains a naturalist's wide interest, particularly in the population regulation of birds. He has conducted research in the Kluane Ranges since 1970. He has degrees in biology from the universities of Guelph,

Toronto, and British Columbia. Wide interest in the Kluane region was stimulated by his articles in magazines and he was a central figure in spearheading public support for the creation of Kluane National Park. He spends much time as a conservation lobbyist for wilderness preservation and wise park management and is the author of many scientific and popular articles on wildlife and a book entitled *Wolves and Wilderness*.

Mary Theberge specializes in pen-and-ink and scratchboard art, and has illustrated her husband's book *Wolves and Wilderness* as well as many children's magazine articles on wildlife, which she authors or co-authors. She is an active participant in her husband's field work, accompanying him each summer on wilderness trips throughout the Kluane region.

Philip Upton, one of North America's most experienced glacier pilots, has been flying in the St. Elias Mountains since 1961 in support of the Icefield Ranges Research Project. The High Altitude Physiology Study began in 1967 and since then he has piloted the Helio Courier in support of the field station at 17,500 feet. He has also flown in support of Arctic Institute of North America projects on the north slope, based at the Naval Arctic Research Lab, Barrow, and Point McIntyre near Prudhoe Bay.

Roland D. Wickstrom is a limnologist with the Canadian Wildlife Service, Winnipeg, and is involved in research and management of aquatic resources in Kluane National Park, Yukon Territory, and Nahanni National Park, N.W.T. He began work in aquatic biology with the Ontario Department of Lands and Forests, working in northwestern Ontario. He later joined the Fisheries Research Board of Canada, Winnipeg, where he participated in projects on the Mackenzie River, N.W.T., and in the Georgian Bay district of Ontario. In 1973 he joined the Wildlife Service, where he began his aquatic studies in Kluane National Park.

Walter A. Wood is a high mountain geographer and mountaineer who has devoted most of his professional life to the St. Elias Mountains. Between 1935 and 1941 he led four expeditions to the Icefield Ranges, followed by Project Snow Cornice (1948-51), and the Icefield Ranges Research Project (from 1961 to the present). He has served as president of the American Alpine Club, the American Geographical Society, and the Explorers Club, and each of these societies has awarded him its highest honor.

William B. Workman is currently Associate Professor of Anthropology at the University of Alaska in Anchorage. Since 1962 he has devoted many of the past sixteen summers to archeological work around the Gulf of Alaska, in southern interior Alaska, and in the southwest Yukon Territory of Canada. Fieldwork in the Yukon, supported by the Museum of Man and the National Museums of Canada, in 1966 and 1968 led to some of the most rewarding and memorable professional and personal experiences of his life and to his doctoral dissertation at the University of Wisconsin. Finished in 1974, this monograph was published by the Museum of Man in 1978.

FURTHER READINGS

Geology

BOSTOCK, H. S. "Kluane Lake, Yukon Territory, its drainage and allied problems." *Geological Survey of Canada*, Paper 69-28, Ottawa, 1969.

BOSTOCK, H. S. "Geology of the northwest Shakwak Valley, Yukon Territory." *Geological Survey of Canada*, Memoir 267, Ottawa, 1952.

CAMPBELL, R. B., C. J. DODDS, G. H. EISBAKER, J. W. H. MONGER, P. B. READ, J. G. SOUTHER, and C. STANCIU. "Operation St. Elias, Yukon Territory." *Geological Survey of Canada*, Report of Activities, Paper 75-1, Part A. 51-70, Ottawa, 1975.

CAMPBELL, R. B., and C. J. DODDS. "Operation St. Elias, Yukon Territory." *Geological Survey of Canada*, Current Research Paper 78-1, Part A. 35-41, 1978.

DENTON, G. H., and M. STUIVER. "Neoglacial chronology, northeastern St. Elias Mountains, Yukon Territory, Canada." *American Journal of Science* 264:577-599, 1966.

DENTON, G. H. "Quaternary glaciations of the White River Valley, Alaska, with a regional synthesis for the northern St. Elias Mountains, Alaska and the Yukon Territory." *Geological Society of America Bulletin* 85:871-892, 1974.

KINDLE, E. D. "Dezadeash map-area, Yukon Territory." *Geological Survey of Canada*, Memoir 268, Ottawa, 1952.

MULLER, J. E. "Kluane Lake map-area, Yukon Territory." *Geological Survey of Canada*, Memoir 340, Ottawa, 1967.

RAMPTON, V. N. ", Lato quaternary vegetational and climatic history of the Snag-Klutlan area, southwestern Yukon Territory, Canada." *Geological Society of America Bulletin* 82:959-978, 1971.

Glaciology

DYSON, J. L. *The World of Ice*. Alfred A. Knopf, New York, 1962.

POST, A. and E. R. LACHAPELLE. *Glacier Ice*. University of Washington Press, Seattle, 1971.

SHARPE, R. P. *Glaciers*. University of Oregon Press, Eugene, 1960.

FISHER, M., (ed.). *Expedition Yukon*. Thomas Nelson and Sons (Canada) Ltd., Toronto, 1972.

BUSHNELL, V. C. and R. H. RAGLE, (eds.). *Icefield Ranges Research Project Scientific Results*. Vol. 1, 1969. Published jointly by the American Geographical Society, New York, and the Arctic Institute of North America, Montreal. Vol. 2, 1970; Vol. 3, 1972; Vol. 4, 1974.

SUGDEN, D. E. and B. S. JOHN. *Glaciers and Landscape*. John Wiley and Sons, New York, 1976.

Climate

Atmospheric Environment Service, Department of Environment, Canada. *Annual Meteorological Summaries*. Prepared annually by Whitehorse Weather Station, Yukon.

KENDREW, W. G., and D. KERR. *The climate of British Columbia and the Yukon Territory*. The Queen's Printer, Ottawa, 1955.

MARCUS, M. G. *Investigations in alpine climatology: the St. Elias Mountains, 1963-1971*. Icefield Ranges Research Project, Scientific Results. Vol. 4, American Geographical Society, New York, and Arctic Institute of North America, Montreal, 1974. (This volume includes 17 research articles dealing with the climate of the St. Elias-Kluane Mountains.)

MARCUS, M. G. and J. C. LABELLE. "Summer climatic observations at the 5,360 meter level, Mt. Logan, Yukon: 1968-1969." *Arctic and Alpine Research*, 2:103-114, 1970.

TAYLOR-BARGE, B. *The summer climate of the St. Elias Mountains Region*. Arctic Institute of North America Research Paper Number 53, Arctic Institute of North America, Montreal, 1969.

THOMPSON, H. A. "The climate of the Canadian Arctic." *The Canada Year Book 1967*. Dominion Bureau of Statistics, Ottawa, 1967.

Ice Age Mammals

GEIST, V. *Life strategies, human evolution, environmental design*. Springer-Verlag, New York, 1978.

GUTHRIE, R. D. "Paleoecology of the large-mammal community in interior Alaska during the late Pleistocene." *The American Midland Naturalist* 79(2):346-363, 1968.

GUTHRIE, R. D. "Re-creating a vanishing world." *National Geographic*. 141(3):294-301, 1972.

Botany

DOUGLAS, G. W. "Montane zone vegetation of the Alsek River region, southwest Yukon." *Canadian Journal of Botany* 52(12):2505-2532. 1974.

HULTEN, E. *Flora of Alaska and neighboring territories*. Stanford University Press, Stanford, California, 1968.

IVES, J. D., and R. G. BARRY, (eds.). *Arctic and Alpine Environments*. Methuen, London, 1974.

PORSILD, A. E. "Plant life in the arctic." A reprint from the *Canadian Geographical Journal*, March 1951, available from the National Museum of Canada, Ottawa.

SAVILE, D. B. O. "Arctic adaptations in plants." *Agriculture Canada Monograph* No. 6, Ottawa, 1972.

WELSH, S. L. *Anderson's flora of Alaska and adjacent parts of Canada*. Brigham Young University Press, Provo, Utah, 1974.

ZWINGER, A. H., and B. E. WILLARD. *Land above the trees*. Harper and Row, New York, 1972.

Birds

BANFIELD, A. W. F. "Notes on the birds of Kluane Game Sanctuary, Yukon Territory." *Canadian Field-Naturalist* 67:117-179, 1953.

DRURY, W. H., JR. "Birds of the Saint Elias quadrangle in the southwestern Yukon." *Canadian Journal of Botany* 54(12):2505-2532, 1953.

GODFREY, W. E. "Notes on the birds of southern Yukon Territory." National Museum of Canada, Bulletin No. 123, Ottawa, 1951.

HOEFS, M. "Birds of the Kluane Game Sanctuary, Yukon Territory, and adjacent areas." *Canadian Field-Naturalist* 87:345-355, 1973.

THEBERGE, J. B. "Bird populations in the Kluane Mountains, southwest Yukon, with special reference to vegetation and fire." *Canadian Journal of Zoology* 54(8):1346-1356, 1976.

Mammals

BANFIELD, A. W. F. "Notes on the mammals of the Kluane Game Sanctuary, Yukon Territory." National Museum of Canada, Bulletin 172:128-135, Ottawa, 1960.

HOEFS, M. "Ecological investigation of Dall sheep and their habitat." *Syesis* (supplement), Vol. 9. British Columbia Provincial Museum, Victoria, 1979.

KREBS, C. J., and I. WINGATE. "Small mammal communities of the Kluane Region, Yukon Territory." *Canadian Field-Naturalist* 90:379-389, 1976.

MARSDEN, W. *The Lemming Year*. Chatto and Windus, London, 1964.

OOSENBRUG, S., and J. B. THEBERGE. "Altitudinal movements and summer habitat preferences of woodland caribou in the Kluane Ranges, Yukon Territory." *Arctic* 33(1): 59-72, 1980.

PEARSON, A. M. "The northern interior grizzly bear *Ursus arctos L.*" *Canadian Wildlife Service Report* Series No. 34, Ottawa, 1975.

THEBERGE, J. B., and T. J. COTTRELL. "Food habits of wolves in Kluane National Park." *Arctic* 30(3): 189-191, 1977.

YOUNG, G. O. "Alaska-Yukon trophies won and lost." *Standard Publications*, Huntington, West Virginia, 1947.

YOUNGMAN, P. M. "Mammals of the Yukon Territory." National Museum of Canada, Publication in Zoology No. 10, Ottawa, 1975.

Fish

SCOTT, W. B. and E. J. CROSSMAN. "Freshwater fishes of Canada." Fisheries Research Board of Canada, *Bulletin* 184, Ottawa, 1973.

Prehistoric Man

JOHNSON, F. and H. M. RAUP. "Investigations in Southwest Yukon: geobotanical and archaeological reconnaissance." Papers of the Robert S. Peabody Foundation for Archaeology 6(1):1-198. Phillips Academy, Andover, 1964.

McCLELLAN, C. *My old people say: a ethnographic survey of southern Yukon Territory*. Publications in Ethnology 2(6). Museum of Man, Ottawa, 1975.

CLARK, A. McF., (ed.). Proceedings: northern Athapaskan conference. 2 vols. National Museum of Man Mercury Series, Canadian Ethnology Service Paper No. 27. National Museums of Canada, Ottawa, 1975.

MacNEISH, R. N. "Investigations in southwest Yukon: archaeological excavations, comparisons, and speculations." Papers of the Robert S. Peabody Foundation for Archaeology 6(2):201-488. Phillips Academy, Andover, 1964.

MORLAN, R. E. "A technical approach to lithic artifacts from Yukon Territory." National Museum of Man, Mercury Series, Archaeological Survey of Canada. Paper No. 74. National Museums of Canada, Ottawa, 1973.

WORKMAN, W. B. "Prehistory of the Aishihik-Kluane area, Southwest Yukon Territory." National Museum of Man Mercury Series, Archaeological Survey of Canada Paper No. 74. National Museums of Canada, Ottawa, 1978.

VANSTONE, J. *Athapaskan adaptations: hunters and fisherman of the subarctic forests*. Aldine, Chicago, 1974.

White Man History

THEBERGE, J. B. "Kluane National Park: history of establishment." In *Northern Transitions*, Vol. 1, Northern Resource and Land Use Policy Study. E. B. Peterson and J. B. Wright, (eds.). Canadian Arctic Resources Committee, Ottawa, 1979.

MARTINDALE, T. *Hunting in the upper Yukon*. G. W. Jacobs and Co., Philadelphia, 1913.

AUER, H. A. *Camp fires in the Yukon*. Steward and Kidd Co., Cincinnati, 1917.

Mountaineering and Climbing

FISHER, M. (ed.). *Expedition Yukon*. T. Nelson and Sons (Canada) Ltd., Toronto, 1971.

INDEX

location of oldest rocks in, 7
oldest known rocks in, 5
youngest known rocks in, 7
Vulcan Mountain, 183
Mountain sickness, 145
Mouse, deer, 82
Muir, John, 155, 157
Muskrat, 83

National and Provincial Parks
Association of Canada, 123
National Museum of Canada, 123
National park reserve, the, 123
National parks, values, 156
Neanderthal man, 44, 47, 51
Neskataheen (Neskatahin), 105, 106,
111, 116
graveyard, 117
Neoglacial Period, 102
Northern Airways, 135
North West Mounted Police, 116-17,
129
Nunatak, 20, 60, 62
Nunatak Fiord, 129

Odell, Noel, 132
Old Crow Flats, evidence of early man
at, 97
Otter, 83

Pacific Ocean, 84
Paleolithic man, 44, 47
description of, 51
Pearson, A.M., 72
Pika, collared, 81
Pike
northern, 91
Pipeline, Haines-Fairbanks, 122
Plants
Androsace alaskana, 62
Androsace septentrionalis, 60
Aphragmus eschscholtzianus, 62
Arabis lemmonii, 61
Arabis lyalii, 61
Artemisia alaskana, 60, 62
Artemisia frigida, 74
Artemisia rupestris, 62
aspen, quaking (*Populus
tremuloides*), 54
Aster yukonensis, 62
bearberry (*Arctostaphylos uva-ursi*),
54, 106
bear root (*Hedysarum alpinum*), 106
birch, dwarf (*Betula glandulosa*), 54,
57
birch, paper (*Betula papyrifera*), 63
blueberry (*Vaccinium uliginosum*),
106
Braya purpurascens, 61
Calamagrostis purpurascens, 74
Carex parryana, 61
Carex scabulosa, 62
Carex filifolia, 74
Cassiope stelleriana, 60, 61
Cassiope tetragona, 61
Castilleja yukonis, 62
Cerastium beringianum, 59
Claytonia bostockii, 60, 62
crowberry (*Empetrum nigrum*), 54,
106

death camus (*Zigadenus elegans*), 60
Draba ruaxes, 59
Dryas octopetala, 60
ericaceous shrubs, 57
Erigeron pumilis, 61
Erigeron purpuratus, 59
Erotia lanata, 61
Erysimum pallasii, 59
false hellebore (*Veratrum
eschscholzii*), 57
fern, bladder (*Cystopteris fragilis*),
59
fern, grape (*Botrychium lunaria*), 60
fireweed (*Epilobium angustifolium*),
54
Fritillaria camschatcensis, 61
grass, fescue (*Festuca altaica*), 57
hawk's beard (*Crepis nana*), 59
highbush cranberry (*Viburnum
edule*), 106
Jacob's ladder (*Polemonium
pulcherrimum*), 60
Labrador tea (*Ledum* spp.), 106
larch (*Larix laricina*), 63
Ledum palustre, 60
Leutkea pectinata, 60
Lewisia pygmacea, 61
lowbush cranberry (*Oxycoccus*
spp.), 106
Luzula piperi, 60
maritime plantain (*Plantago
maritima*), 55
Northern alkali grass (*Puccinellia
nuttalliana*), 55
Oplopanax horridus, 61
Oxytropis arctica, 61
Penstemon procerus, 60
Phippsia algida, 60, 62
pine, lodgepole (*Pinus contorta*), 63
Poa paucispicula, 60
poplar, balsam (*Populus
balsamifera*), 54, 56
Ranunculus nivalis, 60
Ranunculus pygmaeus, 60
rose (*Rosa acicularis*), 106
Rumex graminifolius, 63
Salix glauca, 74
Salix selchelliana, 62
saxifrage, purple mountain
(*Sasifraga oppositifolia*), 60
Smelowskia borealis, 59
Smelowskia calycina, 61
soapberry (*Shepherdia canadensis*),
54, 106
Solidago multiradiata, 60
sorrel, mountain (*Oxyria digyna*), 60
spruce, black (*Picea mariana*), 63
spruce, white (*Picea glauca*), 54, 56,
61
Stellaria alaskana, 59, 62
Stellaria monantha, 59
Stellaria umbellata, 62
strawberry (*Fragaria virginiana*),
106
Thlaspi arcticum, 61
Townsendia hookeri, 61
Vaccinium ovalifolium, 61
Vaccinium uliginosum, 60
Valeriana capitata, 60
willow, greyleaf (*Salix glauca*), 54
willow, prostrate (*Salix polaris*), 60

willow, Scouler's (*Salix
Scouleriana*), 54
yarrow (*Achillea millefolium*), 60
Porcupine, 81
Prehistoric tools, 100-01, 103-04
Project Snow Cornice, 132, 136

Ragle, Richard H., 138
Randall, Bob, 135
Reeve, Robert, 130, 136, 138
Refugium, number of mammalian
species in, 47
Rhinoceros, 46
Rivers
Alsek, 13, 14, 16, 17, 35, 54, 72, 84,
86, 92, 102, 106, 118
Chilkat, 108
Chitina, 126
Copper, 128, 129
Dezadeash, 12, 13, 17, 54, 72
Donjek, 12, 13, 35, 62, 87, 90, 131
Duke, 7, 8, 12, 35, 87
Dusty, 12, 17
Jarvis, 12
Kaskawulsh, 14, 17, 86
Kathleen, 13
Kluane, 16, 86
Klukshu, 72, 73, 105
Liard, 90
Peel, 90
Slims, 12, 13, 14, 16, 35, 55, 118, 123
Tatshenshini, 12, 73, 105, 116
White, 12, 35, 63, 84, 115, 123, 126
Yukon, 84, 86, 90, 129
Russell, I.C., 126
Russia-Great Britain Boundary
Treaty, 126
Ryder, Lloyd, 138

Salmon, 73, 106
chinook (king), 91
kokanee, 92
sockeye, 91-92
Sam, Constable, 108
Schwatka, Frederick, 111, 125
Sculpin, slimy, 90
Service, R.W., 115
Seton-Karr, H., 125
Shakwak Trench, 3, 13
exposure during glaciations and
direction of ice movement in
Pleistocene era, 13
Sheep, Dall, 46, 74, 105
Sheldon, Charles, 118
Shortt, T.M., 123
Silver City, 114, 117
Simmons, George, 135
Sitka, 110
Skagway, 116
Ski-wheels, 136-38
Skolai Pass, 128
Sloth, ground, 47
Soil, Slims River, 97-99
Squirrel
arctic ground, 80-81, 106
northern flying, 81
red, 81, 106
Steele, Colonel Sam, 117

Tanana Valley, 101
Taye Lake Culture, 101-04